IRELAND'S NEW TRADITIONALISTS

Fianna Fáil republicanism
and gender, 1926–1938

IRELAND'S NEW TRADITIONALISTS

Fianna Fáil republicanism
and gender, 1926–1938

KENNETH L. SHONK

CORK **cup** UNIVERSITY PRESS

First published in 2021 by
Cork University Press
Boole Library
University College Cork
Cork
T12 ND89
Ireland

Library of Congress Control Number: 2020945040
Distribution in the USA: Longleaf Services, Chapel Hill, NC, USA

British Library Cataloguing in Publication Data
A CIP record for this book is available from the British Library.

ISBN: 978-1-78205-439-9

Printed in Poland by BZ Graf
Print origination & design by Carrigboy Typesetting Services
www.carrigboy.co.uk

COVER IMAGES – 'Fianna Fáil Has a Plan', *Irish Press*, 15 February 1932, p. 5, courtesy Irish
Newspaper Archives and *The Irish Press*.

www.corkuniversitypress.com

For Claire and Lindsay

Contents

Acknowledgements

I write about the aspirational rhetoric of Fianna Fáil from the 1920s and 1930s – and oftentimes amplify the party's message as it was intended at the time. This act of contextualisation should not be viewed as any validation of, or support for, the party's actions, past or present. Apart from my scholarly interests in Irish history, and as an American of Italian/Germanic descent without any documented Irish ancestry, I have no 'horse' in this race in that my aims are apolitical and should not be attached to any contemporary political dialectics. By extension, my arguments regarding the gendered aspects of Fianna Fáil's aesthetics should not be construed as an attempt to undermine well-founded arguments that Fianna Fáil – or Irish/western patriarchy, for that matter – is any less complicit in creating or maintaining structures of oppression based on gender. Finally, the arguments contained herein, as well as any mistakes or oversights, are my own.

This project has had a long gestation period and has been the product of work at four universities – two as a graduate student and two as faculty. My first serious foray into Irish history began as a master's student at the California State University, Fullerton, where I received guidance and support from Cora Granata, Robert McLain and Jochen Burgtorf. My interest in Ireland during this period was further developed at Marquette University, culminating in the dissertation from which *Ireland's New Traditionalists* evolved. My time at Marquette was joyous, as I was free to explore new approaches to history, utilising myriad theoretical lenses to analyse the past. Julius Ruff, Alan Ball, Carla Hay, Thomas Jablonski and Lezlie Knox were important in my training as a historian. Irene Guenther was generous with her time in discussing foundational historiographical elements of interwar Europe, and her own work has done much to inspire my own. Philip Naylor has provided transformative and insightful feedback on my work, and his encouragement to broaden my understandings of Irish history by incorporating the global and the theoretical has been of tantamount importance to this and subsequent projects. Timothy G. McMahon served as the director of the dissertation on which this manuscript is based as well as advising me throughout the process of completing my doctorate. I cannot imagine a better doctoral adviser than Tim – from his general encouragement and support of my research, to his encyclopaedic knowledge of Irish history and historiography, to his willingness to advocate for my scholarship at all levels to junior and senior scholars (all going a long way to assist an introverted graduate student, now tenured associate professor), thereby helping me to get my 'voice' heard. Since graduating, Tim's interest and support have not flagged and, best of all, he has come to be a great friend. He continues to be a model teacher, adviser and academic.

I have been fortunate to work with a number of people who have offered support in myriad forms, whether it was specific feedback on my work, or words of encouragement throughout the writing process. In no particular order, other than how they come to mind as I write: Marie Moeller, Tiffany Trimmer, Gita V. Pai, Julie Weiskopf, Kate Parker, Matt Chedister, Marti Lybeck, Heather McCracken, Chris McCracken, Gerry Iguchi, Ariel Beaujot, John Grider, Megan Litster, Darci Thoune, Robert Allen, Linda Dickmeyer, Scott Baker, Shannon Suddeth, Tammy Proctor, Eric Edwards, Merose Hwang, Jodi Eastberg, Ann Ostendorf and Heidi Jones. Gratitude must also be extended to the members of the History Authors' Writing Group (HAWG) at the University of Wisconsin-La Crosse for their support in reading and commenting on portions of this project. Many thanks to my students past and present for their questions, feedback and interest in Irish history.

I have had the great honour to be part of the American Conference for Irish Studies, an international organisation of scholars whose unspoken mission has been to encourage and advocate for the work of graduate students and emerging scholars. This includes James Donnelly, Timothy O'Neill, Jay Roszman, Cian McMahon, Michael de Nie, Kristine Byron, Matt O'Brien, Maria Luddy, Margaret MacCurtain and James Silas Rogers. In addition, the scholarship of Jason Knirck has greatly inspired and shaped my own and his support for and advocacy of this project through feedback and encouragement has been invaluable throughout its long gestation. Sean Farrell has been generous in his encouragement and interest, and his unofficial mentorship and honesty has helped in all facets of my academic career. Marianne Elliott has been instrumental in introducing me to the larger field of Irish history. McKayla Stehr has offered unwavering friendship, support and encouragement during the writing process. I owe much to Bairbre ní Chiardha and her extended family for assisting with translations and grammar in Irish, as well as helping to establish a network of kindness strewn across many homes in Galway and Dublin. Special thanks also to my parents Ken and Linda Shonk, and to my extended family, especially Fred and Mary Steiner.

Any work of history is only as good as its sources, and therefore I am grateful to the library staff at Marquette University, California State University, Fullerton, the University of Wisconsin-Madison, the University of Wisconsin-Milwaukee, and the University of Wisconsin-La Crosse. In Ireland, Lisa Collins and Kate Manning at University College Dublin Archives, Mary Broderick of the National Library of Ireland's Ephemerae Collection, Liam Cullen, Head of Research for the Fianna Fáil party, Bertie Ahern for offering to expedite the process in accessing the Fianna Fáil archive, and James Harte and all the staff at the National Archives of Ireland have my eternal gratitude. It has also been a great pleasure to work with the staff at Cork University Press, including Maria O'Donovan and Mike Collins, and copy-editor Aonghus Meaney.

A highlight of my time as a graduate student has been the formation of two exceptional friendships marked by open and honest dialogue on topics ranging from history to music to the general inanity of American life in the early twenty-first century. Both Daniel McClure and Jana Byars are talented historians and teachers in their own right. Jana has been a source of unyielding friendship and joy for nearly fifteen years. Daniel, in addition to being my co-author for a tome on rock 'n' roll and historical theory, has been a generous friend who always has time to talk Ireland, offering feedback and insight on my work and career. His support and encouragement have shaped and inspired my development as a historian.

My time in Dublin conducting research for *Ireland's New Traditionalists* was most enjoyable due in large part to the friendship of Claire Carey, who provided a warm place to stay at her home in Drumcondra – easily my favourite space in Dublin, if not all of Ireland. Each day spent in the archives ended with conversations ranging from Irish history to popular culture. Claire was also very generous with her time in helping me to explore Dublin and Ireland outside of the archives, facilitating my growing love for the country and its people. As a thank you, I dedicate this book in part to her. *Go raibh míle maith agat.*

I also want to express gratitude to my partner Lindsay Steiner. Her love and companionship have provided immeasurable amounts of joy, and it is to her that I also dedicate this book: 'The Earth looks better from the star/that's right above from where you are'.

Introduction

By 1926 Sinn Féin republicanism had become increasingly untenable, as the vestiges of its rebellious transgression – abstention, hunger strikes, physical force insurgency – ran counter to the political trajectory set forth by the Irish Free State (Saorstát Éireann). The political successes of the Free State further undermined any alternative to the democratic processes that had become firmly entrenched in the wake of its creation. Nevertheless, republicanism under the guise of Sinn Féin persisted, unwavering in its abstention and advocacy for nothing less than an independent Irish republic. And though Sinn Féin maintained a core constituency, its ideals and methodologies had become increasingly unpalatable to many Irish voters. Internal divisions regarding the direction of Sinn Féin inspired party president Éamon de Valera in March 1926 to announce his resignation from the seemingly moribund party. Such an action inspired an anonymous commenter to the *Westminster Gazette* to remark that most people in Great Britain had begun to forget 'that Mr de Valera still exists, and now perhaps we may all forget, since he has since resigned'.[1] Though directed at de Valera, the sentiment of this statement might be extended to include the entirety of Sinn Féin's political relevance within the Saorstát.[2] Nonetheless, de Valera remained optimistic that an Irish republic was possible, seeing opportunity within the democratic frameworks of the Free State. De Valera believed that an evolved republicanism under a new name – Fianna Fáil – could challenge Cumann na nGaedheal as the driving force in Irish politics. In explaining his resignation from Sinn Féin, de Valera wrote: 'Somebody has to enter into the conflict. This is the opportune time and I realise that the coming general election is the time . . . if [opposition] Cumann na nGaedheal representatives get firmly fixed and you get the economic interests of Ireland fixed, there will be no place in Ireland for a national political party.'[3] De Valera's statement reveals a number of things that are fundamental to understanding Fianna Fáil's renascent republicanism: first, that de Valera envisioned this as a 'national party' designed to mobilise the energies of the entire Irish electorate; second, that the struggle against Free State hegemon Cumann na nGaedheal was tantamount to a 'conflict' – that is, a struggle to be won, or a problem to be corrected; third, that this 'opportune time' elevated the need for immediate and expedient action; and finally, that economic matters were tantamount to his party's stated goal of an independent Irish republic. Such was the course of action that defined 'Dev's' party from 1926 to 1938 – a plan whose tactics and purview scarcely resembled the aggressive republicanism of Sinn Féin.

That Fianna Fáil succeeded in its efforts to steer Ireland in the direction of an independent republic is an immutable fact, though its level of long-term success is a matter of debate.[4] Nonetheless, many works on the party – and especially in relation to the party's first decade – tend to establish a point of origin for studies on the long-term successes or failures of Fianna Fáil as a governing entity. The focus has tended towards analyses of the origins of Ireland's dire economic predicament in the middle third of the twentieth century or of the Northern Irish 'Troubles' towards the century's end. Fortunately, several recent works have offered important insight into the period 1922–38 and do much to explicate the importance of the Free State in establishing a stable and peaceful independent Irish nation. These studies are valuable in their scope and are indispensable in the re-evaluation of the years precipitating the formation of an independent Éire.[5] Moreover, authors of such works have demonstrated the importance of looking at the Free State era on its own merits, as something of a transitional period between the Home Rule era and the establishment of Éire. Such works have only accelerated a need to reassess the nature of Fianna Fáil republicanism within the context of the Irish Free State, as extant scholarship has done little to broaden our knowledge of the movement beyond the fundamental political and socio-economic machinations during the Free State era.[6] Further, few works have sought to present an understanding of Fianna Fáil republicanism during this period within the larger context of interwar Europe.[7] This lack of an extrinsic perspective informs the direction undertaken in *Ireland's New Traditionalists*. My intent is to widen the breadth of understanding of Ireland's socio-political landscape in the 1920s and '30s by examining Fianna Fáil's nationalist discourse as contextualised within a larger European/Atlantic world zeitgeist. Fianna Fáil was established at a most precarious time in Europe's history, as myriad crises regarding nation and state, economy and labour, culture and gender, modernity and primordialism abounded, and there emerged during this period an array of solutions to the era's general sense of angst. Situating Fianna Fáil within the larger interwar zeitgeist enables – and warrants – an analysis rooted in the same historical lenses unique to Europe in the 1920s and '30s. The aim here is not necessarily comparative, but rather to see Fianna Fáil as a party operating amid the same historical crises faced elsewhere, and to observe and analyse Irish politics through the same lenses applied to other nationalist projects during the same time period. As such, this study examines of its own accord the period between the formation of Fianna Fáil in 1926 and the passage of the Éire Confirmation Bill in 1938.

Situating Fianna Fáil as an interwar movement informs the perspective advanced in *Ireland's New Traditionalists* – a standpoint that deconstructs the machinations of de Valera's 'conflict' as present in the electoral discourse during the party's rise to prominence. In its first decade Fianna Fáil constructed a nationalist aesthetic that served to aggressively force an evolution from Free State to Éire and 'correct' the literal and symbolic imbalance caused by Ireland's historical associations with Great Britain. The tendency to gloss over the interwar period in favour of historical inquiry that favours a broader twentieth-century emphasis has resulted in a missed opportunity to understand how Fianna Fáil functioned within the interwar zeitgeist – a period fraught with anxieties regarding identity, gender, and the efficacy of modernity and the western liberal order. To put it crudely, there was something in the air in the interwar world that enabled aspects of the old order to be challenged or refined, and this general sense of anxiety permeated and shaped the political, social and economic discourses in and outside of Ireland. Thus, the question emerges: how did Fianna Fáil – undeniably successful in achieving the cultural and political aims of its nationalist project – operate within this particular era, distinguishing itself as an alternative to Cumann na nGaedheal's seeming hegemon? Fianna Fáil, I contend, succeeded in part because of its ability to best address the anxieties specific to the interwar period, especially those that relate to gender and the need to reconcile past trauma by connecting past, present and future as a foundational means of nation-building in a democratic state. In other words, the initial iteration of Fianna Fáil that formed the basis of Éire was a party of its time – as it was constructed to assuage the anxieties of the period through the construction of a nationalist party aesthetic that heralded an age of national regeneration.

The party's nationalist regenerate aesthetic contained three fundamental themes. First was the presentation that republicanism – and in turn the nation – needed to be regenerated in a manner that connected past and present in order to bridge the distasteful chasm of disarray caused by recent historical events, including connections to Britain. Second was the need to maintain and reconcile Irish primordialism with the necessities and opportunities afforded by facets of modernity amid the 'failures' of liberal capitalism and internationalist Marxism. Third, that Ireland required a corrective to the socio-cultural and economic imbalances caused by the 'incomplete' revolution that created the Irish Free State. Fianna Fáil's advancement of a mass national and nationalist party was rooted in efforts to address – and, indeed, correct – these crises by directing the vivacities of the Irish people so that aspects of their cultural, economic/labour and consumerist energies were directed towards the reification of the party's vision. In short, Fianna Fáil's nationalist concept was tantamount to a corrective of recent and ongoing historical, economic and cultural crises. The response to these crises coalesced within Fianna Fáil's socio-economic programme and was manifest in a general party aesthetic that offered an aspirational vision of a traditional and modern Ireland built upon an ideal – and idealised – femininity and masculinity. This gendered aesthetic emerged relatively slowly in the party's first five years, finally taking full shape in the 1930s as part of the discourse deployed during the elections of 1932 and 1933, the economic war, and the run-up to the passage of the 1937 constitution. An idealised and aspirational Irish Feminine and Irish Masculine appeared in the electoral material of Fianna Fáil – a construct that served to underscore a new republic made in an image amenable to the party's aim. Fundamental, then, to Fianna Fáil's national regeneration was a symbolic and literal construction of idealised representations of

Ireland. This reimagined Ireland was contingent upon the party's ability to reconstitute and define appropriate forms of Irish femininity and masculinity as modelled by their aesthetic. National regeneration came when the Irish Feminine and Irish Masculine were restored to their 'traditional' role: the man as an active agent of growth using his body to build a new, modern Ireland; the woman as the homemaker, consuming and wearing the native products produced in Irish factories and on the Irish farm. This is not to say that the entirety of Fianna Fáil's nationalist platform contained these particular elements; however, a careful reading of the party's aesthetic during the years marked by the economic war and the lead-up to the ratification of *Bunreacht na hÉireann*[8] does reveal the recurrence of themes that demonstrate a very obvious concern with reimagining and correcting aspects of Irish masculinity and femininity. In many ways, this party aesthetic had much in common with the promotion of mass politics on the European continent. Whether or not it was a conscious mimesis of continental developments, Fianna Fáil was undoubtedly responding to a similar set of crises and thereby established an aesthetic that was commensurate with the larger European zeitgeist. I would argue that it is more likely that the party was actively and explicitly attempting to establish a renascent republicanism rooted in the regeneration of an Ireland constructed upon a functional gendered binary in which the 'true' definition of Irishness could be attained.

Ireland's New Traditionalists is not meant to be a comprehensive history of Fianna Fáil during the years leading up to the outbreak of the second world war. Rather, this project serves to analyse and contextualise the party's nationalist aesthetic as *part* of its efforts to redefine and retrench Irish republicanism as viewed through the lenses of critical gender theory as well as by situating the era within the context of the decades between the wars. Like many of its European contemporaries, Fianna Fáil made full use of print culture and other forms of modern media to convey its message – a message intended to be consumed and enacted by the Irish populace. As such, my aim is to critically 'read' the wide array of visual, aural and print sources made public by Fianna Fáil in the period 1926 to 1938, ranging from party speeches, missives, electoral ephemerae and internal communications, to print media, including *The Irish Press* and *The Fianna Fáil Bulletin*, and in a few minor instances, film.

A careful read of this material reveals not only an effort to reconstitute Ireland along gendered lines, but also a desire to construct a nationalism rooted in a pastoralist, primordial vision of Ireland rushing headlong and fearlessly into the future. The value of such an approach adds greater nuance to our understanding of Fianna Fáil's electoral success.

Much has been written about the propensity of Fianna Fáil to emphasise the so-called backward gaze, but it is faulty to assume that this was the only direction in which the party was willing to look. Michael Mays notes that in the years after the Great War,

> [e]very nation would be forced to fashion its own image, to forge its own presumptively distinctive style, to weigh its circumstances, needs and desires, in order to determine its appropriate form, and to assess the conditions that would make one style preferable to another. If for a moment a revolutionary nationalism capable of embracing an indeterminate future had seemed a possibility, after the Great War, and even more dramatically, after the economic collapse, nationalism would in the end, for all intents and purposes, retreat into the immutability of a serviceable past, refashioning itself in the process in the image of the newly dominant bourgeois class whose values and interests it would come to reproduce. Yet in Ireland – where national self-definition had taken shape – that project was all the more pressing. And that beloved image of Ireland – rural, Gaelic, anti-materialist, retaining an ancient pastoral distinctiveness and simplicity – could only be maintained by turning a blind eye to the difficult realities then in the process of transforming the Irish landscape.[9]

Fianna Fáil neither turned a blind eye to the problems of modernity, nor did it seek to excise all aspects of modernity from its envisioned republic. Indeed, the party placed the pastoral as the goal, but, as its nationalist aesthetic demonstrated, it was willing to accept aspects of modernity so long as they fit within proper frameworks that did not challenge the idyllic republican vision. This is not to say, however, that Fianna Fáil was a paragon of industrial and economic futurism – a cursory read of Ireland's history after the Emergency bears this out. However, the party's aspirational rhetoric of aggressive, masculine industrial vision as buttressed by feminine work, and free of West Britonism, bore the hallmarks of an Irish futurism where factory chimney stacks belched the smoke of progress and where modern tractors tilled and reaped crops to feed healthy Celtic bodies.

The theoretical approach taken herein was informed by a need to add nuance to or to diverge from the strict political histories of Fianna Fáil and of the political climate in the decades following the formation of the Irish Free State. The evidence presented here reveals a party concerned with rebirth – or liberation from Cumann na nGaedheal, the United Kingdom and Sinn Féin. At its core, Fianna Fáil's electoral aesthetic was a continuation of the war of independence and civil war fought non-violently: first as a retrenchment of Sinn Féin and general republican policy, followed by a blitz of rhetorical combat intent on building a fully realised nation that emphasised pragmatism over idealism. The weapons employed by Fianna Fáil? The construction of a political movement and nationalist project that mobilised not only the political and the economic, but also the social and cultural structures of Ireland. Indeed, other scholars have explored the political and economic machinations employed by Fianna Fáil in the party's rise to prominence in the Irish political landscape. More recently, scholars have touched on the interaction between politics and mass culture – a culture intended to be literally and figuratively consumed by the Irish electorate. This analytical approach, shaped by the application of gender theory, enables us to see Ireland from a wider context that is not inherently comparative in nature. Political histories allow for direct comparison and contrast, demonstrating that Ireland was one of a few European states in which democracy grew, as distinct from the rise of right-wing reactionary thought in the guise of fascism and fascistic national organisation. However, martialling gender theory and the fascistic lens as a broader study on the confluence of politics and culture allows us to suss out the anxieties that informed Fianna Fáil's electoral discourse. Thus, the theoretical approach applied herein draws heavily on – and owes a great debt to – the extant political histories. Moreover, the application of gender theory allows for a nuanced analysis of the party's visual culture.

The general historiography on this era tends to foreground the party's legislative agenda, in turn paying little attention to the party's mass

mobilisation efforts. Such works are incredibly valuable, yet their scope
precludes any detailed understanding of Fianna Fáil's nationalist aesthetic
vis-à-vis the interwar zeitgeist. Alvin Jackson contends that Cumann
na nGaedheal failed to create an exclusive constituency apart from ex-
unionists and 'those who profited from commercial ties with Britain'.[10]
Regarding Fianna Fáil, Jackson notes that the party 'was able to tap an
electoral core which was unreconciled to the Free State: it was rather that
the party was able to reconstruct the political chemistry of Parnellism by
combining nationalist fundamentalism with a carefully tailored social
and economic appeal'.[11] The implication is that the Irish public's support
for republicanism was largely dormant, and that Fianna Fáil's nationalistic
aims served as a proper alternative to the stop-gap element of the Free
State and its party of government. As such, Jackson portrays Fianna Fáil
as offering a political pastiche in which the party's rhetoric was simply
a rehashing of seemingly mordant ideologies. Further, he contends that
Fianna Fáil's success was due in large part to Cumann na nGaedheal's
failings in dealing with Europe's changing socio-economic landscape. In
these works, there is presented a clear distinction between Fianna Fáil
politics and Irish culture, and how the former sought to mandate the
latter. Conversely, my goal is to demonstrate the machinations of a party
that attempted – successfully, in the short term, at least – to forge a nexus
between society and economy, culture and nationalist aesthetic, and
gender and power.

A more aggressive and active Fianna Fáil is advanced by Richard
Dunphy, who notes that 'the party did not simply enjoy an electoral
superiority, but succeeded in establishing its intellectual, moral, and
cultural leadership'.[12] Dunphy asserts that Fianna Fáil succeeded in part
because of its ability to balance a new economic and social policy on top
of pre-existing notions of republicanism. In this sense, Dunphy does not
differ much from Jackson, apart from his suggestion that Fianna Fáil was
far more progressive in its vision of Ireland's future. An important element
of Dunphy's work is his contention that the emergence of de Valera's new
republican party to prominence completely restructured Ireland's political
landscape. I am most interested in looking at what Fianna Fáil envisioned
and how it grappled with interwar anxieties, in turn adding to Dunphy's
party history while expanding on Joe Lee's assertions regarding the Fianna

Fáil spectacle. Lee notes that de Valera's party 'succeeded in capturing the market for the emotional resentment of the excluded underdog, who felt that the political "system" was fixed against them . . . [and] Fianna Fáil satisfied the demand for pageantry, and for vicarious participation, among the politically emotive'.[13] Indeed, this viewpoint is largely representative of what has correctly been called a rather oppressive society, especially for women, or what James Smith called Ireland's 'containment culture'.[14] However, a deeper look at the nationalist aesthetic advanced by Fianna Fáil in the years preceding the drafting of the constitution shows a party much more open to incorporating elements of modernity into the national fold. Granted, some saw this as evidence of a continuation of British-style capitalisation of Irish society, but the party's propaganda regarding economic nationalism, as well as the role of women within a 'de Valerian' state, show that Ireland was not the culturally regressive state that it once was. This, however, is not to say that the rhetoric regarding the inclusion of modernity was seamlessly woven into Irish society. Rather, the point here is that Fianna Fáil worked to produce a republican narrative through the incorporation of a gendered aesthetic that fulfilled the need to reconcile – if not intermesh – the backward and forward gazes.

Recent political histories of Fianna Fáil and the Free State are largely concerned with the impact of the Irish civil war in shaping political discourse, as well as questions regarding Ireland's place within the larger European context. The general consensus is that Ireland was largely unaffected by the vagaries of interwar continental Europe, and that civil war divisions defined the future trajectories of Fianna Fáil and Cumann na nGaedheal/Fine Gael. All these studies are carried out with an eye towards the relative successes and failures of the political parties' policies. Most recent works do hint at a nexus of culture and politics, but do not fully embrace the intersection of the two.[15] The result is an incomplete history that allows for a relatively narrow view of Fianna Fáil's efforts to construct a national and nationalist socio-political project. Yet there exists a corpus of material that warrants a study that draws equally from the political and the social – resulting in a point of view that forces us to broaden our understanding of Ireland's interwar period.

Fianna Fáil had the luxury of jettisoning Sinn Féin's self-realising policy of constructing a democratic state relatively independent from the

United Kingdom; the civil war and the formation of the Irish Free State rendered this outdated, if not completely redundant. Alan Zink notes that the development of this Irish democracy – that is, a political entity literally independent from Westminster – was shaped by a 'historically unique set of circumstances which influenced both the content and the context of Irish politics and which partially isolated the country from the mainstream of modern European development. Ireland was thus largely shielded from the socioeconomic, intellectual and political changes of the 1920s and 1930s.'[16] Zink argues that Ireland was somewhat *sui generis* in its political development vis-à-vis other emergent European states.

> The country's path to independence was by no means smooth, being strewn with dissension, violence and internecine strife, yet at no time was Irish democracy itself seriously in danger. This was due to an historically unique set of circumstances which influenced both the content and the context of Irish politics and which partially isolated the country from the mainstream of modern European development. Ireland was thus largely shielded from the socioeconomic, intellectual and political changes of the 1920s and 1930s.[17]

Further, Zink writes that 'Fine Gael and Fianna Fáil were strongly leader-oriented associations which bore little resemblance to the mass parties which had emerged in the urbanized, industrial polities of Europe.'[18] That Ireland diverged from the political developments seen in Europe is quite clear. However, it should not be construed that Ireland was unaffected by the same phenomena that shaped the interwar zeitgeist.

Alvin Jackson notes that Cumann na nGaedheal 'taught their republican successors in Fianna Fáil that they did not need to shoot the British in order to secure political rights.'[19] The bifurcated rhetoric of division constructed during the civil war did make its way into the political discourse of the Free State, as well as Éire, where passions and violence were channelled into democratic functions. Indeed, as explored herein, Cumann na nGaedheal made every effort to present Fianna Fáil as violent reactionaries intent on giving rebirth to the violence and politics of the Irish civil war. Further, Jackson argues that Fianna Fáil's fight with Britain – especially during the economic war – was 'defined in the language and with the vigour of the battlefield [which] possibly helped to acclimatize the retired warriors of Fianna Fáil to the peaceful exercise of state power'.[20] Perhaps, but this is not the lone defining factor that shaped the era's political dialectic, where the assumption is that every facet of party discourse was forged in relation to another. Fianna Fáil certainly presented itself as a bulwark against all that Cumann na nGaedheal/Fine Gael represented, save for the extant democratic framework. Fianna Fáil's electorate-facing aesthetic reveals something else: a party that evolved nationalist republican ideology that could – and did – affect national regeneration.

Gavin Foster examines how the civil war shaped societal and political developments. 'The complex dynamics of Ireland's civil war offer a rich field of study for a more nuanced, culturally informed exploration of the ways that class and status-based hierarchies and interests interacted with nationalist politics and violence and how these combined currents shaped the conflicts, impacts, and outcomes of the revolution's settlement for winners and losers alike.'[21] Foster's work examines the relationship between class- and status-based hierarchies in Ireland where there was a dynamic post-civil-war politics present in Fianna Fáil. Such has been studied. My work does not aim to recreate that, but rather add a level of nuance vis-à-vis Fianna Fáil's efforts to transcend this schism and formulate a culturally-facing national visage. I also consider the social aspects of the civil war in the aftermath of the conflict, from 1923 to the end of the decade, an oft-neglected period which is crucial for understanding the outcomes of the civil war and therefore of the revolution itself. Indeed, this is the context in which Fianna Fáil operated, but one must be careful not to anchor the entirety of interwar Ireland as a reaction to – or at least a creation of – the events of the revolutionary period. That is to say that the politics of this time were certainly informed by larger anxieties specific to the era. The revolutionary period undoubtedly impacted the political landscape in Ireland. This has been demonstrated in the growing historiography of the time, as numerous scholars have addressed this matter head-on. However, Fianna Fáil's electoral aesthetic between 1926 and 1938 reveals something more –that the party was not just intent on 'winning' a civil war replayed in the Dáil and at the ballot box. Fianna Fáil was intent on serving as a corrective to a wide array of ills, both perceived/constructed and real. Indeed, Fianna Fáil in this period was intent on restricting its politics through a public infiltration of the Free State, but it also sought to actively (re)define – so as to correct – the societal underpinnings of Irish society: the Irish man and the Irish woman.

Mel Farrell, like others, ably demonstrates the impact of the civil war on Irish politics – namely the mostly two-party division between the pro-Treaty and anti-Treaty sides. He writes: 'The Irish Free State was of its time. However, aspects of the Irish state's experience of the interwar period are unique to its own political context.'[22] Further, Ireland's 'rapid transition from revolution and civil war to emerge as one of Europe's most stable democracies' is without question.[23] This is due in large part to the successes of the Free State in effectively fostering a peaceful democracy – a peace that owes much to the distaste for approaches to nation-building held onto by the increasingly irrelevant interwar iteration of Sinn Féin. Relatedly, Sinn Féin between 1923 and '26 was being pulled apart by internal strife – a divergence that contributed directly to the formation of Fianna Fáil. Farrell's work adds to the scholarship on the period and does much to illustrate the political dialectics that emerged between Ireland's primary political foes: Cumann na nGaedheal/Fine Gael and Fianna Fáil. While his works focus on the political machinations of the time period, my work focuses on Fianna Fáil's envisaged Ireland. In many ways the approach taken herein is an inversion of political histories in that my reading of the party's envisioned electoral aesthetic helps to foster understanding of how Fianna Fáil sought to not only distinguish itself from Sinn Féin republicanism, but also to reconstitute Irish republicanism in a manner that was not only best suited to operate within the democratic frameworks of the Saorstát, but that would also assuage the socio-economic anxieties of the time.

Recent works by Aidan Beatty and Timothy Ellis demonstrate the value of looking at this time period through a social and political lens that situates Ireland in the broader European, if not global, context – that is, one that examines the intersection of gender, politics, society and economy. Beatty, for example, argues that Irish men had been emasculated by the economics of British rule, finding distinctive similarities between myriad facets of Irish nationalism and Zionism: 'Zionism also utilised gendered notions of martyrdom, nationalist time, physical culture, and special sovereignty. And many Zionists saw language revival, agrarianism and social legislation as key means for achieving national revival . . . this was due to a similar European/quasi-colonial bifurcation shared by Zionism and Irish nationalism.'[24] As regards Fianna Fáil, Beatty notes that the party constructed an electoral aesthetic rooted in agrarian masculinity in a manner similar to Zionist nationalists. Such a comparative study, then, illustrates the tensions and anxieties that informed Irish nationalist tropes, as this external perspective further demonstrates that global – or, at the very least, external to Ireland – cultural and economic factors were drawn from a similar set of experiences. My aim is to add to this growing canon. Timothy Ellis' work on the masculine depictions of Éamon de Valera most closely resembles the approach taken herein. Ellis seeks to 'demonstrate how discourses of masculinity were central to the construction of political power in the Irish Free State, using de Valera as a case study'.[25] Ellis' approach – like Beatty's – helps to illustrate the value of looking at visual culture as a means of understanding constructs of political power in Ireland in the Free State era. Both are of great value in understanding aspects of the intersection between politics and masculinity. However, I wish to add some complexity to Beatty's assertion that 'Fianna Fáil imagined the Irish electorate as a male-only field'[26] and to Ellis' contention that nationalist projects are 'imbued with the rhetoric of masculinity'.[27] Indeed, the works of these scholars have done much to explicate the importance of masculinist imagery in the effort to construct political power. Conversely, the approach taken herein situates Fianna Fáil as utilising its electoral aesthetic as pedagogy – that is, a didactic approach that served to actively define aspects of femininity and masculinity in Ireland.

George Mosse notes that 'analysing the relationship between nationalism and respectability involves tracing the development of some of the most important norms that have informed our society: ideals of manliness . . . and their effect on the place of women; and insiders who accepted the norms, as compared to the outsiders'.[28] His work underscores the importance placed upon the construction of appropriate gendered tropes by nationalist projects to advance the cause of the nation. Mosse adds: 'The dynamic of modern nationalism was built upon the ideal of manliness. Nationalism also put forward a feminine ideal, but it was largely passive, symbolizing the immutable forces which the nation reflected.'[29] By providing 'symbols with which the people could identify', nationalist projects such as the one advanced by Fianna Fáil could harness the immense power of the nation's collective.[30] A gendered corrective was key to Fianna Fáil's success, for the party's electoral dialectic with Cumann na nGaedheal began with the latter's assertions of feminised republicanism, forcing de Valera's party to counter by advancing a masculine rhetoric. As Mosse notes, 'Masculinity provided the norm for society; its symbol had to send out clear and unambiguous signals.'[31] Joan Scott identifies the relevance of gender as a signifier in the 'perceived differences between the sexes, and gender is a primary way of signifying relationships of power'.[32] And, for Fianna Fáil, there were two signifiers of power that needed correction: first, the aforementioned dialectic between itself and Cumann na nGaedheal and the ensuing struggle to 'finish' Ireland's democratic revolution; and secondly, Ireland's colonial relationship to Britain. Philippa Levine notes that such gendered representation of the colonised as 'frail men' was 'more than descriptive; it became a hierarchical ordering of quality, skill, and usefulness'.[33] Thus, to undo this central aspect of colonialism, and build up a nation amid anxieties regarding modernity, it became necessary to construct a new gendered binary that clearly defined aspects of society in a manner suitable to the nation-building efforts of Fianna Fáil. Fundamental to this was the party's effort to define what was acceptable and what was not; what was appropriate to the new nation and what was a threat: it was a corrective to the nation's past troubles, as well as being representative of a new discourse. Fianna Fáil defined and trumpeted acceptable visions of Ireland's Gaelic past while pushing for the nationwide acceptance of modern industry as both a means of reifying independence and isolation, but also of instilling patriotism. Such an effort was akin to Roger Griffin's description of Italy, where the fascists 'sought to bring about [that which] was not "anti-modern", but part of the attempt to create an alternative modernity to rescue society from decline and decadence, an aspiration which in turn gave Fascism's bid for the renewal of civilization a deep affinity with modernism itself'.[34] The effort to construct a truly independent Éire was not simply the result of the party's legislative agenda; rather, Fianna Fáil constructed its new republican rhetoric through the inclusion of people within gendered frameworks, or what Foucault described as the 'way in which sex is put into discourse'.[35]

Ireland's New Traditionalists is about the attempt by a nationalist party to define and correct gender by transforming masculinity and femininity. Further, the purpose here is not to create a history of women or men, per se, but to examine how Fianna Fáil sought to appropriate notions of gender to suit its aspirational republic. This need to extend politics into definitions of masculinity and femininity was a common feature of nationalist projects during the interwar period. Ann Taylor Allen argues that anxieties regarding gender were the result of traumas faced during the Great War and other modes of conflict, whether local or global. She writes, 'The domestic culture of the inter-war era was marked by wartime trauma. Soldiers at the front had often envied civilians, including their own wives, lovers, and mothers, whose life they imagined as easy and safe. They were often suspicious about what the women might have been up to during their men's absence . . . Some pessimistic observers feared the outbreak of a "sex war" which might abolish all distinctions of gender.'[36] These anxieties were manifest in the electoral aesthetic of Fianna Fáil in the Free State era, when the party sought to make a clear distinction between the roles of women and men in the aspirational republic. Maryann Valiulis writes that 'by defining women's primary responsibilities in the domestic sphere . . . political leaders were, in fact, emphasizing women's difference'.[37] In this regard, anxieties were also rooted in the active, public role of Irish feminists in the push for Home Rule and in physical force insurgency up to and including 1922. In doing so, women blurred the concept of what constituted femininity, corroborating Taylor's assertions regarding interwar Europe. Thus, Fianna Fáil worked to redefine, and thereby reiterate, the differences between men and women in Ireland. Such efforts by Fianna Fáil were not necessarily stated explicitly, but even cursory analysis of their politics reveals a patriarchal thrust. Now, it is not entirely innovative to claim that Fianna Fáil was patriarchal in its effort to legislate the place of Irish women. Máirtín Mac an Ghail and Chris Haywood write, 'There is increasing understanding from cultural theorists that if women are configured through traditional representations of femininity, men are also bounded by specific masculine cultural forms. Furthermore, the messages being conveyed in the media aim to promote particular masculine subjectivities . . . There is much empirical and conceptual work to be done in exploring the gendering of men.'[38] This book intends to do just this – to examine how Fianna Fáil sought to liberate masculinity from what it presented as centuries of oppression wrought by the presence of Britain and the Free State's torpid economic development. My aim, then, is to demonstrate how this was part of a larger effort by Fianna Fáil to reconstitute Ireland and Irish society along new ideations of gender that – when engaged in literal and symbolic coitus – could, if realised, propagate generations of 'true' Irish women and men; that this was not just its political platform, but the basis for its national strategy for electoral and party mobilisation.

The party's aesthetic contained themes of tradition (Gaelicism, the glorification of a time before the 'invasion', the primacy of Ireland's Catholicity) and modernity (glorification of growth and industry, the cult of progress), and it had much in common with nationalist parties that emerged in Europe in the first third of the twentieth century. Regarding nationalist movements of that era, Mosse asserts that the 'ideal of classical beauty was co-opted by nationalism, just as nationalism would annex many other political movements and philosophies over the years . . . The visual self-representation of the nation was just as important as the much-cited literature of nationalism.'[39] During its rise to power, Fianna Fáil established an inclusive republican aesthetic that created a definitive vision of a new, modern state. According to Foucault, such a modern state characterised both 'individual and totalizing form[s] of power' and was built upon 'a very sophisticated structure, in which individuals can be integrated, under one condition: that this individuality would be shaped in a new form and submitted to a set of very specific patterns'.[40] Fianna Fáil constructed a nationalist movement that sought to unify the nation through party-sanctioned individual behaviours. More specifically, as is contended below, the party constructed sanctioned norms along a female/male binary that offered both a corrective to past difficulties and a basis for building this new state. As such, the people of Ireland were now asked to direct their energies towards an inculcation of republican ideology into all aspects of their daily life, enabling the party to alter 'the world by reinterpreting it'.[41]

In describing the downfall of Sinn Féin republicanism, Jason Knirck has made special note of the rhetorical dialectic between the supporters of the treaty – Cumann na nGaedheal – and de Valera's party. Central to this was Cumann na nGaedheal's ability to portray Sinn Féiners as feminine and reactionary, and therefore a threat to the peaceful order established by the Free State. According to Knirck, 'pro-Treatyites used gendered arguments and stereotypes to bring republicanism into disrepute. As a result, republicanism became "feminized", tarred with the brush of hysteria, irrationality and undue emotion.'[42] Knirck adds that 'Pro-Treatyites also used images of the irrational, emotional, feminized political figure to castigate women and urge their exclusion from politics. They linked women and republicanism, and much of their seemingly misogynistic policy was also directed against radical republicans.'[43] Notions of sacrifice, emotionalism and reverence for Irish martyrs were a unifying force for the modern republican movement and were central to Sinn Féin's *raison d'être*. Further, these tropes highlighted by Knirck meshed well with British sentimentalities that 'were perfectly happy to find the Irish just the sort of bucklepping, gallivanting rebels they had always proclaimed them to be, the rebel being one reassuringly familiar kind of Irishman whom the liberal, book-buying English had taken fatally to their hearts'.[44] This rhetorical endeavour to delegitimise the republican cause was taken up by Fianna Fáil and served as the basis for the gendered rhetoric of de Valera's party that sought to correct the male/female binary within Ireland. Fianna Fáil worked hard to distance itself from a Sinn Féin weakened by its inflexible ideology. This was manifest in how the party presented itself as logical, peaceful, willing to play by the rules of the Free State, thereby working to undo this feminised stigma. Chapter 1 explores efforts by Fianna Fáil to reorient the party's renascent republicanism. These efforts are evident in the party's early electoral manifestos and internal correspondence, including that between de Valera and his former Sinn Féin compatriots.

That the need to 'correct' and reappropriate Irish femininity, thereby redirecting the political energies of Irish women, was a central facet of Fianna Fáil's nationalist project is discussed in Chapter 2. The problem to be corrected was this: through the guise of such organisations as Cumann na mBan and Inghinidhe na hÉireann, public activism in the guise of dedication to Sinn Féin abstentionism, and through associated hunger strikes and marches, Irish women – and by association, the republican movement writ large – had been politicised to the point that they were viewed as disruptive to the newly formed Free State. Fianna Fáil sought to correct this by clearly defining an aspirational role for Irish women as part of its attempt to assuage anxieties regarding potentially unsettling behaviour that was damaging the republican cause. By reasserting – and thereby redefining – femininity, Fianna Fáil constructed a model of Irish republican womanhood that was best suited for its congress with the model Irish republican man. Central to this was the restorative reconnection between the local and national and the redirection of political activity towards the domestic sphere. As such, Irish women were to adopt a palingenetic aesthetic that was traditional *and* modern. Through consumerist consumption of Irish-produced goods and adornment of Irish fabric, Irish women were crucial agents in the advancement of Fianna Fáil's march towards industrial modernity. Fianna Fáil also advocated for Irish women to embrace *couture moderne* and modern vocations, so long as this was done to reify Fianna Fáil's nationalist vision. Simply put, Irish women were to be paragons of Fianna Fáil's vision: traditional, modern, demure, consumerist and, more importantly, the aesthetic embodiment of a new old Ireland.

Fianna Fáil's attempt to redirect women's political activity into both domesticity and avocation was matched by its efforts to establish a more public and collective role for men. To push an assertive, masculine, economic nationalism proved advantageous to many political movements in the wake of the Great War and global depression of the 1920s and '30s.[45] In an Irish context, as explored in Chapter 3, Fianna Fáil offered an alternative to the liberal/Marxian framework through a blistering attack on the status quo, which the party situated as a vestige of the incomplete independence wrought by the Anglophilistic Irish Free State. Operating as iconoclasts of sorts, Fianna Fáil's activist economic rhetoric can be viewed both as an attempt to rescue Ireland from stagnation and a final push to break the centuries-long supplication to England. In a study of the electoral ephemerae of Fianna Fáil, three themes become evident:

a dialectical discourse in which the party's activist stance contrasts with the passivity of Cumann na nGaedheal's free market capitalism; the portrayal of the party as a dynamic agent of growth marked by its embodiment of the male; and finally, the party as the protector of Ireland – both symbolic and literal – from the trappings of depression and colonialism. Within this rhetorical push, one finds conversations about land, the fetishisation of Irish products and masculine labour, imagery of insemination and reforestation, glorification of industry coupled with a romantic view of Irish pastoralism, and the effort to heal and offer shelter for the sick and weak. As was the case with many fascistic entities, there occurred a dualistic glorification of both the past and the future – an embracement of modernity built upon the glorification of a racial primitivism. Like the Italian fascists' embrace of Futurism and its glorification of speed, industry and Roman iconography, Fianna Fáil trumpeted the glories of progress and movement while maintaining the backward gaze towards Ireland's mythical racial heritage. While the party did not engage in the martial vulgarisms seen in Italy, Germany or Spain, there was a kinship of sorts in how continental parties and Fianna Fáil developed, in that they were products of new thinking that rejected the tenets of the previous age, but, more importantly, situated themselves as being better equipped to deal with the anxieties specific to the age in which they were created. Fianna Fáil was built upon a narrative in which past and present coalesced, so that progress was justified by its racial uniqueness. Fianna Fáil's aesthetic functioned not only to define what was appropriate, and thereby inclusive, but also that which was not suitable or conducive to national regeneration. In this regard, the party ostensibly queered that which did not contribute to its vision. As we will see in Chapter 4, the party presented Cumann na nGaedheal as weak, emasculated and subservient, functioning to serve the whims of its British master. Moreover, the queering of Cumann na nGaedheal as British lapdog enabled Fianna Fáil to strengthen its masculine bona fides by juxtaposing itself as virile and strong. Such a positioning served to reinforce the Irish Masculine as being most suitable for parentage with the Irish Feminine. Moreover, the queering of what the party deemed as overly Anglophilistic served to correct Ireland's narrative arc by actively working to destroy any vestige of English presence.

An astute reader will have noticed a subtle utilisation of scholarship on fascism to underpin the arguments and analyses contained herein. This was not accidental, nor was it an attempt to subtly claim that Fianna Fáil was – or is – fascist. After all, there were the Blueshirts, an overtly fascist party in Ireland.[46] Rather, the intent has been to draw upon fascist historiography as a way to understand interwar Europe and the myriad forces and anxieties inherent therein – and to find solutions to the unique problems of the era. *Ireland's New Traditionalists* is not the first work to dance around the question of Fianna Fáil's similarities with fascist movements. Indeed, Joe Lee contends that 'Fianna Fáil . . . most effectively harnessed [the] potential' of fascism.[47] Moreover, Lee asserts that:

> Some isolated resemblances can certainly be detected between fascist and Fianna Fáil rhetoric. The more strident versions of integral nationalism favoured on some Fianna Fáil platforms could veer close to the fascist variant. Aspects of Fianna Fáil's autarkic economic policy were reminiscent of fascist panaceas. Some Fianna Fáil spokesmen clung to the ideas of an agrarian utopia as insistently as any fascist rhetorician. And Fianna Fáil certainly possessed the type of charismatic leader cherished by fascist ideologies.[48]

At most we can claim that Fianna Fáil was fascistic, for the reasons listed here by Lee. However, Lee's reading of Fianna Fáil as potentially fascistic is largely based on the party's organisational polity. Nonetheless, the point here is not to make any assertion as to de Valera and Fianna Fáil being better at fascism than the Blueshirts or having any relation to the myriad forms of global fascism contemporaneous to the era discussed herein.

My aim has been to use approaches deployed by scholars on fascism as an interwar European phenomenon as an entry point to understanding Fianna Fáil as a product of this era, especially as it relates to the construction of gender as a means to 'correct' an Ireland underdeveloped and oppressed by Britain and the Irish Free State. Ara H. Merjian writes that it is 'through the refractive lens of aesthetics – whether visual or verbal, high or low – that the public and private spheres of fascist life become inexorably intertwined, and where the lines between individual sexuality and collective politics become indistinguishable'.[49] Antliff argues that fascistic political projects emerged from concerns about the dehumanisation of industrialisation, the 'globalization of capitalism', as well as Marxian socialism, which sought to remove individualistic expression in exchange for the greater whole.[50] Building upon Antliff's assertions that fascistic movements did not emerge from a vile, destructive ideology – as many would later become – Fianna Fáil constructed its nationalist efforts at a time when there was a general dissatisfaction with the liberal/Marxian binary, as well as an appreciation of the need for corrective frameworks. For Germany, Italy and Spain, this 'third-way' alternative to liberal capitalism and Marxian socialism was a means to destroy the remnants of the *ancien regime*, or to assuage anxieties regarding industrialisation and the emasculation that followed the Great War.[51]

A study of Fianna Fáil's nationalist rhetoric and aesthetic nationalism finds much in common with movements on the continent. In the case of Ireland, such an approach offered a corrective to the emasculation of colonisation, as well as a framework for Fianna Fáil's plan for a modern state. Further, the party offered a participatory model that Lee contends 'succeeded in capturing the market for the emotional resentment of the excluded underdog, who felt that the political "system" was fixed against them . . . [a]nd Fianna Fáil satisfied the demand for pageantry, and for vicarious participation, among the politically emotive'.[52] Additionally, Lee suggests that Fianna Fáil was most successful in 'exploiting the fascistic rhetoric of nationalism'.[53]

Walter Benjamin asserts that 'the logical result of Fascism is the introduction of aesthetics into political life'.[54] I would add that the aestheticisation of politics was not necessarily unique to fascist states, but instead was a means to cope with anxieties that resulted from the progression of modernity. Lutz Koepnick argues that politics 'becomes aesthetic in fascism because fascism explicitly utilizes the charismatic promise of Great Politics into a viable consumer good, a carefully designed and marketed product that appeals to dormant desires of modern consumers and window shoppers'.[55] Koepnick adds that a political aesthetic of this sort was a 'historically unique endeavor of breaking older bonds of solidarity while simultaneously rendering modern consumerism, including the consumption of charismatic politics, a privileged ticket to national rebirth'.[56] While both Benjamin and Koepnick discuss the inclusion of militancy in the aesthetic of Germany and Italy, the fact that this was not seen in Fianna Fáil's rhetoric adds weight to the argument that the party was not fascist. Yet the inclusion of the aesthetic of national rebirth and 'consumption' of the new nation – or in the case of Fianna Fáil, the renascent republican rhetoric – was fascistic, for Irish politics functioned within the same geo-political zeitgeist as Germany and Italy, and each was informed by similar anxieties.

It can be assumed that the forgetfulness of that anonymous reader of the *Westminster Gazette* discussed above was short-lived, as the success of Fianna Fáil over the next decade did much to rebuff any future questions about the efficacy and vivacity of both de Valera and his party. Such is evidenced in the British parliamentary debates on the passage of the Éire Confirmation Bill in the spring of 1938.[57] In the debate, it is clear that – with few notable exceptions – parliament was no longer concerned with forcing Ireland's hand regarding the custodianship of the Irish Free State. On 4 May 1938, Secretary of State for the Dominions Malcolm MacDonald quoted King George VI's response to the name change that was central to the bill:

> His Majesty's government in the United Kingdom takes note of Articles 2, 3 and 4 of the new Constitution. They cannot recognise that the adoption of the name Éire or Ireland, or any other provisions of those Articles, involves any right to territory or jurisdiction over territory forming part of the United Kingdom of Great Britain and Northern Ireland, or affects in any way the position of Northern Ireland as an integral part of the United Kingdom of Great Britain and Northern Ireland. They therefore regard the use of the name Éire or Ireland in this connection as relating only to that area, which has hitherto been known as the Irish Free State.[58]

But in his response to the eventual passage of the bill, the ardently outspoken opponent of Éamon de Valera, Winston Churchill, stated:

An Irish Parliament, freely assembled, accepted the Treaty by a majority. That Treaty has been kept in the letter and the spirit by Great Britain, but the Treaty has been violated and repudiated in every detail by Mr. de Valera, quite consistently, because he had already rebelled against his colleagues who had made the Treaty in his despite. He has repudiated, practically for all purposes, the Crown. He has repudiated appeal to the Privy Council. He has repudiated the financial agreement. He claims to have set up an independent sovereign Republic for Ireland, and he avows his determination to have all Ireland subject to that independent Republic.[59]

To which William Gallacher replied: 'Good luck to him.'[60] Such was evidence of Britain's attitude towards the attempts by Ireland – via Fianna Fáil – to establish a state independent of British rule. The most interesting element of Churchill's tirade – apart from its obvious vitriol – was the repeated acknowledgement that the current state of Ireland was the result of de Valera's actions. Granted, this might be indicative of Churchill's personal feelings towards de Valera, but the fact that Fianna Fáil had dramatically shifted Anglo-Irish discourse regarding the formation of an Irish republic was irrefutable. Was the economic war won because of Fianna Fáil's mobilisation of female consumers or by its ability to best cloak itself in the rhetoric of manly, active, economic progressivism? Perhaps not. Yet the ability of the party to mobilise an electoral majority of the Irish people to support its efforts to create a republican nation cannot be questioned.

CHAPTER 1

Fianna Fáil's Immodest Innovation, 1926–31

At the 1927 Sinn Féin ard fheis Mary MacSwiney denounced those of her former colleagues who had splintered off to form Fianna Fáil, lamenting not just the move but also their rejection of Sinn Féin's policy of abstention from the Free State Dáil. MacSwiney feared that this new departure, and Fianna Fáil's plan to circumvent the oath of allegiance to the English monarch and thereby enter the Dáil, could destroy an iteration of Sinn Féin that represented the core of dissident Irish republicanism forged in the wake of the Irish civil war:

> Within the past twelve months certain of our colleagues inaugurated a new departure which would involve letting the Republic remain in abeyance for an unspecified time, while on certain conditions, the Free State Parliament is to be worked in the hope of giving that 'Irish interpretation' to its acts, and winning the people back step by step to their true allegiance.
>
> But we have seen where steps and stepping stones have led already. In 1922 when a way to peace was being explored Republicans refused to accept any agreement based on the acceptance of the Treaty position. Why should that be right in 1926 which was wrong in 1922? Yet that is what the new policy involves.[1]

Indeed, what was sacrosanct in 1922 for mainstream republicans was viewed as negotiable in the wake of Fianna Fáil's new departure. For MacSwiney, Fianna Fáil's formation was tantamount to a rejection of the principled stance on the treaty that ended the Anglo-Irish war, and thereby apostacy to republican dogma. Most telling is the final sentence where MacSwiney questioned why Fianna Fáil had changed its stance on the oath. For Fianna Fáil, the answer was not just the passé nature of Sinn Féin abstentionism, but a desire to reconstitute, or at least evolve, Irish republicanism to a level of electoral stability and viability within the democratic frameworks of the Irish Free State. The split from Sinn Féin was only the first step for Fianna Fáil, and this chapter seeks to examine the path traversed by the party in the years leading up to its election into government in 1932.

Fianna Fáil was created by dissident republicans who opted to split from Sinn Féin in 1926. Éamon de Valera led the movement, eventually scuppering Sinn Féin's policy of abstention from the Free State Dáil, rejecting the oath, as well as claims to the legitimacy of the insurgent 3rd Dáil. Fianna Fáil opted to develop an electoral policy that enabled it to participate within the Free State Dáil as a republican alternative to Sinn Féin.[2] Yet, in its infancy, Fianna Fáil expended considerable effort in distinguishing itself as a viable alternative – if not corrective – to Sinn Féin republicanism, and the perceived, if not constructed, Britonism of the Irish Free State. As such, Fianna Fáil's first five years were dedicated to allaying fears regarding its intent, as well as its associations with physical force insurgents. Put another way, Fianna Fáil worked to establish a realistic party narrative and aesthetic that was electorally viable in the Irish Free State, one that rejected the fraught waters of the recent past, while at the same time offered a path towards a fully independent republic. Primarily, the party had to distinguish itself as a variant of republicanism that had evolved away from the intransigent politics of its forbears. This was done in the face of withering opposition from Cumann na nGaedheal and its former comrades at a time when the nation was still recovering from the violence and political schisms of the previous decade. Thus, the party had one eye on functioning within the political wake of the civil war and the other on forging an Irish republic. Such is revealed in the party's electoral aesthetic and ideological underpinning during the period 1926–31.

Fianna Fáil in its first decade expended considerable energy in justifying its existence while at the same time constructing an appealingly electable and viable variant of Irish republicanism suited for the Free State. Apart from its organisational machinations, the party's greatest concern lay within its ability to successfully convince the Irish populace that its renascent republicanism was something more than Sinn Féin *redux*. In short, this chapter is about a party-cum-nationalist movement intent on justifying its place in a new political structure accepted as Ireland's political reality. From its inception, Fianna Fáil had to adopt an electoral aesthetic that consciously shed any physical or rhetorical associations with Sinn Féin abstentionism and physical force insurgency while at the same time working to restate the tenets of republicanism; defend accusations that the party was illogical, illegal, violent, and intent on undermining the security and stability of the Free State; and demonstrate that it could function without disrupting the Free State's burgeoning democracy. In short, Fianna Fáil intended to evolve republicanism, in turn striving to recast the movement as a historically progressive nationalist project.[3] Indeed, Fianna Fáil's earliest hurdles were historical in nature, in that they had to reconcile, correct and even accept the realities of Ireland's recent history, namely the treaty, the Free State, and the bleak future of the 3rd Dáil. Fianna Fáil needed to accept these realities if for no other reason than to demonstrate to the Irish electorate that it had learned the lessons of the recent past, and to evolve, to envision anew and at times to act the conscious amnesiac, selective in its memory of what had gone before. In this regard, the party actively sought to reshape the republican – and by extension Ireland's – narrative, redirecting the backward gaze through selective connections to Ireland's past, but more importantly to forge an imagined future of its own construct. De Valera and his followers needed to reconstitute the very tenets of republicanism if they were to succeed in creating an independent state. Within the relatively popular Free State, this new departure worked in Fianna Fáil's favour, as the party was, in Eunan O'Halpin's words, 'unencumbered by impolitic absolutes, [and was] a party of reality in place of a party of dreams, one in which aspirational rhetoric would complement rather than prevent participation in practical politics'.[4] It is this 'aspirational rhetoric' that will serve as the basis for this chapter.

Fianna Fáil aspired to more than simply remaking Sinn Féin republicanism – they sought to reconstitute the political, cultural, economic and social structures of an aspirational Éire. In this sense, Fianna Fáil had something more on its mind than simply transgressing Sinn Féin and entering the Free State Dáil.[5] Fundamentally, in its earliest years, Fianna Fáil functioned to construct a new national narrative, with 1926 as the birth of a new era that featured a new approach to electoral politics, where Fianna Fáil's voice was *the* authoritative voice in reshaping Ireland's socio-political discourse. Evident within this discourse was a need by Fianna Fáil to offer a corrective: to the 'stigma' of a feminised republican movement, including the equivocation over the oath; to the lingering connection between the Free State and Great Britain, especially related to matters of governance, land and economy; to the perceived extra-constitutionality of Irish republicanism; to the cultural imbalances – along gendered lines – caused by the legacies of Ireland's relationship to Britain. These are the general things to which Fianna Fáil aspired, and a study of its internal and external electoral aesthetic and approach reveals a party concerned with a multi-faceted and nuanced variant of republicanism suited for success within the Irish Free State. O'Halpin categorises the period 1922 to '32 'as a vindication of constitutionality and liberal democracy; as a triumph for decency, for pragmatism, and for modest innovation'.[6] Fianna Fáil, in short, was akin to an immodest innovator, offering a protean republicanism that acted as an advocate of an electoral polity that served as a brake to Cumann na nGaedheal's hegemony in the Irish Free State.

The politics of this era functioned as a continuation of the Irish civil war. They were also informed by the growing pains of a new nation. Bill Kissane applies to Ireland theories advanced by Juan Linz, averring that a political 're-equilibration' occurred, where 'de Valera's transformation of the Free State regime of the 1920s . . . resulted in a political system with a higher degree of legitimacy and effectiveness than that under [William] Cosgrave, without ever departing from democratic rules and methods'.[7] Linz argues that re-equilibration occurs when a nation's democratic principles – or at least one with fundamentally democratic structures – are threatened by some form of a crisis that 'results in their continued existence at the same or higher levels of democratic legitimacy, efficacy or effectiveness'.[8] As such, the Free State period – leading up to the formation of Éire in 1937 – was one of political re-equilibration when

Ireland maintained its democratic foundations through a 'profound transformation of the existing regime, but not [its] democratic institutions'.[9] The politics of this period were indeed marked by two dominant political parties struggling to shape the democratic culture within Ireland. Further, Kissane argues that 'a basic pre-condition of the re-equilibration process lies in the commitment of the new leadership to finding democratic methods for the resolution of particular intractable political problems'.[10] The political rivalry between Fianna Fáil and Cumann na nGaedheal did indeed drive the re-equilibration of the Irish state, in turn securing Irish democracy, yet there is a cultural component underlying this 'balancing' of the Irish state – an immodest innovation that recalibrated the nature of Irish republicanism.[11]

On the surface, the process of re-equilibration does much to explain the ability of Irish democracy to survive the tumult of the post-civil war era. Moreover, this model neatly describes the stakes of the dialectic between Fianna Fáil and Cumann na nGaedheal. Yet, for Fianna Fáil, the struggle was more than mere survival – it was engaged in a process that aspired to reconstitute the Irish state along republican lines. As such, the history of the period 1926–32 is marked by the electorate's drift away from Cumann na nGaedheal, 'believing', as Jason Knirck asserts, 'that Fianna Fáil was the better choice to govern as the revolution faded into memory'.[12] Fianna Fáil's success as an electoral party in the Free State era had much to do with its ability to recast republicanism as constitutionalist – at least in its willingness to remake Ireland through negotiation and electioneering. This, in short, was the foundation for Fianna Fáil's re-equilibration – an opportunity that was advantageous for Fianna Fáil, as the general absence of references to the 'revolution' reified its futurist gaze – towards an Ireland not borne from recent struggles, but an aspirational republic built from the centuries-long association between land and people.

Knirck advances a thesis that Cumann na nGaedheal undercut the republican movement by saddling its republican opposition as a feminised party, marked by irrational, emotional, extra-legal and violent behaviour. He notes that Cumann na nGaedheal made much of Irish women's 'increasingly high profile within nationalist politics and were thus seen as critical cogs in the developing revolutionary machines'.[13]

Moreover, Knirck adds that 'Cumann na nGaedheal politicians struggled to create a Free State/republican opposition and then blurred it with the more recognizable and resonant male/female opposition. In their quest to define a politics that excluded and delegitimized republicans, Cumann na nGaedheal defined a politics that excluded and delegitimized women.'[14] The growing success of Cumann na nGaedheal and, in turn, the Irish Free State represented a victory for that party's gendered discourse. Concurrent with this was the decrease in interest in revolutionary rhetoric, which led to Sinn Féin being further marginalised in the political constructs of the Free State. In turn, Fianna Fáil's response to these attacks by Cumann na nGaedheal also had a gendered component, in that the party seemed to consciously de-feminise its electoral discourse and aesthetic during the Free State period. Given the evidence laid out below, it is nothing if not a major coincidence that Fianna Fáil was so explicit in presenting itself as a masculinist party averse to violence and irrationality. Indeed, as will be shown in Chapter 4, Fianna Fáil returned the favour by presenting Cumann na nGaedheal/Fine Gael as an emasculated, impotent party acting in submission to its British master.

By distancing itself from what R.V. Comerford refers to as 'physical force insurgency',[15] as well as the feminised Sinn Féin, Fianna Fáil in turn embraced an approach to democratic republicanism where logic, the rule of law and a general espousal of legislative insurrection became the means to both distinguish itself from previous incarnations of republicanism and engage more effectively in a socio-political dialectic with Cumann na nGaedheal. Such was the reality for a party revolting 'against the tyranny of the dead'.[16] Fianna Fáil leaders justified their transgression by undermining what they viewed as a multi-faceted British entity with iterations strewn across Ireland in the guise of Dublin Castle, the Free State Dáil and constitution, and in the Irish soil. As such, the period between 1926 and '32 featured Fianna Fáil promoting a party rhetoric which promoted a backward gaze, drawing upon elements of past nationalist movements in order to justify advancing Irish independence beyond the Anglo-inclined Free State. Fundamentally, Fianna Fáil attained legitimacy through its public rejection of the previous decade's militancy, clarifying its distinctiveness from Sinn Féin, and assuaging fears that a Fianna Fáil government would mean further bloodshed –

despite Cumann na nGaedheal claiming otherwise. The party further legitimated itself by advancing a socio-political discourse that advocated reform through legislative practice rather than militant revolution. This approach resulted in the renewed relevance of republican discourse that would provide the foundations for an independent Irish republic.

Fianna Fáil's approach served not only to combat the party's gendered associations; it also created a distinct break from the revolutionary-republican approach of the IRA and Sinn Féin. Given the Irish public's distaste for further bloodshed, there was *de facto* support for the institutions of the Irish Free State. Additionally, Fianna Fáil found it necessary to abandon its top-down authoritarian approach towards attaining a republic, in favour of a more inclusive, participatory movement suitable for operation within an Ireland transitioning to relative autonomy. As Bill Kissane notes, 'After the civil war de Valera did not directly shift from an undemocratic position to a democratic one – he shifted from authoritarianism to ambiguity, and then to democracy'.[17] Further, the entrance of Fianna Fáil into the political fray created a new two-party system which further democratised the Irish populace, at least in terms of attracting potential voters to the electoral dialectic. However, as will be shown in later chapters, Fianna Fáil went much further, constructing a nationalist project that aspired to being the social and economic foundations of Ireland. Indeed, it adopted a discourse that aligned the Irish populace into gendered roles, making them active agents advancing the republican cause.

Fianna Fáil was born as much from the politics of the civil war as from the failings of Sinn Féin republicanism to adapt to the relatively democratic constructs on offer in the 1920s. De Valera's new approach proved effective because the Anglo-Irish trappings of the Free State enabled Fianna Fáil to present its republicanism as a movement of reform and reconstruction, rather than a militaristic movement. What we find, therefore, in a study of Fianna Fáil's rhetoric in its first half-decade, is a party that actively engaged Cumann na nGaedheal in a democratic dialectic, in direct contrast to Sinn Féin's guerrilla style of republicanism that sought reform from without. The most intriguing aspect of Fianna Fáil's reclamation of republican discourse lay within its efforts to recognise and adapt to the changing nature of Irish politics, thereby eschewing connections to past militancy. Part of this change was the emergence of Cumann na nGaedheal as a mass party, effective in its leadership and its ability to create a stable, democratic state. Donnacha Ó Beacháin notes: 'How the citizenry are to be motivated to mobilise from the habitual passivity depends on the quality and quantity of political communication with the electorate.'[18] Moreover, Fianna Fáil was a mass party, which Mel Farrell argues was marked by 'the willingness to form local branches, thereby marshalling followers through the official organizational structures', and by extending 'the influence by "educating" their members in the workings of the political process'.[19] The political broadsides issued by Fianna Fáil during this period were as much pedagogical as ameliorative. Further, they were part of what Joe Lee describes as the 'superior organisational ability' of Fianna Fáil which 'crushed Sinn Féin as a political party within a year'.[20]

Following the Anglo-Irish war and the Irish civil war, republicanism was associated with violence, not to mention quixotic notions of external association and, ultimately, complete independence from Great Britain.[21] Specifically, Cumann na nGaedheal employed epideictic rhetoric to stoke public fear that a republican thrust meant further violence. Thus, de Valera and Fianna Fáil had not only to combat the albatross of militarism, but also the connections to an era from which the people of Ireland sought to escape. As such, Fianna Fáil was to spend the initial portion of the formative era demonstrating that it was *not* Sinn Féin – that it was not irrational, emotional or, most importantly, a harbinger of a new *belle Gaeilge*. Ultimately, because of its ability to reconstitute republicanism as being logical, pacifist and democratic, Fianna Fáil emerged from the shadow of the gunmen to fully engage in the political dialectic of the Saorstát.

MACSWINEY, DE VALERA, AND THE END OF INDEPENDENCE-ERA SINN FÉIN

Sinn Féin, by 1926, had already shown signs of fissure, and the republican divorce was played out in public and in private. An internal civil war of letters between Mary MacSwiney and de Valera reveals the irreconcilable differences between past and present republicanism. The correspondence tells a lot about the diverging ideologies of Irish republicanism – especially as it related to Fianna Fáil's desire to evolve the movement's positionality vis-à-vis abstention and the level to which the party would engage with the Free State. On another level, the letters symbolise a facet of re-equilibration that was manifest in the party's electoral aesthetic, in that the party was intent on accepting as fact the existence of the Free State, in turn rejecting the 3rd Dáil. Kissane notes that 'a basic pre-condition for a re-equilibration process lies in the commitment of the new leadership to finding democratic methods for the resolution of particularly intractable political problems'.[22] The myriad intractable problems faced by Fianna Fáil in 1926 included the oath, the memory – and cost – of the civil war, abstention, the spectre of future republican violence, and republicanism's generally distasteful public visage. In short, Fianna Fáil needed to employ democratically viable methods to address these matters head-on: in the Dáil, on the public rostrum, in the country and in the cities. In essence, Fianna Fáil found itself fighting a discursive battle on two fronts – on the one hand they were challenging the authority and legitimacy of the political frameworks of the Saorstát and its party of government; on the other, they found it necessary to distance themselves from the radical Sinn Féin and the organisations with which the latter was associated.

A study of the struggle between old and new republicans reveals much about the distinctions between the two ideologies and makes clear the approach taken by Fianna Fáil. The largest point of contention between the two parties involved Fianna Fáil's entrance into the Dáil. More than anything else, the new departure polarised the two camps, with each arguing for the legitimacy of rival Dáils: that of the Irish Free State and that of the 2nd Dáil, which had drawn legitimacy from events transpiring before the treaty which ended the Anglo-Irish war. It is fair to say that the political platform espoused by Fianna Fáil was best suited to succeed within the democratic frameworks of the Free State. As such, by juxtaposing the republican movements, one can get a clearer picture of the wider scope put forth by Fianna Fáil.

Mary MacSwiney, in 1927, challenged Fianna Fáil's new approach:

> We fully appreciate the work which Éamon de Valera has done for Ireland and the place which he has won for himself in the hearts of his countrymen. That makes his new policy all the more

disappointing, but not even his personality can commend this compromise to us ...

For it is the proclamation of the Republic in 1916, and its constitutional establishment [in] 1919, that makes the new departure a matter of principle and a step backward.[23]

Ironically, MacSwiney's letter spoke of moving forward together while remaining anchored to the republic of 1916/19. Indeed, she was correct in asserting that the formation of Fianna Fáil represented a new departure, but, in stating that the party was taking a step backwards, MacSwiney's argument embodied the myopia shown by those who remained aligned to Sinn Féin policy.

Writing to fellow Sinn Féiner Michael O'Donnell in 1927, MacSwiney suggested a redoubling of Sinn Féin policy, pinning their hopes on the Irish electorate supporting a united republicanism – going so far as to suggest that Fianna Fáil and Sinn Féin join forces to overtake Cumann na nGaedheal and thereby undermine the Free State. However, as noted above, MacSwiney had defined Irish republicanism in 1916/19 terms, in turn ignoring the realities of the Free State and renewing commitment to the militant anti-Britishness that had long marked Sinn Féin's policy. In a letter dated 25 April, she wrote:

> I believe that united action could be taken and that a majority could thereby be secured, provided that the Republican position can be safeguarded ... In effect, Mr. de Valera is asking the people of Ireland and especially Republicans, to do now what we consistently refused to do in 1922, that is to 'accept the Treaty position, but not the Treaty'. That is impossible for those who really believe in the Republic. Could not F.F. be brought to give up that part of their policy which makes united action impossible? [...]
>
> Though I had no idea of it at the time Mr. de Valera was already discussing the Fianna Fáil policy, so nothing was done.[24]

The last part of this statement is of the greatest interest, for it alludes to the fact that de Valera was already engaged in an ideological split from Sinn Féin as far back as 1922. Indeed, de Valera's rhetoric and decidedly non-military positioning dated back to at least 1919, when he toured the country advancing ideas that he would incorporate into *Document #2*. Further, as MacSwiney's words highlight, Fianna Fáil's greatest challenge among republicans was to justify its entrance into the Dáil in such a manner that it would not appear to be acting the supplicant. In other words, the party could not be seen to be weak and having accepted defeat, nor as angry radicals bringing chaos and disruption to the Free State Dáil. Nonetheless, MacSwiney's letter explicates Fianna Fáil's fundamental need to shed associations with Sinn Féin.

In the months prior to the 1927 election, de Valera travelled to the United States in order to raise funds for what he hoped would be a Fianna Fáil-based newspaper and to raise awareness of and support for his new party. At the same time, MacSwiney worried that de Valera's turn in America had 'muddled thinking', by making speeches that were 'out and out Republican. That and the name – [Fianna Fáil, the] Republican Party – have deceived many.'²⁵ Thus the political campaign for Fianna Fáil against Sinn Féin in the United States was conducted on two fronts – the money-raising effort, and the effort to encourage Irish-Americans to embrace the party's new nationalist project. In other words, the move from Sinn Féin went deeper than just a political shift: it was intent on stealing away the right to be called *the* Irish republican party. De Valera not only sought to redefine the nature of republicanism, but also to co-opt trans-Atlantic networks so that they aligned to – and funded – his vision of the republican future. This action speaks to his effort to evolve the movement towards a new positionality where definitions of republicanism were manifest through Fianna Fáil.

Fianna Fáil's split from Sinn Féin and entrance into the Dáil initially meant that the party lacked the numbers to win a majority in future elections. Fianna Fáil would, at times, find it necessary to form coalition governments in the 1930s and beyond, but these would be constructed as evanescent partnerships with such myriad minor parties as Labour or the Farmer's Party. Despite the republican kinship, Fianna Fáil would never form a coalition with Sinn Féin. This demonstrated de Valera's adamant refusal to be associated with the militant republicans, but it also sheds light on how Fianna Fáil was intent on being seen as offering a different kind of republicanism. The party refused to consider a coalition with Sinn Féin, thus eschewing any possibility of forming a majority in the

Dáil. This may strike one as being rather anachronistic, for Sinn Féin itself was seemingly intransigent in its own policy of abstention from the Dáil. However, a confidential letter written to de Valera by MacSwiney reveals that gestures had been made to reconcile the two parties and put forth a united, republican effort. Less than three weeks after her letter to O'Donnell, MacSwiney wrote:

A Chara:[26]

During your absence [in America] there has been, as I have no doubt you know, a great deal of talk, unofficial of course, about a possible understanding between your people and Sinn Féin. I have been approached on the matter and I have said, and I think most of my colleagues agree with me, *that I see no reason why we could not join together and make a big effort, which I believe would be most successful, or a majority.* The difficulty is the minority position for which directly or indirectly I for one would not stand. It has been suggested that a majority is almost a certainty; that we could negotiate for that and make no stipulation about the minority; *that if afterwards the minority resulted, and your people did things we could not stand by, we would not be responsible.*[27]

Two lines from this excerpt are particularly striking. The first is the aforementioned suggestion that Sinn Féin was willing to retreat from its policy of abstention and enter the Dáil, and the second is the last line, in which MacSwiney conceded the differences between the two parties by suggesting that they would be united as a majority but divided in minority. It appears as if MacSwiney was advocating taking this ideological schism between the republican parties to the level of the Dáil and having the voters decide which of the two they preferred. Conversely, her plan might be seen as a political rehashing of the Irish civil war, in which a united republican cause – however tentative – could destroy the Free State Dáil from within, in turn forming the basis for an independent state. Further, MacSwiney suggested that a minority coalition between Fianna Fáil and Sinn Féin should retain abstention, but in majority, the two could – and should – ignore the oath.

As the letter continued, MacSwiney's tone changed dramatically:

That is what I call a Pontius Pilate attitude, and I will have nothing to do with it anyhow. You have declared that there will be no going into the Parliament unless the oath will be removed. There is not one chance in a thousand that the oath will be removed if you only get a minority. Would it not be worth while telling that to the people, and promising not to use the minority position this time in order that we might join together and rouse the enthusiasm of the people, which seems from all I hear possible to do at this juncture. That is why I write to you . . . [others] may not approve of my writing, but, I feel bound not to lose what seems an excellent chance for lack of this appeal to you.

I have been told that your party are pledged to the minority position, I don't think that argument holds good in view of the situation with which we are faced, and you will forgive me if I say that the argument reminds me very much of Cosgrave's notion of his honour which binds him to keep word faithfully to England though he may break it with impunity to his own fellow countrymen.[28]

The rhetorical flourish of calling de Valera Pilate is in line with the propensity by members of Sinn Féin to position themselves as dogmatic martyrs. In this case, de Valera, like Pilate, is sentencing a visionary to an unfair death, thus demonstrating an ignorance of the True Word. Name-calling aside, it appears that in the second half of the letter MacSwiney rescinds her offer of a coalition, noting that a minority position would do nothing but destroy the republican cause, in turn giving greater strength to Cosgrave and the perception that he and his party sought to maintain ties to Great Britain.

Four days later, de Valera responded in a rather pithy and terse tone:

A Chara:

I received your letter on the 11th inst. I am not going to give a complete reply because I have explained my position so often before.

What you call the 'minority' position of FIANNA FAIL[29] *is an essential part of the whole program, and to give it up would be to cripple the policy as a whole.* Knowing your attitude on this question, and being as convinced that I am right as you are that you are right, I feel that we can only agree to differ.

I do not know what SINN FEIN will do in the matter of preference votes in the coming elections, but we at any rate are determined to see that no Republican votes on our side are lost. It is a pity Sinn Fein cannot see eye to eye with us on our policy as a whole, for I believe that together on that program we would be almost certain of success.

Do Chara,

Éamon de Valéra.[30]

One of the most striking elements of de Valera's letter is that he promotes the idea of Fianna Fáil being a larger, more comprehensive movement that transcended the singular issue of entering the Dáil – a major distinction for a party that elevated electability and national appeal. Whereas Sinn Féin was most successful in the chaotic period between Easter 1916 and the treaty debates, its approach had become outdated the moment the Irish Free State was established. Intransigent zealotry would not succeed in a country tired of war. The creation of a 32-county republic would not succeed as long as unionists dominated in Ulster. A reactionary political discourse would not succeed in a country stabilised by the relative successes of the Saorstát government. De Valera understood that Sinn Féin's variant of republicanism could not work and that the only way to establish a republic was through larger, institutional changes. That is, republicans needed to do more than break the symbolic chains of British authority; they needed to destroy and rebuild the entirety of Irish socio-political and economic master narratives. Operating outside of the Free State, using reactionary methods, could not work within the system accepted by the Irish public. Further, the final two lines of de Valera's letter suggest that he would only reconcile with Sinn Féiners if they embraced his way of thinking. Nevertheless, in the years that followed this exchange, Sinn Féin hardened its militant stance, repeating calls for an armed uprising against the Free State and the British, essentially ensuring its spot in the political wilderness.

'[AN] APPRECIATION OF THE POSITION': FROM DOCUMENT #2
TO PAMPHLET #2

Freedom from tyranny in the guise of monarchism, elevation of the
cult of the electorate, rule of law, and an embrace of human reason as a
progressive force are some of the hallmarks of liberal thought.[31] Philip
Pettit writes:

> Freedom as non-domination, as the French tradition spelled it
> out, required equality and indeed fraternity. It called for a scenario
> in which each could walk tall, secure in the knowledge that no one
> could lord it over them. Each could count on the support of others
> against any would-be dominating power. And so each could look
> others in the eye, seeing a fellow-citizen there, and not anyone
> possessed of special privileges. No one had to live at the mercy of
> another, no one had to hang on the grace and favour of a lord . . .
> [Republicans] thought of freedom as the supreme political value and
> they equated freedom with not being stood over by anyone, even a
> benevolent and protective master. To enjoy republican freedom was
> to be able to hold your head on high, to look others squarely in the
> eye, and to relate to your fellows without fear or deference.[32]

Liberal, democratic thought had permeated into the larger European
master narrative as a foundational aspect of European and western
modernity. To establish a democratic state was to also become a
legitimate partner to the western democracies of the North Atlantic.
Moreover, the espousal of such ideology included a subtle rejection
of freedom as attained by militant or even irrational means. What
distinguished Fianna Fáil from its republican predecessors was the
appreciation of this ideology as a means to an end – legitimacy within
an already-extant democratic framework. This difference speaks to the
fundamental political transformation heralded by the creation of the
Irish Free State. Such a situation opened the way for Fianna Fáil to evolve
Irish republicanism from a revolutionary to a national policy. As such,
an explicit and unwavering public discourse cloaked in notions of logic,
freedom, and the advocacy of the will of the people was a key factor
in allowing Fianna Fáil republicanism to reset the gendered albatross

of its previous incarnation as Sinn Féin. In other words, it became the ideological foundation upon which the new party could most successfully combat the pro-Treaty – but not necessarily un-republican – rhetoric of Cumann na nGaedheal and the Irish Free State.

The ability to present a clear vision of what an Irish republic would entail was a key factor in determining the success of Fianna Fáil. While combating associations with the so-called 'gunmen' was vital in giving peace of mind to those concerned about a renewal of bloodshed, de Valera's party was clear in its intentions to achieve what it defined as an independent state through political means. Viewed through the prism of gendered discourse, the presentation of a new republicanism free from the spectre of revolutionary means represented an overall effort to reset the socio-political narrative of the Free State, where republicanism was restored so as to appear balanced: intellectually and actively anchored in reason and logic (masculine) and free from irrationality and violence (feminine).[33] In justifying its existence, then, Fianna Fáil borrowed much from the rhetoric and ideologies of Enlightenment-era thinkers and movements, finding validation in promoting the will of the people, the rule of law, and the virtues of logic and reason. It was in this sense that Fianna Fáil sought to expand the political debate in Ireland beyond the treaty/anti-treaty dialectic, and create something larger and, indeed, more participatory. In fact, the ideologies of the *philosophes* provided Fianna Fáil with its *raison d'être*; however, they did not necessarily guide the party in establishing its socio-political and economic platforms. As will be shown in later chapters, Fianna Fáil embraced a much more modern approach to widening its appeal – an approach distinct from the nineteenth-century liberal/radical axiom and more in tune with the newer ideologies specific to the early twentieth century. The concern here, however, relates to how de Valera and his followers wedged themselves into the Free State's political climate.

Speaking to the inaugural meeting of Fianna Fáil at Dublin's La Scala theatre on 16 May 1926, de Valera outlined the party's aims in a speech entitled 'A National Policy'. In the early portion of the speech there appeared a section with the subheading '[An] Appreciation of the position', in which de Valera most clearly enunciated the party's new departure.

> We must not allow ourselves to be hypnotised by our own prejudices
> and feelings on the one hand or by our opponents' propaganda on
> the other. To underestimate our strength is even a worse fault than
> to overestimate it. We must not let our opponents dissuade us from
> attempting a task that is well within our power by suggesting that it
> is impossible . . . We must, if we really want to succeed, endeavour
> to judge the situation *just as it is*, measure our own strength against
> it, lay our plans, and then act with courage and tenacity.[34]

Judging the situation 'as it [was]' enabled de Valera and his followers to
construct a policy that abandoned romantic revolutionary pretence and
instead advanced a national project most suited to the realities of the era.
This meant that the party needed to actively confront such issues as the
oath of allegiance, the victory of the treatyites, and in turn to concede
that the civil war was a thing of the past. For Fianna Fáil, political
relevance in the guise of electability was something far more complex
than positioning oneself against the British bogeyman; rather one had
to confront the Cumann na nGaedheal/Free State hegemony and all of
its connections to England – real and perceived. This recognition of the
situation 'as it was', as opposed to what it should be, was one of the key
differences between the pragmatism of Fianna Fáil and the idealism of
Sinn Féin.

Fianna Fáil's most explicit expression of re-equilibration vis-à-vis
its alignment to Free State democracy can be found in a pamphlet
penned by Frank Gallagher under the rather unimaginative title *Fianna
Fáil, Pamphlet #2*.[35] Throughout, Gallagher decried England's nebulous
relationship to constitutionality, in turn connecting such vagueness to
the constitution of the Irish Free State. This rhetorical turn served two
purposes: to call into question the legal, logical and historical validity
of the Free State constitution by way of its perceived Englishness; and
a rather ironic justification for Fianna Fáil's participation within said
government. More broadly, this approach was meant to serve as a brake
on further entrenchment of Cumann na nGaedheal/Irish Free State
hegemony. Citing constitutionalism as a prerequisite for order and
progress, Gallagher wrote:

> A nation may enjoy prosperity and be at peace without international
> alliances; men can be happy and free without being members of
> a party or an organisation. But to the people making up a nation
> agreement is indispensable as to the rules under which their joint life
> is to be lived. Before they can have national or corporate existence
> they must decide upon the fundamental principles by which their
> common affairs will be directed, their common progress and safety
> assured, and their common ideals realised. If such agreement is
> lacking a nation slips back into tribalism.[36]

In this particular statement, Gallagher called into question the validity
of a nation derived from an imposed tradition, as opposed to one that
emerges from the will of the people, essentially challenging the very
authority and legitimacy of the Free State. Further, Gallagher was clearly
advancing the Fianna Fáil party line that sought to establish a discursive
and distasteful Free State/Cumann na nGaedheal–British axis which
in turn invalidated all that had been created in the wake of the treaty.
Indeed, Gallagher ignores the democratic origins of the Free State while
at the same time recognising its position as the current government of
Ireland – a major evolution from Sinn Féin. However, Gallagher situates
the Free State as a submissive, derivative state – note the use of 'they'
to represent a people on the verge of a political wilderness, searching
for a set of common ideals. Gallagher's attack on the legitimacy of the
Free State continued with his assertion that, without a citizenry-derived
constitution, a nation would degenerate into 'a mob at loggerheads with
itself'.[37] 'Where a people have by alien force been denied the exercise of
their liberties,' he continued, 'this unwritten Constitution has a more vivid
reality, a more persistent influence. Because the so-called Constitution
under which such a people are governed is not the expression of their
genius, their individuality, or their ideals, the unwritten Constitution
more than ever dominates the national mind.'[38] The struggle against a
government derived from an imagined or coerced tradition was one of
the hallmarks of democratic thought.

The Whiggish notion of human progress was a fundamental thrust
of Atlantic revolutionaries – an ideal that presented them as being at the
vanguard of human inevitability. In turn, Gallagher noted:

Towards the end of the eighteenth century, when feudal systems
and absolute monarchies began to topple in Europe and America,
the peoples had learned their lesson in much bitterness. They
had learned that there must be one law that was fundamental,
a declaration of rights with which all laws must conform, some
infrangible [*sic*] decree safeguarding humanity of tyranny and
absolutism. The need was so apparent that long before Louis goes
to the guillotine, the popularly chosen Constituent Assembly of
France has adopted the Constitution; long before Britain is driven
out of America the Declaration of Independence, which is also a
declaration of rights, is adopted at Philadelphia long before the
guerrilla war reaches its full vigour and scope . . . in Ireland the first
Dáil Éireann has declared the freedom of the Irish people and its
democratic rights (January 21st 1919).[39]

Apart from the direct connection to the American and French revolutions,
there was an implicit notion that a genuine Irish constitution should be
the inevitable result of the people's movement that began in January
1919. It is also worth noting that Gallagher chose 1919 as the watershed
for Irish independence, thereby side-stepping the revolutionary era of
1919–21. Such was Fianna Fáil's backward gaze that situated the party as
an iteration of a tradition aligned with the constitutional revolutions that
heralded the onset of the modern age. However, this new Irish – Fianna
Fáil – revolution was to be contested at the ballot box and not on the
streets or farms of Ireland. Gallagher added: 'The freed peoples, having
been made wise by long suffering, see into the future and know that the
first act of a liberated democracy must be to lay securely the foundations
of a free national life. The laying of these foundations is completed when
a Constitution is drafted.'[40] But who are these people, and to which
nation do they belong? Using these arguments, the constitution created
in the wake of the treaty and enforced by Cumann na nGaedheal would
hardly suffice; therefore, Gallagher found it necessary to make the case
for a more purely *Irish* constitution. He based such arguments on what
he called the 'force of national tradition'. In order to stave off a return to
tribalism or the continuance of Free State/English tyranny, he suggested
a new constitution be created in the wake of an increasingly powerful

Irish national tradition, something most assuredly not done by Cumann na nGaedheal. Gallagher wrote: 'To devise a basic law for an old nation and in it to ignore the national tradition is folly. But to endeavour to impose a basic law, a Constitution, in flagrant conflict with this tradition is insanity. And so it is proving in Ireland to-day.'[41]

Towards the end of the pamphlet Gallagher made a distinction between the republicanism of Sinn Féin and that of Fianna Fáil. He argued that Sinn Féin lacked the imagination to mount a successful campaign for a new Irish constitution that did not stem from revolution or rely on an abstentionist, and thus divisive, policy. Further, when placed in the context of a national trend towards a truly Irish constitution, the matter of the oath was nothing but a mere tyrannical blockade against the tide of progress. In a section entitled 'An Act of Apostacy [*sic*]' Gallagher stated:

> In face of this analysis it is clear that nobody who believes in Ireland's right to nationhood can take this oath, and that its taking is tantamount to a public act of apostacy [*sic*] to the whole national faith. It is not only an acceptance of, but a most solemn promise to preserve, the instruments forged by Britain for the destruction of that faith. Both 'Treat' [*sic*] and Constitution, violate the *national tradition* and, consequently, cannot lead to peace in Ireland. Yet unless the representatives of the people abjure that tradition and swear to preserve these fomenters of war they are to be excluded from the Free State Parliament. They have no choice, therefore, but to stay out. But as long as they are forced to stay out, the Free State Parliament can be nothing but the headquarters of an *alien domination* holding Ireland for its own profit. History teaches us that such a situation inevitably breeds war. Let the Free State Constitution stand as it now is; let the oath remain. Then the Irish people's only alternative is another national uprising.[42]

For Gallagher, the act of apostasy was not necessarily the renunciation of the Free State Dáil, but rather a clean break from Sinn Féin's policy of revolution from without. Note also Gallagher's assertion of a national tradition – another iteration of Fianna Fáil's backward gaze – wherein Ireland's historical progress was sidelined by the Free State's adherence to Britain's 'alien' domination. Moreover, this passage contains an interesting calculus: that the treaty and the constitution that it enabled were, by association, constructs of alien Great Britain – therefore, the Free State and Cumann na nGaedheal were also alien; further, in a critique of Sinn Féin, abstention and letting the Free State stand meant war. Therefore, Fianna Fáil could negate the threat of war by entering the Free State Dáil and undoing the oath from within. To rebel again would destroy and alienate the 'national tradition'. The path forward was by accentuating Fianna Fáil's democratic bona fides, where the party was a leader of a legitimate movement grounded in reason, peace and law. Gallagher wrote:

> But all doors are happily not yet closed to the people. There is a way out besides the devastating way of the sword. That way is the drafting of a truly Irish Constitution and, as the first step towards the creation of an assembly capable of doing that, the abolition of the oath. These things can be accomplished under the pressure of *public opinion* . . . And if the Irish people united to end the imposition of disgraceful oath and false Constitution [the Free State] would fall as Jericho fell before the clamour of an unanimous action. If the deputies were themselves in the name of the people to uphold an imposed Constitution what force could compel them to act otherwise? None. And the deputies elected by the people are the servants of the people and can be made obey the orders of the people.[43]

Advancing the Fianna Fáil party line that the Free State was a British creation cloaked in Irish clothing, he added: 'The Free State Constitution, like the "Treaty", was made in London and was imposed from London. Documents having such an origin cannot and do not bind the Irish nation. Their origin and their nature are proof that the first duty of Irish nationalists [is] to get rid of them for the nation's sake.'[44] Lest anyone think that he and Fianna Fáil were advocating war, Gallagher made a clear push for future struggles to be fought within the legal and peaceful confines of the Free State Dáil. This push for a legislative thrust that transcended both the oath and the Free State was neatly supported by Gallagher's claim that 'Without a genuine Irish Constitution Ireland must live perpetually wasted by dissension'.[45] *Pamphlet #2* provided a basis for Fianna Fáil's public disavowal of Sinn Féin's physical force insurgency, while justifying intellectually the new party's anti-hegemonic stance. *Pamphlet #2* did more than any other material from this period to distinguish Fianna Fáil from the other republican movements of the early twentieth century in that it placed the party in a position where its ideology was realistic and rooted in the nature of things; a party advancing such a position was, in a word, electable.

Ideology and willingness to accept the trappings of the Free State and the requisite oath were simply not enough to gain votes, nor does the pamphlet on its own explain Fianna Fáil's success in the 1930s. Still, in light of the gendered environment of the 1920s, this pamphlet – representative as it was of Fianna Fáil's electoral rhetoric – did much to shed those elements of republicanism denounced by Free Staters as 'feminised'. Absent from this manifesto were the call to arms; the arguments rooted in emotion; the commemoration of the 'martyrs' of 1916; the pedantic conceit of holding the key to Irish freedom. Instead we find Fianna Fáil aligning itself with the liberal revolutionaries of France and the United States, where constitutionalism and national identity were manifest in the welling up of public emotion. Granted, there is no mention of heads on pikes or of raids on British camps, yet the importance of indirectly aligning the Fianna Fáil movement to the Atlantic revolutions was that it gave the party relevance and legitimacy amid the socio-political atmosphere of Free State Ireland. Put simply, the pamphlet established Fianna Fáil's *raison d'être* as pushing for an Irish constitution to replace the nebulous Free State/England constitution. Moreover, *Pamphlet #2* presages the gendered aesthetic utilised by Fianna Fáil during the economic war. In many ways, *Pamphlet #2* offers a corrective to the feminisation of the republican movement by Cumann na nGaedheal. Though subtext, there is a re-masculinisation present in Gallagher's representative broadside: that Fianna Fáil was a complex and constitutional party, transgressing the Free State from within. It no longer sought to resurrect the 2nd – or legitimate the 3rd – Dáil, but instead worked to serve a heretofore non-existent, yet envisioned, republican constitution. Fianna Fáil's transgression – its re-masculinisation – was done through active and aggressive *political* action; it aspired to be a national party working to correct the incomplete break from Britain and, as will be seen later, to ameliorate Ireland's economic underdevelopment. This was how Fianna Fáil sought to move forward and to function immodestly in the Free State era.

De Valera, in his address to the second Fianna Fáil ard fheis, was most clear in his embracement of a renewed tenor that emphasised logic, rule by law, democratic constructs and progress. People, not ideology, were to be served by this new direction. Early in the speech, de Valera defined the justifications for his party's envisioned republicanism, couching it in terms of national progress and destiny – no doubt a nod to the party's moniker as the soldiers of destiny. De Valera intoned: 'I have often said that behind the State always is the people and the Nation, and if ever you want to build up a real lasting national movement it must be based on the welfare of the people . . . [and] if the Irish people get the right to choose their own governmental institutions without interference, that the choice they would make would be that of a Republic.'[46] This statement represents a marked change from Sinn Féin rhetoric, and served to assuage possible anxieties regarding Fianna Fáil's potential militancy. As such, this break from militancy as a means to an end was better suited for success within the already democratic Free State, not to mention more appealing to a populace ready to move beyond the violence of the recent past. This latter point was made clear when in the same address, de Valera stated that in order to attain a free republic, Fianna Fáil and its followers 'must get a national agreement above that [Free State] constitution as long as it lasts, and the national agreement is an agreement amongst all parties that the representatives of the people, freely elected, free to meet without any political Tests [*sic*] of any kind, may decide by majority rule the national policy for the moment. I see no other way. It is either that way or the appeal to force.'[47] Interestingly, de Valera positioned both the constitution and Cumann na nGaedheal as having a basis in British authority, like Gallagher noting both explicitly and implicitly that neither were of true Irish origin. Further, the rhetoric placed the will of the people as the utmost authority – a power that transcended colonial ties or party affiliation.

In its first national election, Fianna Fáil won forty-four seats, which forced the party's hand regarding its views on the Free State Dáil.[48] The stumbling block was the requisite oath, which, as we have seen, remained as the basis for Sinn Féin's policy of abstention. At the time many, including Mary MacSwiney, viewed Fianna Fáil's entry into the Dáil as an act treasonous to the republican cause, or at least an example of how de Valera and his party had betrayed the movement. Yet, Fianna Fáil's entrance into the Dáil gave the party a major opportunity to demonstrate through actions that it was not Sinn Féin *redux* – that it was hesitatingly willing to play by the rules and operate within the frameworks of the Saorstát. Whereas earlier policy might have resulted in republicans threatening force as a way to combat the oath, the new republicanism of Fianna Fáil grounded its contentions in legal proceedings and critiques of such a requirement.

In response to the killing of key Cumann na nGaedheal party member Kevin O'Higgins on 10 July 1927, which, although unsolved, was blamed on radical republicans, with some implicating members of Fianna Fáil, Dunphy notes that 'Although de Valera strongly condemned the murder, Cumann na nGaedheal, apparently convinced that Fianna Fáil's parliamentary abstention contributed to an atmosphere in which such murders took place, coupled a new Public Safety Act against the IRA . . . with an Electoral Amendment Bill aimed at Fianna Fáil'.[49] One such bill required members of the Dáil to take an oath of office, and provided an early test to Fianna Fáil, namely its willingness to abandon Sinn Féin's policy of abstention. O'Halpin notes that 'de Valera had to choose between being consistent and being constitutional. The decision he made transformed the politics of independent Ireland.'[50] In essence, the acts that resulted from O'Higgins' murder forced the hand of Fianna Fáil and its approach to the oath, as the party would be compelled to address the issue if it were to enter the Dáil legally. As a means to publicly combat the actions of Cosgrave and Cumann na nGaedheal, Fianna Fáil printed the first issue of the *Fianna Fáil Bulletin* on 25 July 1927, in order to claim the actions unconscionable and illegal. Under the headline 'War Upon the People's Peace', the paper read, 'By illegal exclusion of 45 Republican deputies, debarred by police and military force from taking their seats, the Cumann na nGaedheal Party manoeuvred themselves back into office despite the people's emphatic vote. They have now proclaimed war on the public peace.'[51] The same editorial also claimed that these actions had invalidated the Free State constitution of 1923. Under the subheading 'The Last Straw', the author(s) referred to Cumann na nGaedheal and its 'revising' of the constitution as tyrannical, stating that the 'Free State Constitution [can] now be declared to be less fundamental than a [illegible insertion] Emergency Bill but deputies who in the future swear to the Constitution swear in addition to the English King, to Partition and to this latest most ferocious [action]'.[52] The attacks on tyranny may seem more suited to a previous era, but they were vital to Fianna Fáil's claims to legitimacy. By presenting Cumann na nGaedheal in such terms, Fianna Fáil appeared the more rational and less reactionary of the two parties. Further, by appealing to the will of the people, it added a greater sense of legitimacy for its cries of tyranny. Despite this, Fianna Fáil would eventually abandon its legal attacks against the oath, instead choosing to rhetorically sidestep the issue and address it from within the Dáil itself.

In essence, de Valera's party shunned, even marginalised, the significance of the oath as it chose to enter the Dáil, labelling it an 'empty formula'.[53] In an untitled draft of a letter written by de Valera, the Fianna Fáil 'chief' laid out the reasons for the change in policy. On behalf of the Fianna Fáil deputies, he wrote: 'They recognise that this legislation may imperil the general peace, that it disfranchises and precludes from engaging in any peaceful movement all Irish Republicans who will not acknowledge that they owe allegiance to the British Crown.'[54] Herein lay two assertions: first, that Fianna Fáil was placing the will of the people above party conviction, and second, that it had indeed abandoned the policy of abstention. In the closing refrain, de Valera wrote:

> Thus, if the signing of a meaningless political formula [i.e. the oath] is sufficient to secure for them admission to their seats, the Fianna Fail Deputies feel it in [sic] their duty in this crisis to comply with the formality. On the other hand, they feel it is equally their duty to accept the consequences of continued exclusion if entry can only be obtained at the price of the transfer of their allegiance from the Irish Nation to the English King. They feel confident that their constituents, and all Republicans, will support them in their refusal to commit as public representatives what they *must* regard as an act of national apostacy [sic].[55]

The act of apostasy referred to by de Valera and Gallagher was the abandonment of Sinn Féin's hardline stance towards abstention, as well as that party's principled stance on the revolutionary republican Dáil which it had sought to legitimise. It appears that Fianna Fáil was more concerned with the public's distaste for militancy than any perceived contradictions of its representatives entering the Free State Dáil. In short, Fianna Fáil went to great lengths to assure the Irish people that it was in no way connected to the violence that continued in parts of Ireland.

'DEVVY'S CIRCUS': FIANNA FÁIL V. CUMANN NA NGAEDHEAL AND THE PUBLIC STRUGGLE OVER THE GUNMEN

As the party of government from the formation of the Free State up until a narrow loss in 1932, Cumann na nGaedheal took the tactical approach of attempting to weaken support for Fianna Fáil by drawing connections between the latter and the reviled 'gunmen' of the Irish Republican Army. The connotation was that Fianna Fáil was a party of murderers intent on dragging Ireland into another civil war or, worse, a protracted confrontation with Great Britain. A study of the election material used by Cosgrave's party during this era shows that Cumann na nGaedheal continued to portray Fianna Fáil along gendered lines as irrational, emotional, militant, and thus feminised agents of disorder. Conversely, a study of Fianna Fáil's election material reveals a party making every effort to extricate itself from this feminised label, in turn resetting the gendered discourse.

Underlying Cumann na nGaedheal's message was the perceived threat that Fianna Fáil posed to the Free State's sense of law and order. In a continuation from its rhetoric levied against Sinn Féin in the early 1920s, Cumann na nGaedheal positioned itself as custodian of the security and lawfulness of the Irish Free State. This theme continued up through the demise of the party and served as the basis for its dialectic with Fianna Fáil. Such themes were evident in two electoral posters from the 1927 and 1932 elections. The first and most recognisable is a poster depicting a mysterious gunman looming menacingly over an unassuming, quaint rural Irish home. The words 'The Shadow of the Gunman. Keep it from your home. Vote for Cumann na nGaedheal' implied that the party was all that stood between security and the feared gunmen.[56] Another example of Cumann na nGaedheal's effort to draw explicit connections between Fianna Fáil and the feared gunmen can be found in a poster centred upon a drawing depicting a card game and three figures sitting at a table, including de Valera, an upright and decidedly non-threatening 'Saorstát Citizen', and a shadowy figure labelled Saor Éire – Ireland's socialist party – and IRA.[57] The most striking element of the cartoon is the long leg of de Valera featuring the words 'Fianna Fail' stretched out under the table, passing a card marked as 'the Joker' to the spectral IRA/Saor Éire figure. Beneath the drawing are the words 'Fianna Fail's Game. Don't let them cheat you! Vote for Cumann na nGaedheal'.[58] Again we find a continuation of the theme of de Valera working in concert with the militant gunmen who, according to Cumann na nGaedheal, were running rampant through the countryside. It is also worth noting the depiction of the Irish citizen as being of the Free State rather than of Ireland, connoting that the Free State was the apex of Irish citizenry. This is something that would be seized upon by Fianna Fáil in its own rhetoric, as the party would reify the notion of Ireland and its citizenry, thus negating any connections to Britain such as was seen in reference to the Free State.

One of the more recognisable images from this era is an election poster for Cumann na nGaedheal emblazoned with the headline 'HIS Master's Voice'. The phrase was originally used in England and Ireland in an advertisement by the Gramophone Company (later HMV), and by RCA/Victor in the United States, beginning in 1909 and featuring Nipper the dog reacting to a realistic recording of his master.[59] Beneath this was a drawing of a particularly effeminate-looking de Valera, with a Fianna Fáil card hanging from his hand, being held up by a shadowy gunman armed with two guns, each labelled 'IRA' and 'Saor Eire'. The connotation was that de Valera was a passive agent, indeed puppet, of the militant and radical elements of Irish politics. Given the connection with the Victor ad, a more vulgar interpretation can be made, notably that de Valera was the IRA's and Saor Éire's 'poodle'. Further, the phrase 'HIS Master's Voice' suggests that de Valera and his party had been hijacked by extremists, but also that he and his party were really militant extremists

Figure 1.1 Cumann na nGaedheal, *Presented by the artist to the nation. De Valera is now working on another Canvas(s), but what about the price? Vote for Cumann na nGaedheal*, NLI, 1932, EPH F38. Image courtesy of the National Library of Ireland.

hiding under the cloak of a thinly veiled neo-republicanism. Spanned across the bottom was the phrase 'Make <u>YOUR</u> voice heard by voting for Cumann na nGaedheal', implying that a Fianna Fáil government would somehow mean the end of democracy and the return to the perceived lawlessness of the previous era.[60]

The propaganda published by Cumann na nGaedheal also offered more complex characterisations of Fianna Fáil than mere accusations of violence and disorder. In many cases, references to specific elements of de Valera's actions and republican events were included. One such example was an electoral poster that depicted de Valera – 'Fianna Fail' is emblazoned across his long arms – opening a door labelled 'Constitution Amendment Act', allowing the ever-present IRA and Saor Éire gunmen access to a munitions dump containing 'Dumped Arms', 'Mines' and 'High Explosives'.[61] The poster simply reads, 'Don't let this happen. Vote for Cumann na nGaedheal'.[62] Dangling from the Fianna Fáil leader's coat pocket was a paper entitled 'Document no. 2', a clear reference to de Valera's failed alternative to the Anglo-Irish treaty.[63] The connotation here is that the Free State under the leadership of Cumann na nGaedheal was a bulwark on behalf of safety and peace, as opposed to what Fianna Fáil would unleash.

Perhaps the most striking depictions by Cumann na nGaedheal of de Valera as the harbinger of violence came in the form of two posters portraying the republican leader as the orchestrator of the death and destruction wrought by the civil war. The first was entitled 'Presented by the artist to the nation' and depicts de Valera as the artist pondering a work of his own – entitled 'Civil War by E. De Valera' – and features images of war and a city ablaze (see Figure 1.1). Dangling from the painting was a price tag with the figure '£33,000,000', the estimated cost of damages from the prior conflict.[64] Similar in theme, but more striking in its accusation of human cost, was a poster with the title 'The dead who died for an "empty formula". Was it worth it? Vote for Cumann na nGaedheal'[65] (see Figure 1.2). Above was a striking line drawing of a classic image of Erin, dressed in traditional Irish robes, holding de Valera by the arm while pointing to a series of crosses – an image not unlike what was seen in the wake of the Great War – and featuring the names of prominent Irish nationalists who had lost their lives in the civil war. De

Figure 1.2 Cumann na nGaedheal, *The dead who died for an "empty formula". Was it worth it? Vote for Cumann na nGaedheal*, NLI, 1932, EPH F43. Image courtesy of the National Library of Ireland.

Valera has a look of shock and surprise, as well as an effeminate posture. Erin is his complete opposite, looking fierce and stern. The names on the crosses are as follows: Liam Mellows, Erskine Childers, Seamus Dwyer, Sean Hales, Emmet McGarry, Cathal Brugha, Rory O'Connor and Michael Collins.[66] It is somewhat ironic – if not anachronistic – that de Valera was labelled with the death of these men despite the fact that some were executed by the Free State government.[67] The implication, however, was that the ultimate blame for their demise lay at the feet of their political leader.

In a similar vein, a Cumann na nGaedheal poster entitled 'Oh Dry Those Tears!' depicted a weeping de Valera as having the body of a crocodile, eliciting misguided emotion over the destruction brought by the civil war (see Figure 1.3). The subtitle 'The cost of an empty formula' was common in Cumann na nGaedheal propaganda and was a clear signifier of Fianna Fáil's militant lineage. In what is clearly a feminised depiction, through 'crocodile tears', de Valera apologises to a manly Irish labourer about the destruction wrought by the civil war. But in an interesting twist, the worker, wearing an apron labelled 'Irish Industry', complains that war has crippled Irish industry. As £33 million goes up in smoke, the hobbled worker shakes an angry fist at de Valera.[68] The message was clear: emotion and ideology had been the great enemies of industry and manly Irish industriousness. These posters demonstrate one facet of the larger battle Fianna Fáil would have to fight to attain legitimacy with the Free State electorate. It would have been disinguous for the members of Fianna Fáil to simply state that they were not at fault for the civil war. More than anything, the party had to put to bed any notion that its new manifestation of republicanism would in any way rekindle the passions of 1921–2.

Although exaggerated in their claims, these posters were clearly meant to create a sense of unease among the Irish populace about Fianna Fáil's militant past. The posters depicting de Valera as the harbinger of death and destruction – both corporal and financial – were intended to draw a clear line from the civil war to what Cumann na nGaedheal saw as a renamed manifestation of Sinn Féin and the IRA. In essence, the past was used to create a sense of unease about the presence of de Valera on the public stage. But what would a Fianna Fáil state look like according

Figure 1.3 Cumann na nGaedheal, *Crocodile Tears: the cost of an empty formula. "Oh dry those tears!" and vote for Cumann na nGaedheal*, NLI, 1932, EPH F51. Image courtesy of the National Library of Ireland.

to Cumann na nGaedheal? One vision was presented in a poster that declared: 'No goods taken from window! Supplies from goods stores only'[69] (see Figure 1.4). Situated above this declaration was an image of de Valera dressed as a shopkeeper, offering key Fianna Fáil policies disguised as 'goods', such as 'No Oaths Taken', 'High Tariffs', 'Land Annuities' and 'De-Rating Schemes'.[70] To the side of de Valera, standing in a side door, was a masked gunman watching over a store of arms including rifles and 'bombs for jurymen'.[71] In this case, Cumann na nGaedheal was making a literal case that Fianna Fáil was a front for violent revolutionaries intent on bringing violence and disorder to Ireland.

As outlined above, Cumann na nGaedheal sought to position itself as a law and order party, one that maintained peace and accord not only within Ireland, but with England as well. Herein lay Cumann na nGaedheal's second point of attack against those in Fianna Fáil – they were the same old revolutionaries as 1916 and 1921, and their election into government would result in a renewed conflict with Britain. Moving from connotations of past connections with the civil war, Cumann na nGaedheal sought to portray Fianna Fáil as a political branch of the IRA. Considering the connections between Sinn Féin and the IRA – not to mention Fianna Fáil's still ambivalent relationship with the IRA – it wasn't difficult for Cumann na nGaedheal to depict de Valera and his followers as revolutionaries launching a new directive against the Free State and England. In this sense, Fianna Fáil had to free itself from the stigma of the gunmen.

Another election poster, likely from 1932, portrayed Fianna Fáil as a party that lacked the seriousness and integrity to warrant election into power (see Figure 1.5). The very large poster is a mock-up of the type used to promote a travelling circus, in this instance 'Devvy's Circus'. In an unambiguous reference to de Valera's mixed ancestry – his mother was Irish-born and his father was a Spaniard she met in the United States – the words 'Senor De Valera [*sic*]' are in very large print, clearly meant to catch the eye of the passer-by, followed in smaller type with a description of him as a 'World-Famous Illusionist, Oath Swallower and Escapologist. See His Renowned Act: "Escaping from the Strait Jacket of the Republic" Everyone Mystified!!'[72] Above this is a series of phrases, reading: 'Absolutely the Greatest Road Show in Ireland To-Day!' '57–Star

Figure 1.4 Cumann na nGaedheal, *No goods taken from window! Supplies from goods stores only!* NLI, 1932, EPH F57. Image courtesy of the National Library of Ireland.

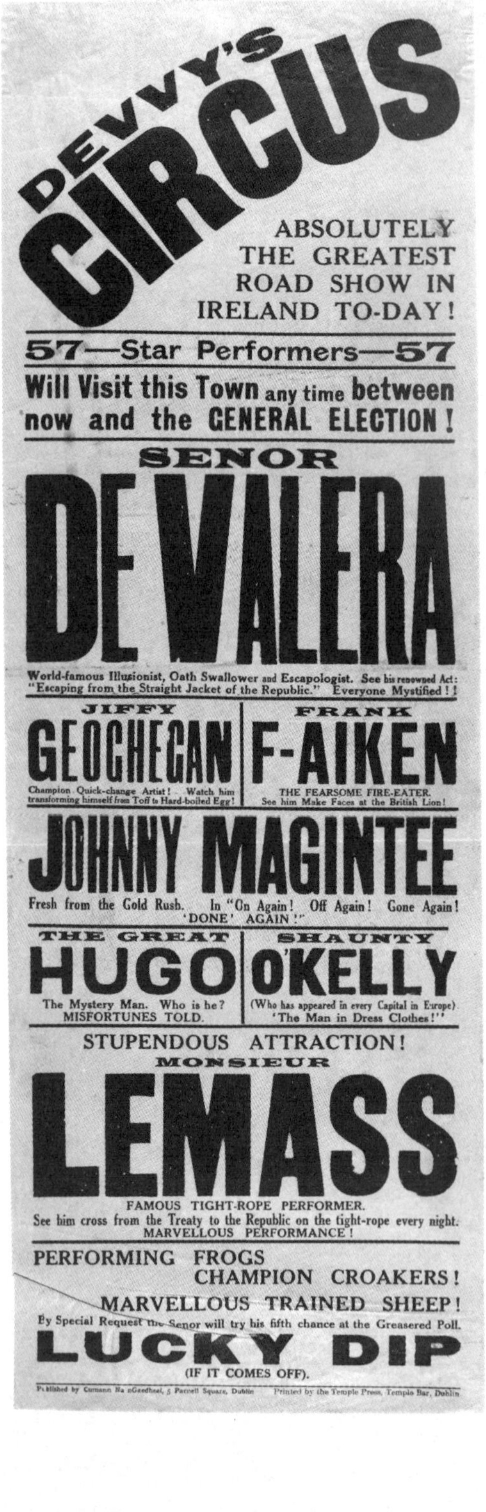

Figure 1.5 Cumann na nGaedheal, *Devvy's circus. Absolutely the greatest road show in Ireland to-day!* NLI, 1932, EPH F50. Image Courtesy of the National Library of Ireland.

Performers' 'Will Visit This Town any Time Between Now and the General Election!'[73] To the observer, the seriousness of Fianna Fáil was being brought into question. Most telling is the phrase 'Escaping from the Strait Jacket of the Republic', which suggests that de Valera is somehow utilising circus tricks – a type of chicanery not described in the poster – to escape from his past as a key figure in the 1916 rising, and the destruction which followed; an anachronistic claim considering that many of the key members of Cumann na nGaedheal were sympathetic to – if not actively involved in – the declaration of the 1916 Republic. Adding to the notion that Fianna Fáil was a party comprised of men willing to change on a whim – and therefore unstable – is the listing of 'circus' performers, all members of the party. For example: 'Frank Aiken: The Fearsome FIRE-EATER. See Him Make Faces at the British Lion!'[74] 'Johnny Magintee: Fresh from the Gold Rush. In "On Again! Off Again! Gone Again! Done Again!"'[75] 'Monsieur Sean Lemass:

Famous Tight-Rope Performer. See Him Cross from the Treaty to the Republic on the Tight-rope Every Night. Marvellous Performance'.[76] The poster concludes with 'Performing Frogs Champion Croakers!' 'Marvellous Trained Sheep!' 'By Special Request the Senor Will Try His Fifth Chance at the Greasered Poll'.[77] This poster is an excellent example of the efforts Cumann na nGaedheal went to to portray key Fianna Fáil figures as irrationally and foolishly anti-British, with a history of vacillating between pro-treaty and anti-treaty stances, or as failures making numerous attempts to awe their followers with deceit and conceit. Most telling, however, was the presentation of followers of the party as thoughtless sheep blinded by the spectacle of Fianna Fáil. Like a circus, Fianna Fáil was being portrayed as mindless, evanescent entertainment, and thus untrustworthy and dishonest.

Another Cumann na nGaedheal election poster, from September 1927, continued the theme of portraying Fianna Fáil as harbingers of an empty rhetoric that would ultimately yield no results. It depicts a large chicken with a stereotypical rendering of de Valera – stern, large nose, glasses – looking sadly upon a cracked and empty eggshell, across which is written: 'The Empty Formula'[78] (see Figure 1.6). Below the egg are the words 'The hen that took 5 years to lay an egg, and then it was empty. Vote for Cumann na nGaedheal'. In light of the assertion that Cumann na nGaedheal exerted great effort to feminise the republican cause, there are two notable facets of this particular poster. The first is the advancing of de Valera and his party as the unpleasant and illogical choice, depicting a hen – a female chicken – who is, moreover, infertile. The second is the portrayal of Fianna Fáil's platform, born of the treaty debate and civil war, as being just as empty in 1927 as it had been in 1922. The conclusion for the Irish voter, therefore, is that de Valera and his 'hatched' republicanism remains hollow in 1927, but, most importantly, as there is no 'chick', the party's ideals can never mature – indeed, they never truly existed in the first place. Additionally, the depiction of de Valera as a hen brings to mind Angela Bourke's assertion that 'In storytelling, and in written reminiscences of rural life, we also find a recurring analogy between resistance to the keeping of hens and resistance [by men] to women's speech. That hens make too much noise, and that women talk too much, is a familiar theme in men's traditional storytelling.'[79]

Figure 1.6 Cumann na nGaedheal, *The hen that took 5 years to lay an egg, and then it was empty. Vote for Cumann na nGaedheal*, NLI, 1932, EPH F44(A). Image courtesy of the National Library of Ireland.

Ex-Unionist (after the election): Mr. Cosgrave has not been returned, but our money has been well spent. As you will see, it has been employed by Cumann na nGaedheal to defame the natives far better than we used to do it.

Figure 1.7 Bee, 'Ex-Unionist', *Irish Press*, 15 February 1932, p. 1. With thanks to Irish Newspaper Archives and *The Irish Press*.

Although they were in power, the level of vitriol expounded by Cumann na nGaedheal suggests that Cosgrave's party saw Fianna Fáil as a serious electoral threat. Even in the early days of the party, the presence of Fianna Fáil became a lightning rod in which all aspects of the political debate revolved around the republicans' rhetoric. In other words, the republican movement, whether it was Sinn Féin or Fianna Fáil, remained a powerful force throughout the life of the Irish Free State. Furthermore, the issue of republicanism's fate was indeed the central element directing Irish political debate. Yet in the years leading up to its electoral triumphs in 1932, 1933 and 1937, Fianna Fáil had to constantly weather severe attacks that were formed along gendered lines. Accused of being irrational, violent, treasonous and equivocating, the party embraced a public discourse that incessantly distanced itself from the type of republicanism that had been made irrelevant by historical events, and, by extension, undermined the propaganda and rhetoric of the pro-Treaty Cumann na nGaedheal.

It took Fianna Fáil roughly four years to adequately respond to Cumann na nGaedheal's lampooning, explored above, and when it did so, it addressed the charges of violence and irrationality. A cartoon from the 15 February 1932 edition of the *Irish Press* demonstrates the manner in which Fianna Fáil would not only mock Cumann na nGaedheal's accusations, but also weaken the effect of such posters as 'Devvy's Circus' and 'The Shadow of the Gunman', which appear in the cartoon (see Figure 1.7). The artist 'Bee' depicts an 'Ex-Unionist' standing before a room filled with well-fed, monocled and formally dressed males and saying: 'Mr. Cosgrave has not been returned, but our money has been well spent. As you will see, it has been employed by Cumann na nGaedheal to defame the natives far better than we used to do it.'[80] Simply put, Cumann na nGaedheal's broadsides had little impact on Fianna Fáil, other than to shape the party's rhetoric and create a foundation from which it could launch its own attacks.

'UNSCRUPULOUS PROPAGANDA': FIANNA FÁIL'S REASONED REPLY

As shown above, Cumann na nGaedheal utilised a particularly pointed aesthetic attack on the electability of Fianna Fáil. Initially, Fianna Fáil deflected these accusations by responding with speeches and pamphlets – such as *Pamphlet #2* – relying mostly on public events and the consequent print media reports to engage Cumann na nGaedheal. To be sure, Cumann na nGaedheal's efforts to associate Fianna Fáil with the 'gunmen' had achieved some success, as evidenced by the direct references to these accusations within Fianna Fáil's own election propaganda. One such example is a poster titled 'Unscrupulous Propaganda', with the subtitle 'Here is a copy of a leaflet issued by Cumann na nGaedheal during the elections'.[81] Centred on the poster is a copy of a Cumann na nGaedheal leaflet, bookended by the words 'You Know the Facts'. The text of the Cumann na nGaedheal piece reads: 'Shot dead. A Cumann na nGaedheal Candidate and a Detective Officer were on Sunday in Leitrim. Shot Dead. While canvassing for support. You can rout the gunmen by supporting Cosgrave & Redmond and voting Blythe Brady'.[82] The bottom of the poster reads: 'Do you think a party that would stoop to such methods is worthy of your support? Vote for the Fianna Fáil candidates'.[83] Although there are similar examples of Fianna Fáil repudiating the claims of its opponents, de Valera and his party utilised a much more public, perhaps more cerebral, approach in responding to the claims of Cosgrave's party.

For instance, at the party's first ard fheis in November 1926, Éamon de Valera stated:

> I have never said, and am not going to say now, that force is not a legitimate weapon for a nation to use in striving to win its freedom. I know that in history it is seldom that foreign tyrants have ever yielded to any other. I have believed, and still believe, that if a nation held in subjection by a foreign power were to exclude altogether the idea of using physical force to free itself, it would in effect be handing itself over as a bound slave without hope of redemption. It is a long wait they destine themselves to who rely on their tyrants spontaneously suffering a change of heart.
>
> <u>But a nation within itself ought to be able to settle its polity so that all occasion of civil conflict between its members may be obviated</u>, and NO NATION WHICH EVEN PRETENDS TO FREEDOM WILL SUFFER A FOREIGN POWER TO IMPOSE CONDITIONS WHICH MAKE THE ADOPTION OF SUCH A POLITY IMPOSSIBLE.[84]

In this short passage, de Valera is able to construct a rhetorical distinction between the republicanism of Sinn Féin and that of his own party. By acknowledging the legitimacy of force as a means of escaping foreign tyranny, he lauds the efforts of previous revolutionaries, yet at the same time he is clear in noting that this was effective in the past but has no place in Fianna Fáil's vision for Ireland's present. In the next paragraph de Valera firmly states that force has no place in Ireland, thus acknowledging the belief that he and his party view the nation as being in a transitional phase between colony and complete independence. The significance of such a position was that it allowed Fianna Fáil to develop a socio-political and economic discourse that would operate within the frameworks of the Irish Free State, thereby abandoning the abstentionism and militancy of Sinn Féin and other hardline republican offshoots.

Returning to *Pamphlet #2*, we find another rejection of violence as a tenable option for establishing an Irish republic. With the civil war still fresh in the public's mind – not to mention being incessantly resuscitated by Cumann na nGaedheal and republican militant groups – Fianna Fáil had to clarify its role in the causation and fighting of the war. Gallagher contended that the root cause of the civil war was not militant republicanism, but rather that the treaty 'had already filled the nation with dissension'.[85] He further asserted that the treaty 'outraged the national tradition by destroying Ireland's age-old nationhood and substituting for it that which has for centuries been most loathsome to Irish nationalism – the domination of the British monarchy'.[86] In a clever twist that played into the anti-British rhetoric of Fianna Fáil's nationalism, Gallagher did not blame Cumann na nGaedheal for orchestrating the civil war, but rather claimed that the party was duped by the duplicity of Prime Minister Lloyd George. Under a heading entitled 'A Constitution Based on Civil War', Gallagher wrote:

> Had Prime Minister Pitt sat in Mr. Lloyd George's place when the Constitution was under revision in London in 1922, he could not, in the circumstances of the time, have produced a document better calculated to divide our people. The Articles of Agreement for a Treaty which in the Preamble are made the real Free State Constitution had already proved their power not to unite the nation but so completely and thoroughly to divide it as to make Civil War possible after six months. How better could any British statesman secure the permanent weakening of Ireland by internal disunion than by declaring that to be the fundamental law which had already cast the whole nation in conflict and confusion[?][87]

What Gallagher did, in essence, was to establish a causal link between Britain and the civil war, implicitly questioning the courage and wisdom of those Irishmen responsible for the treaty and the resultant constitution. Further, Gallagher's assertions undermined the Free State constitution as being inherently divisive. Indeed, the most significant element of this passage was Fianna Fáil's attempt to establish a very public disconnect between itself and the outbreak of the war.

From its inception, Fianna Fáil sought to foster a new socio-political and economic dialectic that moved beyond the militancy of the previous decade. As such, the formation of the party could be presented as the beginning of a new era in Irish history; thus, the time between 1926 and 1937 served as a transition from the civil war era to that of a fully independent state. In many ways, Cumann na nGaedheal represented an Ireland that was born of the civil war and treaty debate – not to mention retaining some connections to Britain – whereas Fianna Fáil advanced a movement that sought to break from this narrative, in turn creating a new republican master narrative. De Valera's closing speech from Fianna Fáil's first ard fheis made this break explicit. Speaking of a leaderette in the *Irish Independent* from that morning which accused Fianna Fáil of representing a shadow of the once-bloody fight, de Valera responded: 'I ask who is responsible for its remaining? I simply point to it as an objective fact . . . Those who complain that the "shadow of the bloody fight" remains must point their accusation elsewhere. It remains because human nature is what it is, because national aspirations are natural to men. I have done nothing but point out the facts.'[88] While justified at certain times – even in Ireland's past – force was a means to an end, but in de Valera's view, the Free State precluded the need for further bloodshed. Militancy and force – in the figurative rather than literal sense – was something that was not without place in the rhetoric of Fianna Fáil. Indeed, militaristic organisation and activist rhetoric were to be key elements for de Valera's party as it advanced its nationalistic republican cause throughout the decade. In referring to the renascence of the republican movement, de Valera stated: 'We have rallied ourselves and have already made wonderful progress in rallying the whole of the national forces. These forces were scattered, but they were not annihilated. In a short time they will be as stout an army as ever, and every success will increase their morale.'[89]

Still, in relation to its political dialectic with Cumann na nGaedheal, Fianna Fáil republicanism needed to be made distinct from Sinn Féin republicanism. Although the rhetoric of the party aligned Fianna Fáil with a continuum of nationalist heroes, it had to tread carefully around its problematic associations with Sinn Féin and the more recent past.

Whereas Cumann na nGaedheal sought to draw an unequivocal line connecting Fianna Fáil to Sinn Féin, de Valera and his party sought to add greater nuance to the past. Building on his speech from the first ard fheis, de Valera made a much more explicit statement regarding the connections – or lack thereof – between Fianna Fáil and Sinn Féin in 1927. At the party's second ard fheis, de Valera stated:

> To free a country that has been in the oppressive grip of a big Empire for seven centuries is not a light task. It can only [be] performed if we are firm and conscientious and if we feel that we can start again and build up from the foundations. We are building up solidly from the foundations, and we have built up and established to-day – and I hope it will prove to be an organisation of destiny – an organisation which is a fitting *successor* to the great Sinn Fein Organisation which existed from 1917 to 1921.[90]

The last sentence here is rather curious, considering that de Valera was president of Sinn Féin *after* 1921, yet it is more understandable if we view it through the prism of his vision for Fianna Fáil. In essence, de Valera is claiming that Sinn Féin had ceased to be vital after 1921 with the formation of the Irish Free State, for the militancy that created it was no longer essential to the greater cause of creating an independent republic. Therefore, Sinn Féin was no longer a viable entity within the frameworks of the Irish Free State. Yet it was on this incarnation of Sinn Féin, the united revolutionary entity that had opposed the foreigner, rather than the abstentionist/militant Sinn Féin of the mid-1920s, that de Valera sought to build his party's historical foundation. At the very heart of this speech was the notion that Fianna Fáil marked a new departure for the republican movement, as well as an implicit recognition of the legitimacy of the Saorstát.

The acceptance of the Free State as a real and functioning entity provided the starting point for Fianna Fáil in its efforts to operate as a 'slightly constitutional party', for the very machinations of the organisation were rooted in the plan to form a majority within the Free State Dáil and then destroy it from within, thereby creating a new Irish state. As such, Fianna Fáil – from its inception – wrapped itself in the cloak of innovation, a truly new departure for the Ireland of the 1920s and beyond. In the same speech given in 1927, de Valera was explicit in his claims that the party was formed with an eye towards the future:

> The circumstances, however, in which this organisation has to perform its task, are not the same circumstances as those in which we had to fight then, and if we are going to succeed it will be using at each particular moment, as I have often said, the methods which seem best at that moment for the success of our task. When circumstances change, methods must change; but the thing that has not changed is the aim, and that aim is to secure the complete freedom of this country; and we know that, no matter how they might alight it as a mere form, the form in which that aim will express itself is that of an independent republic.[91]

The themes of rebirth and renewal are essential to understanding the nature of Fianna Fáil's renascent republicanism in the formative era. Party leaders envisioned their new project as the beginning of a socio-political and economic trajectory headed towards establishing a state independent of both the long *durée* of the British conquest and also the short *durée* of the Irish Free State. Thus, Fianna Fáil would concern itself with constructing an innovative and expedient party discourse suitable for the exigencies of both the Irish Free State and interwar Europe.

The examples above make it clear that those in Fianna Fáil were cognisant of how they were cast as irrational militants by Cumann na nGaedheal. As such, de Valera's party was explicit in its effort to distinguish itself from the militant republican past. Knirck has demonstrated that Cumann na nGaedheal did much to build strength within the Free State by casting the republican movement in feminine terms – a trend continued through the image of Fianna Fáil as the harbinger of a renewed commitment to the policy of the gunmen. As has been shown, Fianna Fáil went to great lengths to distance itself from this association. Another aspect of the party's discourse can be found in its promotion of a logical, delayed-Enlightenment approach to such controversial issues as its entrance into the Dáil and the ensuing battle over the oath of allegiance. From one perspective, this can be seen as a gender neutralisation of sorts, in which the party sought to dissolve any feminine connotations while embracing a more active, reasoned masculine cloaking.

On 9 November 1932, de Valera addressed the sixth Fianna Fáil ard fheis – the first since the party had formed a coalition government in the Free State Dáil. The speech reflected the entrenchment of the party's republican approach, but it also foreshadowed its embracement of a policy of action towards institutional change. De Valera stated:

> This organisation of FIANNA FAIL was founded primarily to provide a path to peace and to the ultimate victory for which a common understanding and an agreed national policy is the first essential. The pillars on which the policy of the organisation rest are: the acceptance of the vote of the majority of the people's elected representatives as deciding national policy, and the abolition of the oath which at present prevents a section of our people from having representation in the representative assembly.
>
> Recent elections have shown that the people have come to appreciate the fact that we are really the Party of peace, and that our programme is the one which promises the most satisfactory solution of the national problems with which we are confronted. It is not improbable that before the next Ard Fheis assembles the representatives of this organisation will have placed upon them the responsibility of guiding the nation and governing that portion of it included in the twenty-six counties.[92]

In essence, this speech serves as a rhetorical transition from the period 1927–32 when Fianna Fáil was fighting for legitimacy in its dialectic with Cumann na nGaedheal. Further, the speech confirmed that the notion of republicanism and the will of the people – an Irish Enlightenment of sorts – had become an indisputable fact. By looking backwards, Fianna Fáil was successful in its bid to rightly align itself among the pantheon of Irish nationalist efforts, at the same time avoiding the pitfalls of the unpopular and distasteful associations with militant republicanism. Put simply, Fianna Fáil had succeeded in creating a political discourse suitable for operation within the Irish Free State. However, as de Valera implies, the problems of governing in 1932, as well as the overall goal of attaining an independent state, necessitated that Fianna Fáil adopt innovative measures to attain such a lofty ideal.

The threat of gunmen and the gendered discourse of Cumann na nGaedheal had been effectively neutralised by the machinations of Fianna Fáil in the period between its formation and its election – as part of a coalition – into government in 1932. This was in large part due to the ability of the party to effectively deflect the attempts made by Cumann na nGaedheal to construct a direct link between the two republican movements. Indeed, the positions taken above explain how Fianna Fáil was able to withstand the slings and arrows of Cosgrave's party in such a manner that it was able to attain electoral legitimacy within the Irish Free State. However, this alone does little to explain the *appeal* of Fianna Fáil as an alternative for the Irish voter. Lest one think that Fianna Fáil was solely Whiggish in its intent, one need only examine the party's policy during its initial period as head of a Free State coalition government. Notions of logic, reason and constitutionalism served largely as agitprop so that the party could carve itself a niche within the Free State's political realm. This backward embrace of eighteenth-century ideology represented only a portion of Fianna Fáil's larger discourse. Much of the material covered in this chapter depicts the party's more generalised and nebulous ideologies, with little indicating actual practice. Further, the call-back of Enlightenment-tinged rhetoric offers precious little insight into how the party would or could deal with the specific problems affecting Ireland in the interwar years. Yet as it moved towards greater relevance, Fianna Fáil began to espouse innovative socio-economic and political approaches free from the nineteenth-century liberal/conservative/radical triad. Attempting to place the party within this model fails to recognise the interwar zeitgeist that informed Fianna Fáil, not to mention offering the party great opportunities to succeed. By eschewing the politics of external association, revolutionary separatism or bastardised commonwealthism, Fianna Fáil manufactured a reconstituted nationalist project that sought to envelop all aspects of Irish life in an active, newly gendered movement.

'Bright days are coming! In Quaker grey': Fianna Fáil and the construction of the Irish Feminine

There appeared in the 7 June 1933 edition of the *Irish Press*, on the page of the paper primarily dedicated to women, a column that blurred the lines between advertisement, republican aesthetic and political action. It was hardly surprising to see political content in the paper; the *Irish Press* began publication in 1931 with monies raised in part by Éamon de Valera. Colloquially – and correctly – known as the 'house organ for Fianna Fáil',[1] the paper not only trumpeted the party's cause, but also served to enter into public discourse the party's nationalist directives. This particular advertisement, however, further obfuscated the lines between journalism and business, as it was printed in a font that was indistinguishable from the rest of the newspaper. The first in a serial feature, the editorially tinged advertisement was titled 'Morning in the Irish Home' and asked, 'Is yours a real Irish Home? Are you doing everything a patriotic Irish man or woman should do to support the industry of your own country? We shall show how you can have a real 100% Irish home not only without entailing any sacrifice, but with immediate advantage to yourself in the matter of quality and price.'[2]

This advertisement for Dromona Soaps typifies how editors of the *Irish Press* sought to direct the gaze of its women readers in a manner most amenable to Fianna Fáil's national project during the interwar years.[3] Seemingly benign, the advertisement strikes at the heart of domestic aspiration and consumption, channelling (republican) political energy towards the party's vision of an economically solvent and independent

Ireland. The advert does more than reify feminine domesticity in Ireland – it seeks to conflate rudimentary consumer habits with political action. Indeed, the *Irish Press* was hardly an innovator in this regard, but novelty did occur in how Fianna Fáil-cum-the *Irish Press* sought to direct the conscious and subconscious political energies of Irish women. Beginning in 1931 and continuing up to 1938, each edition of the *Irish Press* dedicated a portion of its third page to women's issues, including fashion, cooking and dietary advice, guidance on social graces, child-rearing, and pastimes.[4] Among the large-circulation newspapers of Ireland, this attention to women was unique to the *Press*, if not wholly original. A similar type of page had been a feature of the *Dundalk Examiner*, a paper associated with Frank Aiken,[5] and the transition from a local to a national focus parallels Fianna Fáil's nationalist endeavours to create a broader, nationalist movement. Introducing a political charge to an advertisement for a common household product was not at all unusual for the portion of the *Irish Press* dedicated to matters feminine.

The appearance of a story indicates a fundamental awareness – if not understanding – of events and trends occurring within and without Ireland. In this regard, the newspaper is a malleable reactive force, reporting on developments from around the world. Editorial decisions to include stories reflect a sense of what consumers of the *Irish Press* were interested in reading. Conversely, a recurring series of articles – such as the women's page – is indicative of what the editors felt its readership *needed* to read. Given that the *Irish Press* was founded by de Valera and was often in lockstep with Fianna Fáil policy, we can conclude that the regular appearance of the women's page was indicative of how the party sought to construct an idealised Irish woman. Anne Dolan, examining a May 1935 issue of the *Irish Independent*, notes that a single day's edition 'captures a place that seems hungry for the newest, the most modern of everything'.[6] She adds, 'It is clear even in the columns of easily passed over classifieds that this Free State thought itself, or was cajoled by the advertisements to think itself, an up-to-the-minute type of place. No frugal, homespun Ireland here.'[7]

In the years 1931 to '37 – a period dominated by the economic war with Britain – the *Irish Press* served as the place where Fianna Fáil sought to direct – and indeed control – the Irish Feminine gaze so as to define the political energies of Irish women. The prescribed behaviours set forth in the daily newspaper were a corrective, wherein the party sought to both define the fundamental tenets of Irish republicanism and also direct the political energies of Irish women in a manner that suited the party's nationalist aims. Fianna Fáil was founded at a time when the republican movement had been marginalised as being irrational, emotional, violent and irrelevant in the Free State. The predominance of women as the leaders of Sinn Féin became increasingly associated with the violence and public handwringing surrounding the events that preceded the foundation of the Saorstát.[8] In short, the republican movement had become synonymous with reactionary violence, and was widely perceived as emblematic of a distasteful recent past. In the years immediately following the party's inception, Fianna Fáil had to combat associations with violence and the reactional femininity embodied in such personages as Constance Markievicz or Kathleen Lynn, among many others. Republican leaders, then, attempted to construct a nationalist aesthetic that repositioned feminine political agency in a manner that also supported nativist industries – real and aspirational. Fianna Fáil used its journalistic and electoral endeavours to shape and redirect the political energies of Irish women such that they supported the party's nationalist aims. Through a fetishisation of nativist Irish products, by means of directed consumption and an attempted categorisation of female avocation and *couture*, Fianna Fáil sought to construct an idealised and emulative model of womanhood restated: the Irish Feminine.

It would have been counterproductive to Fianna Fáil's nationalistic aspirations to relegate women to an apolitical home, for women were positioned as vital producers and consumers both in, and of, a republican Éire.[9] The redirection of feminine political energies was one half of Fianna Fáil's gendered reconstitution of a nationalist discourse that was to provide the basis for the party's renascent republicanism and, in turn, its nationalist aspirations. On one hand Fianna Fáil sought to construct an active economic and industrial plan that situated Irish men – and Irish masculinity writ large – as progenitors of a new Irish state, providing the necessary seed and labour to construct a self-contained, modern, agrarian-industrial state. In this version of the future, Irish women were on one hand envisioned as purse vessels of the Gaelic-Catholic-Irish republican triumvirate, while at the same time radical consumers and purchasers of fetishised Irish products, thereby creating a domestic, republican aesthetic in which all manner of daily life was designed to work towards the progression and reification of Fianna Fáil republicanism. In both their public and domestic lives, these constructs of the idealised Irish Feminine were to be Ireland's new traditionalists: demure and chaste custodians of Ireland's primordial idyll; active producers and consumers of domestic products grown in Irish soil and manufactured in modernist factories by the Irish Masculine; adorners of modern, yet traditional fashions woven from domestic wool and festooned with colourfully patriotic flourishes; comfortable in their role as mother and housewife, yet wily enough to succeed in urban avocations associated with modernity. Once realised into existence, the Irish Feminine and Irish Masculine could then engage in the act of a symbolic national coitus upon which a new Ireland could be based.

There is little need to argue with the contention that there was a culture of repression for women in Ireland. Fianna Fáil operated outside public policy frameworks to reify, or even dictate, gendered tropes regarding the appropriate behaviour of Irish women in the domestic and public spheres, thereby adding to the already extant pressures and dichotomies placed on women by Catholic-Irish patriarchy. When contextualised within the gendered reconstitution of Irish republicanism, as well as the radical protectionism of the economic war, Fianna Fáil's envisaged role for Irish women appears slightly more nuanced than previously believed. True, de Valera once stated that 'everyone knows there is little chance of having a home in the real sense if there is no woman in it, the woman is really the home-maker'.[10] These words notwithstanding, Fianna Fáil advanced a particularly nuanced and relatively modern version of Irish domesticity and public life; one that afforded women a vital role in the party's cause, in turn refocusing the energies of republican-minded – patriotic – women into a form more acceptable to the party's aims. These goals were to be attained by encouraging women to actively – but cautiously – participate in acts of everyday living that served to reify and advance Fianna Fáil's nationalist vision. Indeed, such a vision was in no way feminist or even progressive – my intent is not to 'rescue' Fianna

Fáil from justifiable accusations of repression or misogyny. Moreover, the dichotomy of being traditional yet modern can be viewed as either a further example of women being tasked with the burden of serving as custodians of primordial traditionalism *and* an aspirational Irish futurism, or as an example of a party that acknowledged the reality of an engaged and politicised female electorate keen to wear modern fashion or work outside the home.

Whatever its intent, a study of Fianna Fáil's aesthetic reveals a somewhat more nuanced relationship between the party and Irish women voters between 1931 and '37. This association was part of an overarching effort to redefine the republican movement in the hope of creating a new nation-state rooted in Fianna Fáil frameworks. The 1937 constitution did, in fact, codify the domestic role of women; yet the *Irish Press* and other Fianna Fáil material presented a more complex and active role – for all women regardless of their level of political endeavours. That role in part defies, or at least complicates, the idealism advanced in Article 41.2.1 of *Bunreacht na hÉireann*, that 'In particular, the State recognises that by her life within the home, woman gives to the State a support without which the common good cannot be achieved'. It is more accurate to say – if we consider these statements and policies within the time period and juxtaposed with the Irish Masculine discussed in the next chapter – that women were meant to be vital contributors to the construction of an independent state, however much that vision may have borne the hallmarks of paternalism and a repression in which women were seen as little more than clever homemakers. There was – for at least a brief period leading up to the writing and ratification of the 1937 constitution – also a perception that women could in fact embrace elements of modernity and modernism while contributing to the construction of an Irish republic.

Works on 1930s Ireland have brought to light the repressive nature of Fianna Fáil policy as embodied in de Valera's call for a primordial femininity in, for example, his 'comely maidens' speech.[11] This divide in the relationship between women and policy in 1930s Ireland clouds the historical context within which Fianna Fáil reconstituted itself. Indeed, Cumann na nGaedheal instituted policies that can be construed as repressive of women, but the distancing of Fianna Fáil from its feminist-friendly Sinn Féin roots is certainly striking. Yet, as Nancy Curtin has written of the generation of the United Irishmen, 'Republicanism . . . was a manly calling . . . But women could also exert themselves as heroines exemplifying republican virtue, reflecting as a redefinition of femininity that complemented and supported new ideals of masculinity.'[12] What I would suggest, however, is that Fianna Fáil's idealised Irish Feminine was rooted more in political and economic expediency than in an overarching need to set the course of women back two hundred years. Considering its origins, and the curbing of 'attacks on women's citizenship and employment after 1937',[13] Fianna Fáil's vision for women in Ireland was largely informed by its desire to successfully reconstitute an Irish state free from the vestiges of a perceived West Britonism enabled in part by Cumann na nGaedheal, the oath, the annuities and the ports. Maryann Valiulis writes:

> Women were critical to the Free State's definition of itself as a pure and virtuous nation. The important question was, what role would women play in the new State? In the struggle for independence, women played a vital role in organizations such as Inghinidhe na hÉireann and Cumann na mBan. They ran guns, sheltered IRA men on the run, churned out propaganda, served as judges in the new established Dáil courts, and in general, did what needed to be done.
>
> However, with the establishment of peace – at least in the twenty-six counties – in the eyes of both Irish political and ecclesiastical leaders, Irish women needed to be returned to the home. The need was to re-establish a traditional gender ideology which sees the hearth and home as women's rightful sphere. Their citizenship, their participation in the State, would be directly related to the home.[14]

There is much truth to Valiulis' argument, but one must add some nuance to such claims. She further contends that motherhood was elevated to a level of primary significance, as it afforded a 'political status'[15] and 'according to the dominant discourse of the period, women did not have a public identity, nor did they belong in the public sphere.'[16] This perspective largely reflects what has been commonplace in the historiography of women in de Valera's Ireland, or, as Caitriona Clear writes, that the words 'de Valera's Ireland . . . convey an oppressive, stagnant, uncomfortable social environment for women'.[17] Yet, a careful study of Fianna Fáil's aesthetic as embodied by the Irish Feminine shows that – at least in its aspirations – the party envisioned a more complex and more modern view of women. Indeed, the palingenetic situating of women as both traditional and modern reveals the party's ideated view of women but also its need to accept the more public role of the contemporary Irish woman.

There occurred a plethora of legislation enacted that sought to create what James M. Smith calls Ireland's 'containment culture'.[18] Smith, like others, sees policy regarding women continuing in an unbroken manner from the Carrigan Committee, through the Legitimacy Act, and Criminal Law Amendment Act, to 'protect' women through repressive government action. Similarly, Tom Inglis notes that 'although women played a crucial role in the struggle for independence, once this was gained, the new Free State began to pass legislation that helped confine women to the home'.[19] Indeed, there is little need to argue with any contention that there was a culture of repression in Ireland; Fianna Fáil also operated outside public policy frameworks to reify, or even dictate, gendered tropes regarding the appropriate behaviour of Irish women in the domestic and, to a lesser extent, public, sphere. In other words, at the same time that de Valera and his colleagues were publicly praising the silent Irish domestic, their party was constructing a different and relatively active supporting role for Irish women. Indeed, de Valera in a 1929 speech stated that the people of Ireland might 'have to wear somewhat less fashionable – though by no means less serviceable – shoes, or hats or hosiery'.[20] These sentiments may have been the reality for women under the guise of Fianna Fáil, yet a deeper analysis of the party's propaganda reveals a much different, if not contradictory, intention for the party in the years between 1932 and '37 – years shaped by the economic war. Women were indeed politicised by the party, but in an untraditional manner more in line with the types of feminised politicisation seen on the European continent. Moreover, as Clear writes, 'it is inaccurate – to say the least – to depict de Valera's Ireland as a graveyard of women's rights . . . The very fact that women's rights were constantly being debated, defined and defended indicates that they were very much alive.'[21]

Louise Ryan and Margaret Ward write that 'Anti-colonial nationalist movements have frequently employed gendered ideologies that position women in "traditional" roles within the domestic sphere'.[22] Yet the manner in which Fianna Fáil envisioned women was not as simplistic as their mere relegation to the home. Instead Fianna Fáil advanced a rhetoric that offered women what it saw as a crucial role in its cause, in turn refocusing the energies of republican-minded women towards actions that were more acceptable to the party's aims. This was done by encouraging female participation, via expressions of everyday living in the city and on the farm, through their outward appearance and consumer habits. Such aims were reflective of a much more nuanced relationship with women that was part and parcel of an overarching effort to redefine the republican movement. Ryan and Ward further note that 'women have been a continual part of nationalism, not just occasional players who can be easily summoned and dismissed'.[23] I wish to add to this by noting the tentative, if not completely guarded, political agency offered to women by Fianna Fáil in the years leading up to *Bunreacht na hÉireann* – the constitution drafted by de Valera in 1937. Although not the complete repression or degradation claimed by some, this vision was an effort to politicise the women of Ireland in a manner consistent with the nationalistic aims of the party. Indeed, the constitution of 1937 did codify the domestic role of women, giving credence to Clear's depiction of what it meant to be a woman in de Valera's Ireland. But when contextualised within the time period and juxtaposed with the masculine image on which Fianna Fáil sought to base its economic policies, it is more accurate to say that women were *envisioned* as being vital to the construction of an independent Irish state. What is striking, however, is that while the hallmarks of paternalism and repression were evident in the party's rhetoric, there was, for at least a brief period of time, the perception that women could embrace elements of modernity while serving the Irish state.

Fianna Fáil therefore constructed a palingenetic femininity in which elements of modernity were blended with the primitivist elements of cultural nationalism. Such was evident in how the party sought to shape the Irish Feminine not only into an emulative model for a regenerated Irish state, but also as avatars for its aspirational economic war with Great Britain. The Irish Feminine was to become the physical and outward countenance of appropriate and meaningful expressions of both Irishness and femininity. Such was evident in the *Irish Press*, where the party created a socio-political framework which allowed for women to physically embody traditionalism and modernism in public and at home. Elizabeth Francis Martin writes that, 'Like the mothers of the American and French Revolutions before her, the Irish woman was idealized as the vessel of the race, and her fulfilment would come from the realization of her children's dreams and achievements, not her own.'[24] But what was that envisioned role, and to what extent did it advance and support the party's efforts for a new republic?

Elements consistently present in the *Irish Press* point to a conscious effort to fabricate and model an aspirational, yet achievable, model of approved femininity. Of particular emphasis were matters related to contemporary fashions, the domestic woman as wife and busy homemaker, and, as the economic war raged – as a republican consumer. The shift from activist revolutionary to subtle republican fits within the paternalistic, logical and rational nationalism of Fianna Fáil in the 1930s. Female readers of the *Irish Press* were encouraged to be frugal – except when purchasing Irish products; modern yet traditional; subdued yet fashionable; patriotic and unquestioning. Indeed, there was room for women inside Fianna Fáil's vision for Ireland, and according to the *Irish Press*, compliance meant following the party line regarding fashion, occupation, domesticity and consumerism.

If one were to question the importance of the *Irish Press* in advocating Fianna Fáil's renascent republicanism, one need only to take into consideration Sean MacEntee's declaration that the paper 'was established in order to put the Republican position before the people, in order to keep the Republican flag flying, in order to put a Republican Government in the Dáil and in order to give a Republican Constitution to the people of Ireland.'[25] O'Brien notes that 'Cumann na nGaedheal severely under-emphasised the cultural identity of the Irish people, and it was this omission that later allowed Fianna Fáil via the *Irish Press* to exploit the hunger for cultural cohesiveness.'[26] The *Irish Press* then served as the means by which Fianna Fáil sought to define the national narrative through focusing their readers' gaze through the message of the paper. Regarding women, 'The paper made a special emphasis to recruit female writers and was the first newspaper in Ireland to appoint a women's page editor.'[27] Yet, the question remains as to what this relationship between Fianna Fáil, the *Irish Press* and the readers of the women's page was, and how it related to the republicans' vision for women in the Free State. While general themes remained consistent up to the passage of the 1937 constitution, the emphases of the women's page underwent noticeable changes that largely reflected the dictates of Fianna Fáil policy. In this short period, the page became increasingly political, offering Irish women a more prescribed framework of approved behaviours and avocations. As such, the women's page in the *Irish Press* offers a clear indication of Fianna Fáil's emerging definition of both the private and public norms for women.

'I'M GLAD I'M NOT BEAUTIFUL!': REDIRECTING THE ENERGIES OF IRISH REPUBLICAN WOMEN

As discussed in the previous chapter, the party exerted much effort in distancing itself from the militant iconography of Sinn Féin, in turn abandoning – in not evolving from – certain aspects of civil-war-era politics. Such a position demanded that de Valera and his followers break any public ties with the agents of the advanced nationalist press. As a result, Fianna Fáil had to construct its own nationalist narrative that reconfigured its relationship to past – and potential – republican women. Whereas in the time of Sinn Féin's greatest prominence, female nationalists had a huge amount of influence on republicanism, Fianna Fáil set out to channel and refocus their energies. Eve Morrison writes that, despite being home to an influential feminist movement, 'Ireland was just one of several European countries to prioritize the return of women to their traditional domestic roles as a means of restoring order and normalcy in the inter-war period'.[28] This was particularly apparent in the *Irish Press*' daily page devoted to the interests of women. Especially in the early years of the *Press*, the clear narrative thread that heralded the intelligence of women also sought to refocus their energies away from the public sphere. For example, in the 15 September 1931 issue – printed in the paper's first month of publication – there appeared a brief article entitled 'Women Are Clever!' that was written by 'An Admiring Man'.[29] In part it read:

> Women are too clever for words!
>
> Think of having to prepare food, look after three or more children, rush out to admire a man's handiwork in a garden, dust a house, make beds, dole out tea and cakes at eleven o'clock, lay a table, and serve a dinner – ALL IN ONE MORNING! . . .
>
> Think of taking a new length of cloth, and CUTTING it to make a dress that can be worn without shame in the broad light of day!
>
> Think of boiling gallons and gallons of milk every year, without ONCE letting it boil over.
>
> Think of making money last a week without a reserve upon which to draw should you over-spend one day!
>
> Think of lighting a fire EVERY day for the best part of eight months!
>
> Think of these things, oh ye men, and then say that women aren't clever IF YOU DARE![30]

This article justifies claims regarding Fianna Fáil's elevation of the woman domestic confined to the home so as to reify a 'traditional' gendered, heteronormative 'duty'. Yet, when contextualised with the party's overarching republican rhetoric, sentiments such as the contention that women were in fact clever became understandable as part of an all-encompassing effort to recast and redirect the consumerist aspect of the feminine gaze. The role of women in the home – as clever as it could be – coalesced with the party's economic and political policy in a manner that invigorated and supported Irish industry. Through a constructed vision of domestic harmony, the idealised Irish Feminine was endowed by Fianna Fáil with the agency to provide the kinetic energy necessary to speed the wheels of the Irish economy.

On 14 September 1931 an article written by 'A Plain Girl' appeared on page three of the *Irish Press* under the headline: 'I'm Glad I'm Not Beautiful'.[31] Defending her non-beauty, the author wrote:

There'd be so much to lose for one thing . . .

It's such a nuisance being beautiful, and I'm naturally lazy. And it's expensive, too. I have never to 'bury' my face in the cold cream jar or lie like a statue for hours with sticky stuff spread all over my neck and features. While Kitty, my beautiful sister, spends two hours every night ironing out her face and chasing imaginary wrinkles round her nose. *I hop into bed and sleep soundly. My face costs me nothing but a cake of soap and a dab of powder* . . .

The happiest day of my life was when Michael whispered, 'I love you'. If I had been beautiful perhaps I should have wondered . . . Golden hair and eyes like two big stars can act like magic in the moonlight, but a snub nose and a big mouth can't be camouflaged. Michael saw what he was getting, anyhow. So I married him.[32]

Fianna Fáil's envisioned *cailín* was one that valued earthy, conspicuous practicality, and was plain and frugal, present but not showy. The ideal republican woman at this point was the opposite of the Sinn Féin activist: passive; seemingly – or least outwardly – apolitical; demure, and amenable to a life of domestic heteronormativity. In this regard, this chapter serves to correct and resituate the fundamental nature of Irish femininity as envisioned by Fianna Fáil. Viewed in isolation, this falls into line with Fianna Fáil's propensity for regressive containment of feminine agency. This is the (not so) comely maiden – a base *tabula rasa* on which a reconstituted Irish femininity could be constructed to suit the idealised notions of the Fianna Fáil Irish Feminine.

The women's page in the *Irish Press* was not without its contradictions. Although at times women were encouraged to add Irish flourishes to the latest fashions – as will be shown below – in its earliest incarnation, the *Press* intoned that women embody and consume facets of the heretofore. As it were, Irish republican women were to cast their gaze to the past, strengthening cultural and historical ties to the present. In many ways this backward gaze bypassed the vulgarities of the recent past in order to reconnect the present to an imagined past when traditional Irish life was unsullied by the oath, the treaty and West Britonism. Such can be seen in an article – on the same page as the 'Plain Girl's' piece about the joy of not being beautiful – entitled 'Shall We? A Quintet that Shows

HOW the WIND Blows', in which women were told that 'styles are, at any rate, a definite return to the "good old days" . . . The modern girl's clothes will be grandmother's clothes and so exempt from criticism, and that will be that.'[33] The article does not explicate the nature of the criticism from which the ideal Irish woman would be exempt, though it could certainly be implied that these forces of cultural denunciation included the Catholic Church and a Fianna Fáil anxious about the active presence of republican women in the Saorstát. Further, the piece declares that 'hand embroidery, the hall-mark of the womanly woman, will be used in taffetas and faille on the bustle frocks and the designs will be of the rosebud and forget-me-not school, not the futuristic!'[34] Clearly an exhortation to avoid the excesses and vanity of the styles of the day, it recommends subtly that women should not be overly concerned with the trivialities or fluidity of contemporary fashions. An exemplar of this traditionalist trend can be seen in the 1 October 1931 edition of the *Press* (see Figure 2.1).

The glorification of foregone trends was not limited to fashion and cosmetic flourishes. An article in the 21 October 1931 edition of the paper implored women to add 'Old-Time Touches in New Decorative Schemes'.[35] In part, the article read: 'The back-to-our-grandmothers trend in fashions is naturally reflected in home decoration, and to be thoroughly up-to-date you must introduce old-time accessories into your furnishing schemes.'[36] Indeed, there is present here a classist element, as the houses presented as aspirational are most certainly those of people with the means to decorate them.[37] It is hard to imagine that the authors of this article had in mind the homes of those afflicted by the Famine or land agitation. Nonetheless, what is most significant here is the construction of an imagined, idealised past where the demure homemaker praised traditional over modern. The article further suggested that women use inherited objects to decorate their houses, and if they were not fortunate enough to have received such articles, then they should 'haunt auctions or [to] search in antique shops for attractive specimens which are rare enough to take quite a lot of finding and make the hunt the more exciting'.[38] Here, Irish women were to do more than gaze towards the past – they were to purchase, restore and replenish their home with literal icons or totems to the past. Their homes were to be personal galleries or pedagogical spaces where the present could directly connect to the past. There is little doubt that the women were being encouraged to embrace elements of the previous decades so as to avoid showiness, in turn embracing simplicity rather than conspicuousness. Moreover, women were encouraged to draw connections to their familial Irish past, and to find excitement not by marching or fighting for the republican cause, but by hunting at auctions and browsing antique shops. The republican revolution would not be won by carrying banners featuring Tone, Pearse and Connolly – among others – or through public support for imprisoned hunger strikers, but by reconnecting with the fundamental Irishness found in physical remnants of a more civilised age.

Fianna Fáil, as discussed in the previous chapter, expended great amounts of energy in its efforts to distance itself from the republican ethos of abstentionist Sinn Féin. As such, the women's page of the *Irish Press* served to recast feminine political agency away from Sinn Féin militancy and towards a political domestic activism where creating the 'all-Irish home' and voting

In Brown And Beige

A cape of unusual line in sherry brown velvet, with a fox collar.

The cape lining is in beige satin, which makes the cuffs also of the gown.

This, of the finest texture brown and beige small check, has a new pleat arrangement in front which, while definitely slimming, makes for freedom in walking.

Figure 2.1 'In Brown and Beige', *Irish Press*, 1 October 1931, p. 3. With thanks to Irish Newspaper Archives and *The Irish Press*.

– for Fianna Fáil candidates, of course – served as the apex of political activism for Irish women. Missing from articles in the *Irish Press* were the topics found in the advanced nationalist press, where ever-present calls for militaristic action and revolutionary tomes were often penned by noted women who maintained the anti-treatyite cause years after the end of the civil war. In the *Irish Press*, women were directed to become

domesticated harbingers of Irish primitivism – that is, to be the direct connection to an imagined Irish past. Such was the intention of an article that advanced the 'Vogue of the Demure', where 'Quakerish demureness' adorned with 'Irish linen' afforded a 'pleasing simplicity'.[39] This effort to reconstruct the appropriate role of women was commensurate with Fianna Fáil's initial concern to bridge the problematic associations with the militarism that Cumann na nGaedheal had pinned upon Sinn Féin. Thus, it is not surprising to find the party – at least before the 1932 election – still advancing rhetoric overly concerned with a backward gaze. After its election into government, however, Fianna Fáil became far more concerned with a type of Irish futurism rooted in the advancement of a modern yet traditional Irish Feminine that served Fianna Fáil's nationalist aesthetic by working towards victory in the economic war. Nevertheless, the recurring themes – albeit fraught with contradictions – of a sense of 'old-fashionedness' certainly suited a party so obviously anxious about its past associations and the means by which it could incorporate women into the national movement.

In the earliest editions of the *Irish Press*, numerous pieces glorified the pastoral and the harmony of the home and garden. For instance, in an article appearing on 22 September 1931, author Emily Dowling wrote:

> Life is not easy in the country any more than in the town, but in the country sorrow and death are eased. We live closer to the earth, we sink more quietly into its arms.
>
> It is the consciousness of this, perhaps, that makes our homing imaginations fly, not to a building made of bricks and mortar, cut to State measurements and equipped with telephones and lifts, but to some little house softly-moulded of red earth, with a hood of brown thatch and a floor of beaten clay.
>
> In its friendly shelter we hope to find the healing of peace.[40]

The anti-government tone of this article is manifest in the screed against mandated building regulations, as well as a seeming distaste for the trappings of modernity. As such, Dowling glorified the country as a place of idyllic Elysium where one could breathe a 'freedom which is not to be found in cities'.[41] Sentiments such as this were frequently expressed throughout the first three years of the *Press*, and they were contrasted only by ponderings on modern fashion that had an air of 'if you must'. For Dowling, the joys of city-dwelling were attributed to the whims of youth, yet she wrote that 'in the hearts of the most of us there is a secret yearning for the country, for some remote land of our dreams'.[42] Further, Dowling noted that 'it is a pity the young who leave it so callously do not realise this. It is a pity they are not taught to appreciate more fully the blessing of being country-born, to see more clearly the delights with which they are surrounded.'[43] Dowling clearly insinuated that it should be the burden of the older generation to educate younger women about the joys of pastoral living, thereby shortening the period by which women 'matured' into understanding their expected role in Irish life. Explicit elements of Irish nationalism are present, yet there is no question that the women of Ireland were being directed to return to their primeval heritage via the elevation of the Irish sod, and the Irish Feminine was to focus her gaze upon the beauty of the Irish landscape, distancing herself from the unpleasantness of the cities and all their associations, including political activism. In the early days of the *Irish Press*, it was beyond question that women were to be apolitical, leaving such business to the men emblazoned and lionised on the front pages of the paper.

The writers and editors of the *Irish Press* were intent on reintroducing Irish women to the joys of domesticity and the inherent tranquillity that it provided. A series entitled 'Modern Furniture in the Home' was somewhat misleading, as it had little to do with incorporating artistically modern furniture. For instance, readers of an article written by a 'Home Specialist' about the dining room were told: 'The room where we eat our meals should have dignity as well as conviviality. There should, therefore, be harmony in furniture and atmosphere.'[44] Readers were advised that 'overcrowding with furniture is worse in a bedroom than anywhere, for it destroys that atmosphere of rest and contentment that should mark a bedroom. Decide first what furniture you MUST have, and then decide WHERE each piece should go.'[45] As for the kitchen, similar advice was given regarding spacing of furniture and practicality, yet the opening sentence neatly summarised the message: 'The kitchen is really the housewife's workshop.'[46] After decades of feminist discord where political activity was a matter of public spectacle – not to mention the connotations this had for Fianna Fáil – the allegory of domestic harmony fell into line with the party's efforts to re-establish traditional gender ideologies.

Citing the work of Constance Markievicz's 'Woman with a Garden' in *Bean na hÉireann*, Karen Steele notes how Markievicz sought to 'reclaim the garden's political potential for both women and nationalists by composing features that allegorically described how readers could resist domesticity *and* imperialism through the most visible icon of the Ascendancy class, the garden'.[47] Twenty years later, Fianna Fáil utilised the garden to shift the gaze of Irish women, albeit in a fashion much different to what Markievicz had intended. In its early run the *Irish Press* featured a regular column entitled 'The Woman Gardener', where readers were offered sage and practical advice designed to improve the lives of the Irish family. Far from being the allegory on rebellion and resistance, these articles instead encouraged women to create a garden that established calm and tranquillity, as well as serving the practical purpose of decorating their traditional homes.[48] One such example came from a 5 January 1932 article entitled 'Harmony Between House and Garden', which warned that a 'seeming unimportant point which many house-owners overlook when they lay out their gardens is that of harmony between the building and its plot of land. There should be some tangible relationship between the layout and materials of the garden and the size and composition of the dwelling.'[49] By 'avoiding the incongruous' and planting a 'garden that "belongs",[50] the garden and the entire house would exude 'pleasing sympathy and unostentatious charm'.[51] Another purpose of the garden was that of practicality and general improvement of the Irish diet, as evidenced in an article subtitled 'Grow Your Own Vegetables'. It claimed that 'the housewife who studies food values sets a high standard of health for her family, and at the same time practises sound domestic economy'.[52] More than just being concerned with economics, the article claimed that 'as a people, we do not eat enough vegetables, and those we do eat have little variety. Potatoes and cabbage seem to exhaust our imagination.'[53] Potatoes and cabbage, of course, serving as signifiers of poverty, not to mention the horrors of the Famine. Additionally, women were encouraged to accept 'the Virtues of Herbs'.[54] Apart from improving the diet of the people of Ireland, the purpose of the garden – according to the *Irish Press* – was to occupy the minds of women year-round. For example, in an article entitled 'Still Much to be Done', women were warned, 'when everything in the garden looks lovely, when plants are gay and full of promise, the gardener is apt to "sit back" and feel that she may call halt for a time. But there is still much to be done', whether it be fertilisation of chrysanthemums or planning for 'Next Year's Strawberries'.[55] Such efforts would make it rather difficult to participate in public marches or republican militancy – if not both. Two weeks later, on 18 August 1932, readers were given even more specific instructions on how to busy themselves by constant pruning, tidying up borders (not a metaphor), and being mindful of the removal of pests.[56] From planning for autumn planting in June[57] or 'Jobs for July',[58] the remaking of the home was an occupational concern for the women – a far cry from the allegorical means of anticolonial resistance.

In September 1933 an article penned by C. O'R. waxed lyrical about the inherent beauty and value of 'An Irish Home in Adrigole', a home that represented 'the backbone of the Irish nation [and] will move every reader with its beauty and its truth'.[59] At the time, Fianna Fáil was trumpeting its efforts to construct new housing for Ireland's rural population. The article described the home as being in disrepair, cared for by the embodiment of the party's traditional ideal who wished to emigrate to America, but who remained in Ireland because 'she has an ailment which will not pass the emigration authorities'.[60] This woman and her children 'expect little out of life, and consequently are not easily disappointed'.[61] Despite the hardships, the reader was told that 'there is a wonderful faith in these people that supports them like a breastplate. *Biodh eagla ort agus ni baoghal duit.* That is how they walk, in fear and righteousness.'[62] The article depicts an Ireland beset by the social and economic underdevelopment wrought by Britain and then the Cumann na nGaedheal-led Free State. As presented here, the Irish homestead has fallen ill, and poverty, emigration and lowered expectations are tempered only by the strong faith and will of the Irish people. Fianna Fáil presents itself as being able to restore to Ireland strong faith and will *and* a strong home – that is, strong both in the literal and metaphorical sense. Herein lies the intersection between domesticity and political activity: the Irish Feminine had the opportunity – and indeed power – to correct the obscenities of Irish history through her homemaking, thereby reifying

Fianna Fáil republicanism and, as will be seen in the next chapter, supporting the Irish Masculine. As it was presented in the early years of the *Irish Press*, Fianna Fáil was to provide growth and hope, thereby instituting an optimism in the Irish future. Through the *Irish Press* it appeared that Fianna Fáil became more resigned to relegating home and garden advice to just that – advice. More important was the overarching theme of confining and defining the energies of Irish women. Even at this early stage women were still seen as the harbingers of the primitivist Gaelic archetype fashioning home and garden as well as their bodies in a manner that reflected and reinforced the party's feminine ideal: domestic, cognisant of the beauty of the Irish past, demure and passive. Most important, however, she was to embody that approved Irish model.

'YOUR UNIFORM': FASHIONING JANUS

It would, nonetheless, be faulty to assume that Fianna Fáil's sole vision of women was that of the muted domestic. In consecutive issues of the *Irish Press* published in October 1931, two articles appeared where fashion was the primary concern for women of distinct vocations. On 17 October a short entitled 'Fashions in Irish Tweed' could be found, accompanied by a photographic example. In part, the article declared 'Tailored Modes for the Business Girl. Suits of the jumper persuasion fashioned in fine weave Irish tweeds are decidedly the vogue. They are, too, definitely practical propositions for the business girl'.[63] This recognition of professional and public women was careful to ensure that such fashion was subdued and 'neutral' in colour, namely blacks and whites.[64] This is but one example of a trend in which nearly all articles that discussed clothing for public wear promoted the use of muted colours and modest tailoring. High fashion for the visible woman – whether in daily business or in society – was meant to be of 'midnight bloue [*sic*]',[65] ensembles in 'Three shades of brown',[66] long wraps of 'White and Nile blue'[67] or 'Coats with a Military Air . . . [or while] Brown and its Near Relations Still Dominate Day and Evening Wear'.[68]

In fact, a study of the numerous small articles on modern fashion reveals that Fianna Fáil advocated acceptance of fashionable clothing inspired by designers in Paris and New York. Many of these articles

Figure 2.2 'Fashions to Please', *Irish Press*, 6 April 1934, p. 4. With thanks to Irish Newspaper Archives and *The Irish Press*.

were filled with such adjectives as 'smart', 'distinctive' or 'original', and the clothes were often noted for their unique and noticeable flair – a conspicuously public adornment for Irish women that was perhaps meant as a counter to the Sinn Féiner picketing in the streets of Dublin, advocating a seemingly outmoded means of politicking. An advertisement from 6 April 1934, for instance, cements the notion that the *Press*, and by association Fianna Fáil, were willing to concede to women the luxury of wearing the latest fashions. This advertisement was unique in the sense that it boasted about the paper's fashion advice, noting 'Fashions to please/every purse are advertised/in *The Irish Press*. Whether you need – tailored suits, frocks, evening dresses, lingerie, silk stockings, smart shoes, a chic hat or gloves. *The Irish Press* will tell you WHERE to buy them. HOW much they cost. And, for your convenience, you can order by post'[69] (see Figure 2.2). Indeed, the party – via the *Irish Press* – was advocating modern fashions, but there was also an underlying sense of direction and instruction in these advertisements. While the fashions were of the *vogue*, restrictive guidelines regarding colouring, fabric and design were evident throughout (see Figures 2.3, 2.4).[70]

CAPE EFFECTS . . .

Here are two attractive capes— the one in white organdie, worn over a blue and white muslin frock; the other in dove-grey faille— with hat to match—is worn with a dove-grey crepe dress

Figure 2.3 'Cape Effects . . .', *Irish Press*, 16 August 1933, p. 5. With thanks to Irish Newspaper Archives and *The Irish Press*.

Steele noted that in Constance Markievicz's series 'The Women of '98' a recurrent theme was 'what to wear in the revolution'.[71] The heralded clothing of past feminine revolutionaries was something to be envied and perhaps emulated by Irish republicans in the 1910s and '20s. Steele adds that such clothing 'suggest[s] that Markievicz's own Easter Rising uniform, a green Irish Citizen Army coat and a hat with the ostrich plume feather, was selected not merely to express her "theatrical flair" . . . but also to establish a connection with earlier militant women fighting for Ireland'.[72] Such ostentatious displays of feminist rebellion were duly shunned by Fianna Fáil, as evidenced in a January 1932 article from the

ON THE JOURNEY

T HIS trim suit would make ideal travelling wear. It is in light weight Irish tweed in shades of brown, red, and fawn, and the scarf and hat are made of the same material. The inverted pleats in the skirt give a slim line, as well as freedom of movement.

Figure 2.4 'On the Journey', *Irish Press*, 9 November 1933, p. 5. With thanks to Irish Newspaper Archives and *The Irish Press*.

Irish Press in which women were told: 'As regards colours, the following may be worn with safety: navy blue, black, brown, rich wine red, dark green . . . [and] can be introduced by suitable trimmings. The colours to

be avoided are light blues, vivid reds, yellow, pale green, white.'[73] Later
that year, readers were told 'Bright Days Are Coming! . . . in Quaker
grey'[74] (see Figure 2.5). Indeed, while this may have been reflective
of fashionable trends of the period, the recommendation to wear
conspicuously dark clothing – referred to once as 'Your Uniform'[75] –
was repeated over and over again. Conversely, in a foreshadowing of the
economic war, women were encouraged to accessorise their dark clothing
with such things as yellow frocks made of Irish tweed. These were the
fashions of the Fianna Fáil revolution: modern clothing worn outside the
home was haltingly transgressive. Colourful plumage was encouraged
so long as it was produced in Ireland; modern fashion acceptable if only
made of muted and unostentatious colouring or patterning; attention-
getting *couture* only in the sense that it drew attention to the individual
woman's adherence to Fianna Fáil normativity.

The attempt to dampen notions of aggressive femininity through
outward fashions and behaviours and domestic equanimity continued
throughout the early run of the *Irish Press*, yet there appeared a distinct,
if not explicit, change in tone. Added to these sentiments was a greater
embracement of a muted *couture moderne* marked by nativist Irish
flourishes. As such, to the 'vogue of the demure' was added the vogue of
the Gael. In a slight change of nuance, women were encouraged to be less
coy regarding their patriotic aesthetic. While the concern of Fianna Fáil
in the period between 1927 and '32 was about justifying the party's *raison
d'être*, the party's *cause belle* – namely the economic conflict with Britain
that began in 1932, as well as the push for a formal break from colonial
ties – instead guided the period that followed. This shift was slowly
reflected in the manner in which the readers of the women's page of the
Irish Press were encouraged to dress. By early 1933, women were depicted
as the physical and aesthetic representations of Fianna Fáil's republican
aesthetic. Perhaps this shift indicated the party's newfound sense of
legitimacy, fuelled by its electoral 'triumph' in 1932, which essentially
signalled the end of Fianna Fáil's need to distance itself from the shadow
of the gunmen. In essence, the encouragement of women to outwardly
embrace Irish republicanism served as a transition between the time of
the demure and the following period in which women were promoted as
consumers of the aspirational Irish republic.

Bright Days
Are
Coming !

These two outfits would make pleasant spring wear. The first is in Quaker grey fine wool for the frock, with a darker grey jacket and felt hat.
The second has a coat, skirt, and cap in light navy featherweight tweed, with a beige cloth bow at the draped neckline of the coat and smaller one on the cap.

Figure 2.5 'Bright Days Are Coming!', *Irish Press*, 10 March 1932, p. 3. With thanks to Irish Newspaper Archives and *The Irish Press*.

In contrast to the muted if modish clothing of the public female, the domestic woman was encouraged to wear practical clothing that meant 'easy work'.[76] Whereas the articles on *la mode* were small asides, those geared towards housewives were far more substantive:

Everybody else has an outfit – it is taken for granted that the baby, the school-child, the sports-girl, the bride and all the others must have 'special' clothes. But nobody seems to suggest a sane practical outfit to ease life for the woman who does her own housework.

The maidless housewife smiles ruefully over the articles in the magazines imploring her to be dainty at all times! How is she going to slip into fragile be-ribboned underclothes at seven o'clock on a cold morning when she rises to make the family's breakfast? Besides, after a morning's housework, the fragile things would be fit only for the wash-tub and the work-basket.

The housewife's main need is something she can get into quickly; something durable, for she has plenty of mending without having perishable lingerie of her own to add to it; and something neat in appearance.[77]

The solution? A cretonne frock free of 'ribbons and lace' that allowed for unencumbered housework. These two contrasts – the muted businesswoman/socialite and eager and energetic housewife – served as *the* two models for appropriate behaviour for Irish women per the *Irish Press*. There appeared a duality in the fashion ideals promoted by Fianna Fáil, where conceptions of femininity were defined by primordial *and* modernist tropes. Though Fianna Fáil tended to promote the muted domestic as the norm, there was a certain level of acceptance of such aspects of modernity as the professional woman and modern fashions. Such double vision was a common trend amongst nationalist parties that sought to operate outside the interwar economic frameworks, instead opting for a third way – unencumbered by nineteenth-century dogmatism – that allowed for the intersection between past and modern.

'WIN THE ECONOMIC WAR – BY PLANNING!' WOMEN AS PATRIOT CONSUMERS DURING THE ECONOMIC WAR

The politicisation of women became much more apparent in the *Irish Press* during 1933, when the once innocuous articles on fashion and domesticity started calling for direct participation in Fianna Fáil's economic war by leading the charge towards financial self-sufficiency.

Figure 2.6 'Breakfast in the All-Irish Home', *Irish Press*, 10 June 1933, p. 5. With thanks to Irish Newspaper Archives and *The Irish Press*.

No. 6 of a Series

Look for this Trade Mark

IRISH WOOLLENS ONLY IN THE ALL-IRISH HOME

The buyer of all-Irish products is in a particularly happy position when purchasing any kind of woollen goods. Irish Woollen Mills have long been famous for the magnificent quality of their tweeds, blankets, suitings and serges. The finest materials in the world are yours by just insisting on the products of Irish mills.

it means you are getting genuine Foxford goods . . .

Foremost among fine Irish Woollens come the products of the Providence Woollen Mills at Foxford. In this up-to-date factory are made the superb rugs, tweeds, serges, and blankets (white and coloured) that have made the name Foxford so famous.

Blankets from Foxford—warm as toast, light and cosy as an eiderdown. The young housewife finds the years passing by, but her Foxford blankets remain ever new.

Well dressed men and women to-day must have Irish tweeds. Those who appreciate really distinctive tweeds of the finest quality, insist on being shown the latest Foxford patterns.

When buying rugs, blankets, tweeds, and serges always look out for the "EYE" Trade Mark, denoting Foxford products. They don't cost nearly so much as you'd expect to pay for such distinctive goods.

FOXFORD

RUGS · BLANKETS SERGES · TWEEDS

Nos. 1 to 5 of this series showed why Cream's Soaps, Denny's Bacon, Corcoran's Mineral Waters, Blue Band Margarine, and Harrington's Paints, should all be used in the ideal Irish home. Further advertisements will deal with other all-Irish products. Cut out and keep these advertisements for reference when shopping.

MADE BY
PROVIDENCE WOOLLEN MILLS, FOXFORD

Telegrams: "PROVIDENCE, FOXFORD."
Telephone: FOXFORD 4.

Figure 2.7 'Irish Woollens Only in the All-Irish Home', *Irish Press*, 24 June 1933, p. 5. With thanks to Irish Newspaper Archives and *The Irish Press*.

In an article published on 9 June 1933 entitled 'Does Beauty Mean Nothing to You?' the authors queried the reader: 'Life is poorer for us and our children because we wear badly designed *cotton* fabrics, use badly balanced cretonnes in our homes and put terrible wall papers on our walls.'[78] The article continued, encouraging Irish women to strip their walls bare of foreign-produced wallpaper, replacing it with Irish-made paint, and to accentuate their windows – always open to the beauty of the Irish nation – with fine Irish lace. Additionally, the emphasis on 'badly designed cotton fabrics' was a clear condemnation of British-imported cotton and fashions designed in London. Later that year, the call went out to the women of Ireland to 'Win the Economic War – by Planning!'[79] Facilitating this planning was a serial guide to Irish products published throughout 1933. Over the course of the year, women were encouraged to serve Denny's bacon for breakfast, as 'The prosperity of your country depends on the way in which each of you supports its industries', and to 'Make *your* home one a patriotic Irish man or woman would be proud of'[80] (see Figure 2.6). Beyond bacon, women were told to purchase Irish margarine, mineral water and 'Irish Paints for brightening the All-Irish Home';[81] and, bridging the gap between fashion and patriotism, to wear 'Irish Woollens only in the All-Irish Home'[82] (see Figures 2.7–2.9).

Urrey Chocolates would provide a little luxury for the family, and iron gates presumably constructed in Irish factories served to protect hearth and home. Irish children would be comforted and healed by 'All-Irish Preparations', and medicinal and toilet items should 'be Irish whenever possible' and be of the 'highest quality obtainable'.[83] Finally, this poem appeared in a column entitled 'The Irish Ideal Home' on 6 December 1934:

> The ideal home has room for no complaints;
> 'Tis painted spick and span with Irish paints,
> From roof to ground, no trace of dust is seen;
> Tis cleansed with Irish goods, and therefore clean,
> And those who in this ideal homestead dwell,
> By Irish food are fit and well.
> Though hygiene paves the way, they rightly think –
> Good health's maintained on Irish food and drink
> Thus, hygiene, health and happiness are found
> In every home where Irish goods abound.[84]

Morning in the All-Irish Home   No. 1 of a Series

IS yours a real Irish home? Are you doing everything a patriotic Irish man or woman should do to support the industries of your own country? In this series we shall show how you can have a real 100% Irish home not only without entailing any sacrifice, but with immediate advantage to yourself in the matter of quality and price. Take for instance the morning toilet—do you know that household and toilet soaps, shaving cream, etc., as good as the finest imported products are now made in Ireland and at no extra cost?

"Cleanliness is next to Godliness"

CREAN'S "DROMONA" Toilet Preparations serve their purpose in helping the truth of this proverb. Not only do they cleanse, but their perfume, texture, lathering properties, shape and colour, all combine to give that "Good to be Alive" feeling first thing in the morning.

And there is another point—Crean's are 100% Irish, 52 weeks every year—not 51% Irish for one week.

Dad of course has first run in the bathroom. Hard to know whether to use Dromona Shaving Cream or Soap. They're both so good. The same in the bath. "Dromona" Bath Soap with its floral perfumes or one of the medicated range (Carbolic, Pine Tar. Lanoline, Castille)—all Giving the *fit feeling*

HURRY UP DAD GIVE A FELLOW A CHANCE

THEN the boy. Looking forward to the time *he* can shave—dad seems to enjoy it so. Plumps for Pine Tar for his wash—loves the lather.

Mum and the girls say there is nothing like "Complexion" or "Cream" Soap. Although Bouquet and Floral come close. They know they not only clean, but refresh and retain the health of their Irish complexions.

Ask your chemist —he knows

DROMONA

Shaving Soap or Cream—Bath Soaps

"COMPLEXION" "CREAM"
"FLORAL" "BOUQUET"

Medicated Soaps

★ This is the first of a series of advertisements designed to show how you can have everything of the best in your home while buying Irish goods only. Cut out and keep each advertisement in this series. You'll find them very helpful in your effort to make yours a real All-Irish Home.

Figure 2.8 'Cleanliness is Next to Godliness', *Irish Press*, 7 June 1933, p. 5. With thanks to Irish Newspaper Archives and *The Irish Press*.

Referred to as the 'Nation's Bursar', Irish women were expected to combat British colonialism, and in turn support Fianna Fáil nationalism by contributing to what was hoped to be an increasingly self-sustaining Irish economy. After all, shopping and bargain-hunting were deemed the 'most popular pastime for women'.[85] And although this was a far cry from the intellectual and active involvement of republican women prior to the formation of de Valera's republican party, there was nonetheless an indication that women did indeed have a relatively active role in Fianna Fáil's envisioned republic. Although the association between nationalistic consumerism and the economic war began in earnest in 1933, the connection between republican efforts and the advocacy of goods of Irish manufacture had its origins in the first Fianna Fáil ard fheis when the following resolution – put forth by Robert Bondfield of the Dublin City *craobh* (branch) – was passed: 'That F.F. should start an Irish Industrial Revival Campaign, by urging its members to buy nothing but Irish goods, and, also as far as possible, to have propaganda distributed throughout the 32 counties and to see that every Craobh set up committees to deal with the same'.[86]

The appeal to women and their significance to the economic war[87] can be found in a statement made by Éamon de Valera around this time:

> I make a special appeal to the women of this country . . . if they want to help us win this war, that every time they go out to buy an article they will try to get an article of home manufacture. I used to say that we could get back our cotton and silk trade, but until we can get Irish cotton and silk we ought to be content with Irish woollens. We can get our artists to design costumes for our women much more appropriate in our country and climate than the fashions imported from Paris, London or New York.
>
> I know that we can work up a tremendous enthusiasm here by sanctioning deeds of violence in certain directions, that we could get up a war atmosphere in which we would all be at fever [pitch], and we would get in that way a sort of artificial enthusiasm. But that wears off. That state of exhilaration might evaporate as it evaporated in certain conditions before.[88]

Figure 2.9 'No. 10: Footwear for the All-Irish Home', *Irish Press*, 8 July 1933, p. 5. With thanks to Irish Newspaper Archives and *The Irish Press*.

This particular speech, likely to have been given in 1932 or thereafter – note the present tense of the reference to winning 'this war' – was de Valera's most explicit call for the form of political activity advocated by Fianna Fáil. It was more than just a call for support of the party's protectionist policies, as de Valera was rallying Irish females to become active agents in the Fianna Fáil spectacle: working, sewing, buying, wearing and enthusiastically advancing the cause of a free republic.

De Valera's intentions were mirrored in a call for the creation of the Woman's Industrial Development Association (WIDA), 'an endeavour to co-ordinate the activities of town and country'.[89] According to a report of the inaugural meeting that took place in late February 1935, the goal of the WIDA was to establish markets for country products in the city: 'Quantities of fireside articles are made in the very midst of the country; markets should be found for them in Dublin and other big towns.'[90] Days later an article appeared marking the progress of the WIDA, noting that it had 'left the ranks of small organisations and has become the national voice of the consumer, an active agent for the sale and purchase of Irish-made goods, and with the proposed new organisation that voice will make itself heard over all Ireland'.[91] The article further noted plans by the Dublin branch of the WIDA to 'hold a mannequin parade of Irish clothes . . . which promises to be one of the most interesting exhibitions of what can be worn in the way of all Irish garments that has ever been held'.[92] Although a limited number of women were indeed granted a sense of political agency via the mobilisation of their consumption habits, the very fact that the *Irish Press* would deem it appropriate to publicise the WIDA demonstrates a clear link between the party and its envisioned role for women in Ireland. The intersection of fashion and nationalist intentions neatly coalesced in the push for an Irish *vogue*, which in turn would support the isolationist elements crucial to the intended results of the economic war.

The relationship between economics and nationalism was apparent in the advocacy of the WIDA, yet there was a noticeable, if not unique, call for a larger cultural nationalism seen in the organisation's material.[93] For example, in covering the 'All Irish Dress Parade' from March 1935, which called for an increase in fashion designed in Ireland, the author A.K. stated:

Goodness knows we have enough tweeds, woollens and linens of all sorts to cover us from Rathlin to Mizen Head. What we want are people to show us how it would be done. How it should be done gracefully, with art and style and that subtle touch that is the difference between being covered and being 'dressed'.

The French have a word for it, many words.

When Irish designers and dressmakers can catch up with the Irish manufacturers of beautiful dress goods, then we shall have a word for it too. At present the designers, with one or two exceptions, are left at the post, while the manufacturers are well away.

We send tweeds and wools all over the world, while we have no one at home to show us how they should be worn.[94]

Accompanying the event were the 'Misses Sheridan [who] sang songs and duets in Irish and English with harp accompaniment and gave a very entertaining finish to the show'.[95] Of note is a short film clip available from British Pathé that documented 'Some of the Irish creations at the Mannequin Parade held under the auspices of the Women's Industrial Association'. Titled 'Mannequins "wear Irish"', the film, credited as being shot in 1933, shows women and children modelling clothes ranging from the modern fashions outlined above to more modest examples and, of course, a virginal bride in white.[96]

After a later show in May 1935, the *Press* declared the event to have 'effectively demonstrated what could be done when brains and good taste were combined in the production of garments'.[97] The show further 'attracted people of all classes of the community to the hall and was more representative in this respect than any all-Irish dress display yet held at Ballsbridge'.[98] According to the article, the following persons 'occupied seats on the platform': Seán T. O'Kelly, Seán Lemass, Dr and Mrs James Ryan, Frank Fahy, Tomás Ó Deirg and Senator Mrs Wyse Power.[99] The dignitaries at the meeting represented some of the most powerful and prominent members of Fianna Fáil – clearly an effort by the party to publicly advocate on behalf of the WIDA. Whether or not the WIDA was an outgrowth of Fianna Fáil, the mere fact that the organisation existed and was trumpeted in the *Irish Press* clearly demonstrates the manner in which the party sought to politicise the women of Ireland through the embracement of a cultural aesthetic in which they were to be both producer and consumer of the republican thrust.

By 1935 the home advice articles became even more overt in their recommendations that Irish women incorporate Irish-made products into their home projects. This harks back to de Valera's 1929 call for 'greater sacrifices [that] have been made for the preservation of the Irish nation . . . As we stand today, the nation cannot survive without Protection'.[100] Indeed, the protectionism advanced by Fianna Fáil was anchored in economic policy espoused by Seán Lemass, but it also underscored the party's proclivity to present itself as a masculine protector of Irishness, and by extension, the basis for the Irish Masculine explored in the next chapter. However, as noted above, this protectionism was more fluid than portrayed, for the party demonstrated malleability with regard to the modern woman adorned in modern fashions, so long as she espoused sublimated support for Fianna Fáil policy. In turn, these domestically manufactured products, such as the crocheted cosy-cover discussed in an article by Sheila O'Brien, were meant to utilise Irish linen and feature Gaelic designs. O'Brien's pattern called for a 'half-yard primrose-coloured Irish linen', and was meant to be 'a most acceptable gift for every woman who possesses a tea-pot, and, of course, every woman does!'[101] Later that month there was a pattern for a turtleneck jumper, which 'worn with a hand-woven Irish tweed skirt and a belt . . . completes a very smart Spring outfit'.[102] For a readership trained in creating the idyllic Irish home, the slight change in advice advocating the greater presence of Gaelic symbols in the home was simply an added level of nuance. Thus, the Irish Feminine was to help win the economic war – and indeed serve the larger cause of an all-Irish Ireland – by embracing a functional pastime that promoted a constructed aesthetic idyll.

The interwar period was rife with social commentators expressing anxiety about the lack of physical strength of both men and women. Much of this was rooted in the rather obviously debilitating impact of the Great War, where both combatants and civilians bore the physical and mental scars of the conflict. Less obvious was a sense of unease around the impact of modernity upon gendered norms, for example the fact that women were forced to assume laborious tasks – manufacturing, management, agricultural – that had been normalised as being 'men's work'. This caused anxiety amongst the era's political movements that exerted much effort towards controlling and restoring traditional gender norms. Such is evident in attempts to reconnect Irish women with the primordial. Conversely, in the interwar years, political movements – including Fianna Fáil – proved malleable when it came to physical activity as a means to serve the nation and in turn to bear the brunt of an Irishness restated. In short, the Irish Feminine was to be domestic, but also physically fit, as being so served the interests of the nation-cum-Fianna Fáil. Beginning in 1934 and continuing into early 1936, periodic articles also encouraged female physical activity and personal health, which would augment Fianna Fáil's gendered consumerism. Weekly columns appeared that educated women about fitness, so that they could lose their 'double chins' or 'thin those ankles'.[103] Evident of consumerist nationalism, women were told that 'If everyone ate an Irish apple a day, this homegrown fruit industry would soon be on its feet'.[104] Women were encouraged to take up the new trend – as seen in Germany – towards such outdoor physical activities as hiking or engaging in a game of camogie, or *camoghuidheacht*, dubbed 'Irishwomen's National Game'.[105] In this sense, women were encouraged to literally participate in expressions of Irish primordial nationalism as filtered through the Gaelic Athletic Association by means of exercise and the training of their bodies amid the physical beauties and restorative properties of the Irish landscape. Moreover, the channelling of feminine energy into the nationalist cause was in direct contrast to the passivity encouraged in 1931 and '32. This increased malleability suggests that Fianna Fáil's policy towards women was more fluid and rooted in political expediency than previously believed. It also suggests that Fianna Fáil was willing to back away from its initial repressive rhetoric regarding women, which the party felt had been necessary if it was to combat Cumann na nGaedheal's rhetorical broadsides.

'THE GREATEST CAREER OF ALL': PUBLIC VOCATIONS FOR IRISH
REPUBLICAN WOMEN

In 1935 a new thematic trend emerged – one that was concerned with the vocations of the modern Irish woman, which again suggests that Fianna Fáil's stance towards women's work was more nuanced than previously appreciated. Concerns regarding the vocational role of women had appeared in the *Irish Press* as early as December 1933 in an article headlined 'What Shall We Do with our Girls?'[106] The author, apparently a woman but listed only as D.F., queried: 'Are women going back to where they were twenty-five years ago? . . . Retrogression on the part of our sex would indeed be a step in the wrong direction.'[107] Noting that poor economic conditions were threatening to flood the job market with women, the author stated that the problem could be solved if 'Irish capital were diverted into home industries . . . [and] it requires small breadth of vision to see that this country must save itself by endeavouring to supply the nation's needs as far as possible, from within its own boundaries'.[108] According to D.F., possible vocations for women included accountancy, catering, auctioneering, publicity work, and law, where 'solicitor in preference to the Bar' was recommended.[109] Despite the tentative acceptance of women in the workplace, the author cautioned:

> In Ireland, of course, we regard religious vocations and marriage as the highest careers for women, but it is impossible to ignore the fact that for many reasons a big proportion of women do not marry.
>
> In justice, therefore, we cannot deny the intelligent woman, with the necessary qualifications and possessing industry and ability, the right to be economically independent and have the free choice of a career. In the minor commercial positions undoubtedly women are a menace to men. This arises from the fact of men themselves refusing to pay an economic wage, and taking advantage of a glut in the labour market. If a living wage were paid and the standard of service raised, the inefficient and pin money woman would be eliminated.[110]

Once again, we find propaganda in the *Press* operating at the intersection between party politics/legislation and gendered tropes, as Fianna Fáil was clearly positioning women away from jobs meant for men. Clear writes, 'The ban on women doing certain kinds of industrial work in the mid-1930s was a pragmatic attempt to prevent new industries from hiring female labour (by definition cheap) in preference to paying breadwinner wages to men, rather than an explicit attempt to limit women to the home.'[111] Such policy was not unique to Ireland, as many nations, in response to the depression, sought to direct female workers away from such traditionally male vocations as manufacturing or construction. Yet, in light of the gendered labelling utilised by Cumann na nGaedheal against its republican rivals, the desire to refocus and redefine feminine energies had implications beyond economic recovery in that there were nationalistic intentions in what Fianna Fáil was advocating.

Moreover, it should not be forgotten that, in addition to its intent to attain electoral success, Fianna Fáil was in the midst of a wide-ranging and all-encompassing effort to construct a new Irish state while the world was mired in an economic nadir. Daly has cited Fianna Fáil's concern with female employment as a means of 'reversing population decline and creating employment, in part because the post-1929 international recession had meant a virtual end of emigration from Ireland – the safety valve of previous generations'.[112] However, the economic safety valve and paternalistic misogyny were not the sole reasons for Fianna Fáil's policies regarding women's vocation. As with the examples given above regarding fashion, homemaking and consumerism, the direction in which the party sought to guide women through the *Irish Press* was part of its construction of a new nation.

Thus, it is evident that the women's pages of the *Irish Press* were constructed in such a manner as to guide women in a direction that best suited the aims of the party. Critically, Fianna Fáil was attempting to redefine notions of femininity and female existence to fit within its newly constructed Irish narrative. Beyond just mere politicisation, Fianna Fáil sought to make everyday life an extension and daily reiteration/reaffirmation of a new existence where party affected all aspects of normative behaviour. Mary Cullen has noted that many works of history '*do* treat the masculine role as the human norm, presenting a past of male agency and leadership and female passivity and dependency'.[113] In the case of Fianna Fáil and the *Irish Press* in the years leading up to the constitution of 1937, there was a distinct effort to construct a certain level of socio-political agency for women, at least in the sense that the party sought to make indistinguishable the political and the socio-cultural. In the Ireland that Fianna Fáil was seeking to construct, political activity was not solely limited to household work or preordained occupations. As such, relegating women to such roles was not simply a means to restore heteronormativity, but also to appropriate women into Fianna Fáil's nationalist project.

As prelude to a running discussion on women in the workforce, Sighle ní Chinnéide editorialised in 1935 that women needed to work because of the socio-economic realities that Ireland faced in the 1930s.[114] This implied that Fianna Fáil was able to concede the point of women in the workplace so as to secure a purely Irish workforce, yet it still maintained an attitude reflected by writer Nan Mahony, who declared housekeeping to be 'the greatest career of all'.[115] A series of editorials appeared in the *Irish Press* in early 1935 regarding women in the workforce, coming at a time when there were increases in labour force participation by women throughout Ireland.[116] This very short-lived journalistic debate marked a fascinating turn for the *Irish Press*, as women writers were becoming both more visible – in that they were given featured by-lines – and decidedly political.[117] Ní Chinnéide's editorial from 18 January 1935 opened by noting that a 'certain hostility towards the woman worker has crept in amongst us'.[118] She added: 'While professing to have women's best interests at heart, quite responsible people now advocate the exclusion of women from public employment, that they may be thereby inclined to return to their pre-war life as the cherished wives, sisters and mothers of bread-winners.'[119] This latter point referred specifically to the Great War – note the absence of allusions to the Anglo-Irish war or Irish civil war – having necessitated the increase in female labour, and is of great interest, for it asserts that chaos and instability had created a problem that needed remedying. Ní Chinnéide further cited capitalism and the industrial revolution as both curses and blessings for women because they afforded female labourers an opportunity to demonstrate their vocational worth but also created the low rates of pay that 'for women workers [was] the main cause of the real injustice'.[120] Thus, ní Chinnéide claimed, the concept of female labour in a Catholic nation such as Ireland needed to be rethought to better suit the realities of post-war modernity, such that 'when equal pay for equal service becomes the rule, then only will the fathers of families obtain the preference to which they are entitled'.[121]

In essence ní Chinnéide argued that a system of equal pay would correct the imbalances created by capitalism and the Great War, not to mention provide 'honest work for all citizens, men and women', a message not unfamiliar to followers of Fianna Fáil's rhetoric. Ultimately, ní Chinnéide used feminist language to codify the role of women in the Ireland envisioned by Fianna Fáil. Rhetoric aside, there was no arguing that ní Chinnéide was readily defining the accepted place for women in the Irish economy: the primacy of the domestic ideal ('Women are generally the first to admit the married man's prior right to employment'); republican provision of work; and most importantly, the positioning of women in a manner that supports but does not challenge the nationalistic aims of de Valera's party.

Responses to ní Chinnéide's article were published the following week and were duly divided by gender. Among the male responses listed under the article header 'Women Must Work While – Men Must Write – These Letters' were statements that centred upon the notion that motherhood was an 'innate ambition of every female', or that cited the importance of a stable and orderly home.[122] Such sentiments clearly reflected the themes present in the earliest editions of the *Irish Press*. For example, a letter written by Sean Gearoid Traynor queried:

> If the solution of the difficulty is to be found, we must put back our clocks not twenty years, but forty or a hundred, if necessary. Who minds going back a little anyway? Certainly not the enthusiastically-minded political economist. Better to be dubbed a personified anachronism than look for a solution in a future that seems to be landsliding further into the political mire. If our men could find enough to do, our women should be happy in consequence. The fables say they were happy long ago.
>
> Let us first provide employment for our men; and if our unemployment queues are filled to overflowing with women we shall only have to pity them in their self-created misery. Back to their homes! If instinct does not tell them this we shall be forced to devise a place of sending them to some desert island where, like Mark Twain's immortal company of charwomen, they can eke out an existence by taking in each other's washing.[123]

Another reader made an implicit reference to the problems of emigration and late marriage and claimed that women's apathy regarding employment was due to single status, as they tended to 'concede the prior right of employment to husbands which they have denied to potential fathers of families.'[124]

Ní Chinnéide responded to these writers logically and dispassionately:

> My main thesis – that in this modern man-made world women must, of necessity, find work outside their homes – remains unchallenged. Instead of trying to disprove this fact your chief male correspondent indulges in a glorious onslaught on a number of absurd unchristian theories which have no place in my original article . . .
>
> In Ireland the great body of women workers is composed of – (1) Elderly spinsters whose hopes of matrimony have long passed away; (2) Girls in their twenties who will, for the most part, marry eventually; (3) Those comparatively few women who wish to exercise their undoubted right, as individuals, to remain single; (4) Widows; (5) Mothers with ne'er-do-well husbands. These classes of people will always be with us, and it is for them, primarily, that the plea for fair play was made; that, in the Ireland to-morrow [*sic*], they may not be deprived of their hard earned right to occupy those positions for which by ability, education and training they are best fitted.[125]

Ní Chinnéide's response remained the final word on the subject and can be seen as most representative of Fianna Fáil's position. Indeed, ní Chinnéide accepted – if not advocated – the primacy of the male in the workplace, yet there was still a rather progressive element to her arguments. Having women in the workplace, she argued, was an inescapable facet of modernity as well as the nationalist project.

Indeed the 'ní Chinnéide exchange' was a precursor to the series of articles that appeared throughout 1935. This series began a mere four days after ní Chinnéide's riposte to her critics and explored the career options for young Irish women who were neither interested in nor perhaps able to dedicate their lives to housekeeping. The introduction to the series promised that career women from all fields would assess their careers in these articles, 'giving you solid data, [and] will add to them the benefit of her own wise advice and experience.'[126] However, the rest of the article was filled with warnings regarding these professions, as Nan Mahony declared that housekeeping was the career in which she was most interested. She added that 'the intelligent girl, with a trained mind, makes a better housekeeper than the girl with good biceps but not mind',[127] insinuating that the professions to be addressed in future columns might, in fact, lead women back to the home. This passive-aggressive approach was indicative of Fianna Fáil's position regarding professional women, in that so long as their vocational choices fitted within their approved frameworks – as well as accepting the primacy of domesticity – then women were 'free' to enter Ireland's workforce.

The careers given read like a list of so-called 'traditional' jobs for women: nursing;[128] domestic economy teaching;[129] civil service – not if you planned to marry, however;[130] technical teaching;[131] woman of the land;[132] professional *bean tighe* (housekeeper);[133] waitress;[134] librarian;[135] telephonist;[136] and draper,[137] among others. Exceptional columns exploring careers as doctors, pharmacists and journalists were largely written in a way that was discouraging, noting the long hours, difficult road and general hardships in attaining these positions. Indeed, there must have been difficulties for women entering these roles, yet in light of the general sentiment encouraging women towards domesticity, the bias against professional women was clear.[138] Moreover, the lack of politicisation as well as the emphasis on careers as Ireland's caregivers fits with the larger trend regarding careers for women, not to mention Fianna Fáil's concerns with promoting what might be called a 'contained feminine'. This series on women's vocations was, therefore, part of the much larger trend by Fianna Fáil to balance modernity with its primordiality. Moreover, it was representative of the party's effort to establish acceptable frameworks for women who did not fit within that of the much preferred domestic.

1936 marked a further, more radical departure with regard to the representation of women in the *Irish Press*. Throughout the year there was an explicit move away from the heavy-handed articles on fashion and domesticity that featured from 1931 to '35, as there now appeared on the women's page an intersection between women and Irish politics. On 21 March 1936, the *Press* announced the reconstitution of the women's page, re-emphasising its concern for both the domestic and public lives of women.[139] That year also saw a regular feature entitled 'Women in the News', which included a focus on the philanthropic and social activities of prominent Irish women. Another innovation was the increased presence of female writers, whose articles were often accompanied by photographs of either the author or the subject of said column. The 11 March 1936 edition of the *Press* saw the first recognition of feminist organisations, with a 'Women in the News' column that announced the formation of *Mná na hÉireann* (Women of Ireland) and *Mná na Poblachta* (Women of the Republic). The article neither promoted nor condemned the groups, stating only that they were purely republican. Articles written by Hanna Sheehy Skeffington, a long-time advocate of women's rights, heralded a push towards the construction of a new Irish feminism, which – informed by the horrors of the first world war, a conflict she had demonstrated against – promoted pacifism and a greater sense of gendered equality.[140] When viewed within the political context of 1936, Fianna Fáil's association with Skeffington's vision of feminism enabled the party to better defend against claims by their enemies of communistic leanings. This trend towards appealing to a more explicitly politically aware readership can be seen as setting the foundation for the paper's front-page headline of 4 November 1936: 'Mr De Valera Outlines the New Constitution'.[141]

What, then, was the Irish Feminine? Maryann Valiulis writes that 'The ideal Irish woman then – the self-sacrificing mother whose word was bound by the confines of her home, a woman who was pure, modest, who valued traditional culture . . . a woman who knew and accepted her place in society – served the purposes of the ruling Irish élite'.[142] Nothing in this chapter disputes this notion, apart from the level of agency granted to Irish women to express themselves as (Fianna Fáil) nationalist and demure flapper. In the years leading up to the passage of *Bunreacht na hÉireann* in 1937, the *Irish Press* served as the most consistent example of Fianna Fáil's effort to define acceptable definitions of femininity. As the 1930s progressed, the party's idea of the female norm changed, reflecting both its electoral successes and its increasingly sure-footed sense of the aesthetics of private and public life. Granted, there was a distinct whiff of paternalism, if not misogyny, in legislation put forth by Fianna Fáil in the 1930s, yet, in the party's envisioned Ireland, women were to be both the physical embodiment of the nation, and the main consumers of its products. This was the level of agency *granted* by Fianna

Fáil in its overarching efforts to establish an independent republic. Additionally, women were not just relegated to the embodiments of the primordial notion of both femininity and Irish national identity. Like the male – whom Fianna Fáil defined as upholders of traditional, Catholic manliness, and as the muscle behind the modernisation and industrialisation of Ireland – the female of Ireland was also encouraged to accept and utilise aspects of modernity in the effort to construct an Irish republic. Such evidence stands in direct contrast to de Valera's call for a nation of comely maidens, instead being more representative of the participatory ethos so common to third-way governments throughout Europe in the interwar period.

'You do your part, and we'll do the rest': Fianna Fáil's aesthetic masculinity[1]

Du
ring the economic war Fianna Fáil martialled a masculine aesthetic, portraying the party as a model to which Irish men could aspire. This politicisation of the body served to correct what the party viewed as centuries of decay at the hands of the British, and more recently, the leadership of the Irish Free State. Central to Fianna Fáil's mythic core was a crisis of gender wherein the literal and symbolic manifestations of national, regenerative coitus between the Irish Feminine and the Irish Masculine had been corrupted in a way that stunted the island's social and cultural development.[1] As such, the economic war provided Fianna Fáil a means to redirect the political and socio-economic energies of women, thus enabling the fabrications of the party's idealised Irish Feminine. By participating in the party's economic functions – consuming Irish goods, engaging in industrial labour and harvesting Irish crops – Irish men were to rebuild, regenerate and work for the benefit of *Ireland*. In doing so, the Irish Masculine's spiritual and physical transformation served to facilitate the rebirth of Ireland from the moral decay wrought by colony and commonwealth. Fianna Fáil sought to create a new order that was best suited for active national regeneration by enveloping into its nationalist aesthetic the fundamentally masculine forms of industrial and agricultural work.

Elements fundamental to Fianna Fáil's aesthetic masculinity are found in an editorial cartoon that appeared in the January 1937 edition of the *Fianna Fáil Bulletin* entitled 'Time Marches On!'[2] (see Figure 3.1).

"TIME MARCHES ON!"

Figure 3.1 'Time Marches On!', *Fianna Fáil Bulletin*, January 1937, p. 7.

The image is divided into two distinct pieces: the first depicts Cumann na nGaedheal leader William T. Cosgrave – dressed in the dandyish togs of a servant – bowing down to, and laying a wreath upon, a gravestone marked 'Decay, 1649–1932'.[3] In the image, Cosgrave embodies the supporters of the Irish Free State, which Fianna Fáil had begun to categorise as being subservient to Great Britain, and thus antithetical to the interests of the Irish people.[4] The year 1649 represents Oliver Cromwell's conquest of Ireland, while 1932 marks Fianna Fáil's national electoral victory, insinuating that the latter was tantamount to a successful decolonisation and resultant national rebirth. Offering condolences to Cosgrave is a very haggard and decidedly elderly depiction of John Bull. Atop the gravestone is a 'Cup of Bitterness' filled with bills of legislation that seem to represent Cumann na nGaedheal's willingness to retain direct ties to Great Britain.[5] In sum, Cosgrave – the physical embodiment of both Cumann na nGaedheal and the Irish Free State – is cast as an emasculated submissive, bowing before his 'true' master as he/they mourn the loss of West Britain. Situated to the right of this is the visage of a new Ireland, where a more optimistic and less moribund image of the country is offered: a rising sun guides large numbers of Irish workingmen marching towards dynamic and operative factories evidenced by the smoke emerging from their respective smokestacks. Ships are docked near the factories and can be assumed to be awaiting cargo that will be exported throughout the world. Cast between the rays of the new day's sun are the words 'GROWTH, 1932–1937', marking the new Fianna Fáil era.[6] The juxtaposition of the two images reflects the fundamental nature of Fianna Fáil's mythic core: that of national decay wrought by those submissive to the whims of Great Britain; and the need for national regeneration brought by the restoration of manhood to the Irish workingman. This cartoon from the *Fianna Fáil Bulletin* presents the party's national corrective in action. More broadly, the image represents five aspects fundamental to Fianna Fáil's masculine aesthetic. First is the explication of a mythic core centred upon the notion of national degeneration wrought by Britain and its submissive, the Irish Free State. Second, Fianna Fáil's charismatic form of politics in which the nationalist party actively led efforts to correct decay and torpidity through masculine leadership. Third, the need to restore the connection between the local and the national, the farm and the city, by way of a nativist economic system that reconciled the Irish past with aspects of interwar modernity. Fourth, the Janus-like effort to forge a nation rooted in both primordial and modernist means, where the restoration of the whole man occurred through the restorative nature of work. Fifth, the casting of the party as the protector of Irishness and vital to the growth and regeneration of Ireland's future. These fives aspects are essential to the execution of Fianna Fáil's aesthetic and are evident, in myriad forms, of party discourse: the amplification, if not fabrication, of the annuity crisis central to the economic war; the party's efforts to logically undermine and thus invalidate the Free State's perceived subservience to Britain; the presentation of the party as an active agent of growth; and as a seminal agent necessary to the process of national regeneration. In short, the party offered itself as a model of masculine action – a body to emulate as vital to the party's renascent vision of Ireland.

The cartoon 'Time Marches On!' embodies Fianna Fáil's mythic core, where the party presented Ireland and the Irish people as having suffered from stunted economic and political development during the period of both direct British authority and the Anglophilic Irish Free State.[7] Those myths served to agitate the nation, compelling the Irish electorate to embrace and participate in Fianna Fáil's nationalist spectacle. Indeed, it is not novel to state that Fianna Fáil was explicitly anti-British in both rhetoric and polity. However, viewed through the prism of responses to interwar European phenomena, Fianna Fáil's aesthetic reveals a layer of anxiety regarding a crisis of gender. The previous chapter explored the way the party sought to redirect the political energies of Irish women towards domestic and public behaviours, including consumption of Irish goods, in a manner that best suited the nationalist aims of Fianna Fáil republicanism. By creating a prescribed role for women suitable for country and city, traditional and modern, 'Dev's' party offered an idealised form of womanhood intended to correct a corrupted form of Irish femininity that ran counter to the party's national regeneration. Parallel to this was the sense that the presence of Britain – colony or commonwealth, literal or symbolic – had served to emasculate the Irish Masculine by co-opting his energies so that the fruits of his labour would serve the foreign crown. 'Time Marches On!' presented this corruption as having stemmed from the fundamentally submissive and subservient nature of the Cumann na nGaedheal-led Irish Free State. Cumann na nGaedheal, then, was rhetorically neutered, which prevented it from being able to effectively produce a truly Irish offspring. By advancing this crisis, Fianna Fáil put itself in a position in which it might offer an alternative to the decay and degeneration central to the period between 1649 and 1932. As will be demonstrated below, Fianna Fáil offered a corrective that utilised economic policy as central to restoring the Irish Masculine to its role as active progenitor. For Fianna Fáil, its efforts marked a watershed between national decline and national regeneration, for the party was to be the active agent of change that sparked renewal of the Irish and created a new nation.

The Irish Masculine cannot be disassociated from Fianna Fáil's attempt to create a charismatic form of participatory politics in which Irish men, through the simple task of going to work and producing for the nation, reified the essence of the party's Ireland. The socio-political dynamism advanced in Fianna Fáil's aesthetic offered a visionary ideal where all facets of modernity – industrial labour and output, agricultural production, global trade, family structures – represented an observable victory of the Irish over the non-Irish; the victory of the active masculine over the passive and effeminate. As the *consumption* of domestically produced goods functioned to help redirect the political agency of women in a manner that reified Fianna Fáil's envisioned Irish republic, the *production* of Irish goods by Irish men served a similar function in the nation's regeneration. In this sense, the very function of industrious, kinetic labour actively served the party's aims. Such is evidenced in 'Time Marches On!', where growth and activity stood in direct contrast to the decay and bitterness. Moreover, the image situates the party as the sun, a symbol utilised many times over in the myriad newspapers sympathetic to the renascent republican party. Fianna Fáil was the state, the economy and the source of growth; it served to lead Ireland through a 'third way' that avoided the torpid, individual-crushing tendencies of capitalism as well as the distastefully antinational collectivism, not to mention anti-Catholicism, of Marxism. Viewed one way, Fianna Fáil presented itself as a movement that transcended day-to-day politics and instead envisioned itself as the purveyor of life and growth, providing sustenance for a new Ireland.

Fianna Fáil was tasked with overseeing Ireland's economy at a time when interwar nationalist groups deemed the nineteenth-century liberal/Marxian divide as either ineffective or incompatible with the opportunities afforded by the machination of the age. As much as the rejection of the economic order fomented the fetishisation of futurism – speed, industry, mechanisation, rejection of the torpid and old – calls for national regeneration necessitated a careful, if not ahistorical, backward gaze. This approach, as enabled by Ireland's historic connections to Britain, allowed the party to advance an economic policy unencumbered by nineteenth-century constructs. As such, it is important to situate the party's economic ideology within the larger trends of the 1920s and '30s to gain greater insight into how the party forged this inseparable link between party, people and policy. About interwar Europe and the rise of 'third way' principles, Walter Adamson notes: 'Modernity needed a secular surrogate for the increasingly moribund cultures of traditional religion. One that could serve as the basis for a stronger form of human community. To regain this community, cultural practices retrieved from preindustrial societies needed to be infused into modern industrial and political settings.'[8] Fianna Fáil presented its work as an attempt to impart a command of means – a distillation of nationalistic efforts into the everyday. The party transcended class and history, as it was neither encumbered by Marxian trappings nor beholden to a liberal-capitalist lineage; rather, its immediate concerns centred on problems not salvageable by nineteenth-century ideologies. Brian Girvin notes that 'these policies coincided with and reinforced a conviction within Fianna Fáil that a new age had begun: one in which sovereign Ireland would finally break the historic connection with the United Kingdom and establish a specifically Irish dimension to social life and the economy'.[9] This was done through the creation of a complex nationalist party aesthetic that served to mobilise the electoral energies of the Irish people while seeking to progress efforts towards national regeneration.

Between 1932 and '38[10] the socio-political and economic constructs of Ireland were reimagined by the consciously nationalist efforts of Fianna Fáil. The recasting of Irish republicanism under the guise of de Valera's party coalesced around its larger discourse, such that all aspects of the Irish polity came to be viewed in direct relation to the renascent movement enabled by the economic war. Joe Lee notes that 'the annuities controversy provided the focal point of Anglo-Irish conflict in 1932. The issue fused emotional and economic appeal in an optimum electoral manner for de Valera.'[11] Having then been twice elected into government in 1932, Fianna Fáil seized its opportunity and initiated an economic campaign that sought to promote Irish industry through protectionism, in turn weakening ties to Britain and thus invalidating the entire purpose of the Free State. This socio-cultural analysis of Fianna Fáil's economic aesthetic adds a level of nuance to a historiography that tends to focus on the efficacy of the party's policies. Further, these works do little to place Ireland within the larger context of interwar Europe – namely as party to the fascistic critique of modernity. For example, Mary Daly demonstrates Fianna Fáil's public rhetoric of protectionism and its overall effort to ensure that Irish-funded businesses were given a clear path to success.[12] While Daly examines the failure of the party's efforts to limit – if not eliminate – foreign capital in the name of promoting Irish industry, she does not go far enough to wed the relationship between legislation and party rhetoric. Viewed simply as legislative initiative, the Control of Manufactures Acts 'only served to artificially boost a protected Irish capitalist class, who benefited from the profits of a protected market, but were incapable of using these profits to underpin genuinely innovative investment'.[13] Where the acts were more successful, however, was in how they underscored Fianna Fáil's activist economic ambition.

Scholars have indeed examined the connection between Fianna Fáil policy and its nationalist ambitions during the economic war. For example, Brian Girvin notes that Fianna Fáil's economic and political policies were mutually inclusive, and that the economic war 'provided the opportunity to reduce Ireland's dependence on the United Kingdom and to reorganize the economy along lines more congenial to [Seán] Lemass's developmental nationalism'.[14] 'Fianna Fáil', he contends, 'provided an interventionist framework within which Irish sovereignty could be asserted in economic and social policy'.[15] Daly supports such an assertion, noting that native industry and entrepreneurial investment advanced by the Control of Manufactures Acts of 1932 and 1934 were promoted despite 'no evidence that hostility to foreign capital investment in Ireland predated the establishment of the Irish Free State, perhaps because the scale of such investment was insignificant'.[16] While much of Girvin's work analyses the level of economic success which the republicans in power attained, my concern is the way in which Fianna Fáil utilised its economic positions as a means of advancing its nationalistic cause. We will shortly explore the transition of Fianna Fáil from a party concerned with the acquisition of power, to a party exercising that power.

Like many nationalist projects of the early twentieth century, Fianna Fáil policy and propaganda were largely constructed upon a binary in which activity and passivity were delineated within gendered constructs. It is my contention that the Irish republic that emerged in the latter 1930s was a Fianna Fáil construct – a product of the party's efforts to recast Ireland's socio-political and economic frameworks. However, Fianna Fáil's intended path towards an Irish republic would have been fruitless had it not been for the democratic foundation established by the Free State. The same democratic constructs that had invalidated Sinn Féin's physical force methods enabled the reconstitution of republicanism as advanced by Fianna Fáil. As such, it is important to reiterate that nearly everything Fianna Fáil did during the economic war up to the creation of Éire in 1937 was part of a larger effort to discursively dismantle the perceived connections between the Free State and Great Britain. This is not to say, however, that Fianna Fáil was absolutist in its self-aggrandisement, especially after its time in government beginning in 1932, for the party did effectively govern the Free State while it continued its nationalistic push. This paradox was not lost upon the members of the party, and as Chapter 1 demonstrated, it was a key factor in its appeal to the Irish voter. The economic war with England is an example of how Fianna Fáil needed to cast itself as an agent actively seeking to restore a masculine air to its polity. Although the economic war and its core issue regarding annuity payments owed to England had rhetorical origins in early Sinn Féin policy, the 'war' began in earnest shortly after the Ottawa Conference. Using the private correspondence of Sean T. Ó Ceallaigh[17] as a guide, it appeared as if the British were willing to make economic concessions, so long as Ireland chose not to pursue its aggressive political agenda. It is thus clear that the whole sequence of events was politicised so as to be a key component of Fianna Fáil's mythic core. The sticking point between the two sides was indeed political, thus enabling the economic split to fester as the decade wore on and making it increasingly difficult to distinguish between the political and economic questions. De Valera and his followers worked to turn a tariff issue into a larger, national issue of republicanising Ireland, where economics, politics and Irishness became intermeshed. Of course, other political groups, such as Sinn Féin, Saor Éire and the Irish Labour Party, were largely constructed around economic aims, yet they were minority parties encumbered by an adherence to a party dogma that undermined any broad, national appeal. Conversely, Fianna Fáil's rejection of any singular economic dogma – not to mention its central position in government – enabled it to parlay its fluid economic policy into political gain. The economic war was tantamount to a conflict of political will, and was constructed knowingly and purposefully, as opposed to something that was a long-developing, multi-faceted series of complex events – and part of the nationalist creation of Fianna Fáil. In short, O'Kelly's reading of the situation emboldened the party to take a defiant, masculine stance, where it was the manly protector of Ireland's land and people. This is not to say, however, that Fianna Fáil 'created' a conflict with Britain over land rights and annuity payments or that Britain's imposition of tariffs on Irish cattle occurred at the behest of Fianna Fáil. All told, these factors contributed to an outwardly aggressive economic policy that Fianna Fáil advocated as part of its larger socio-political rhetoric, in turn allowing the party to cast itself as the transgressor against Britain, thus further presenting itself as being *the* party that was actively working to construct a political agenda most beneficial to the Irish people. In addition, Fianna Fáil headed into a prolonged economic conflict based on the conceit that Britain was willing to concede many of the points for which Ireland was 'fighting'. Having established operable boundaries in terms of its relations with England, Fianna Fáil was free to advance a hyper-masculinised economic nationalist visage rooted in a positionality underpinned by anti-British bravado and through the advancement of an activist economic policy. Stated simply, this 'conflict' with Britain was a calculated gamble.

Fianna Fáil's willingness to depart from Sinn Féin's political intransigence and its efforts to directly engage with Britain in an economic conflict did much to scupper the feminised stigma attached to the republican movement. Outwardly aggressive posturing notwithstanding, the party – as demonstrated above – did not act in haste; its political manoeuvrings vis-à-vis nationalist politics were accomplished in measured steps. Having successfully deflected claims of being harbingers of renewed violence and conflict with Great Britain, Fianna Fáil began its fight against the land annuities. The annuities totalled about £5 million per year and, Kevin O'Rourke points out, were a significant part of the Free State's 'GNP of roughly £150 million annually'.[18] In language that mirrored the logical and pacifistic tones of its early years, Fianna Fáil couched its rhetorical battle against the annuities in appeals to law, national tradition and reason. Distinguishing Fianna Fáil's public discourse on the annuity issue was an underlying sense of manly activism and guardianship that was central to the party's economic efforts in the years marked by the economic war. Instilled with confidence from its experience at Ottawa,[19] the party aggressively – but cautiously – sought to sell the economic war to the Irish people, for it now hinged its nationalist future on whether or not it could successfully mobilise the Irish people for its 'war'.

'THEY ARE NOT A TRIBUTE': A LOGICAL ATTACK ON THE
ANNUITIES

Fianna Fáil issued a pamphlet in late 1932 that laid out its opposition
to the annuities. The document elucidated ties between the party's
nationalist platform and its economic policies. Further, one finds that the
party's socio-cultural ideal was so interlocked with its economic policy
that one aspect served the other, so that no one single element could be
removed from the larger effort. For example, refusing to pay the annuities
was presented as both a simple matter of principle and a stimulus to
native Irish industry. Continuing this trajectory, Fianna Fáil argued that
this money would be a boon to the Irish worker, would further propagate
the Irish Masculine, and – as seen in the previous chapter – provide an
aspirational model for the Irish Feminine. There was also significance to
the fact that Fianna Fáil was suggesting that it could turn the annuity 'tax'
into Irish capital, for this rhetorical fight was both self-serving and self-
aggrandising. Such sentiments are reflected in the opening paragraphs of
the imaginatively titled *Ireland's Right to the Land Annuities*:

> The amount paid to Britain in respect of Land Annuities is
> £3,000,000 a year. The total amount so paid since the Treaty is just
> £20,000,000. These Annuities are not legally or morally due to
> Britain. 'Northern Ireland' retains the Annuities arising in the Six
> Counties. [The] Free State is equally entitled to do so.
>   We cannot afford to make Britain a free gift of £3,000,000 a year.
> To do so means continued emigration for our young people. It
> means unemployment and impoverishment for those who remain
> at home. **If this money were kept at home it would be sufficient
> to relieve agricultural land and buildings of the entire burden
> of local rates** (stated by Mr. Blythe to be £2,000,000), and there
> would be £1,000,000 a year left for general economic development.[20]

This passage implies that payment of the annuities was an act of
capitulation by those who paid them – namely Cumann na nGaedheal
– and also an act of betrayal to the Irish people in the sense that it
contributed to the centuries-old problems of emigration, domestic
poverty and subservience to Britain. Further, Cosgrave's party was

implicitly depicted as incapable of fostering growth – an emasculated neuter ineffective in efforts to foment an Irish state free from its historical master. Conversely, Fianna Fáil made claim to a monetary alchemy of sorts, where it, and only it, could make the money work in a manner suited to benefit the Irish people and Irish state. Moreover, Fianna Fáil situated itself as being the only party willing to openly defy Britain in order to correct certain aspects of Ireland's recent past.

While Cumann na nGaedheal did not necessarily condone the payment, it did take a dramatically different approach to the annuities. For Cosgrave and his ministers, the annuities were viewed more as an obligation whose repayment would ensure Ireland's future solvency, which of course speaks to the party's efficacy in the 1920s. Such was seen in Cumann na nGaedheal's *Fight Points for Cumann-na-nGaedheal Speakers and Workers, General Election 1932*, which explained the annuities as follows:

> Land purchase is therefore a purely business affair governed by the same principles of morality and good faith as obtain in the cases of similar transactions in everyday commercial life. The farmer received the loan to buy out his farm from private individuals who took up the Land Stock guaranteed by the British Government and is bound to repay the loan first as he would be bound to repay a loan from his Bank for the Agricultural Credit Corporation.
>
> The land annuities, in other words, represent debts which purchasers under the Land Code in this country have contracted to pay other individuals **for value received. They are not a tribute like German Reparations of a contribution to any Government.**[21]

Far from being the weak-willed supplicants to British whims, Cumann na nGaedheal's position more or less was grounded in securing the Free State's financial future in that paying off the debts would ultimately earn economic independence for Ireland. Further, the party believed that paying the debts would avoid upsetting Ireland's largest trade partner – and any position otherwise would represent a 'Communistic Proposal'.[22] Regarding Fianna Fáil's policy of retention, Cumann na nGaedheal held the position that 'nothing could do more to destroy the credit of the country, the national character of the people, or their confidence in each other, than the proposal to evade the payment of a debt, honourably and openly entered into'.[23] To back out of such payments would be irrational and tantamount to 'communism', or at the very least, a basis for renewed conflict with England. Indeed, Cumann na nGaedheal offered a calculated and realistic approach to the annuities – such was necessitated by its political origins, and by maintaining prudence and caution so as to not upset the delicate balance of trade between the Free State and Britain. In other words, Cosgrave's party needed to protect not only its policy, but also its political legacy. This conservative approach played into the hands of Fianna Fáil, who could offer pipe-dream hypotheticals about an Ireland built upon economic republicanism.

Given its willingness to enter the Free State Dáil, it is somewhat surprising that Fianna Fáil invalidated the machinations of the entity within which it operated. Such an issue was raised in one section of the *Ireland's Right to the Land Annuities* pamphlet, introduced with the question 'Free State Ministers ask why Fianna Fáil does not proceed against them in the Courts for illegally exporting the Annuities'.[24] However, as seen above, Fianna Fáil often couched its contrarianism in democratic terms. In response to its own question, the party's position regarding its extra-legal stance on the annuities was stated as follows:

> The answer is that they [the Cumann na nGaedheal ministers] and their Parliamentary majority are the makers of the law, and they have safeguarded themselves by inserting in the Land Act of 1923 a provision entitling them to hand over the Annuities. While the provision remains, no redress can be obtained against them in the Courts. Section 12 of the Land Act of 1923 must be repealed; but it will never be repealed until Cumann na nGaedheal and its supporters are placed in a minority in the Free State Parliament.
>
> *Fianna Fáil's appeal, therefore, is not to the Courts, but to the electorate.*[25]

However dubious this position might be, the importance of this stance lay in the manner in which Fianna Fáil sought to invalidate all aspects of Cumann na nGaedheal's policies – a position that was promoted by the party from its inception, most notably in the arguments regarding entrance into the Dáil. Moreover, the party's appeal to the 'electorate' speaks to the democratisation of the Fianna Fáil nationalist spectacle that sought to provide for the Irish citizen a means to attain a level of agency within the party's regenerative efforts. Of course, Fianna Fáil's national organisation only existed – and succeeded – because of the democratic frameworks of the Irish Free State. The party and its participatory ethos would not have been as effective or appealing if it were more transgressive in nature, inasmuch as the party was far more moderate than Sinn Féin republicanism. In addition, this passage represents an evolution from Fianna Fáil's early efforts to establish itself as more gender-neutral – that is, less illogical and violent in its political discourse. During its early incarnation Fianna Fáil anchored its polity in a rational, legalistic framework inasmuch as the party was willing to distance itself from earlier variants of Irish republicanism. This approach was applied to the economic war, where legalist and nationalist arguments were utilised in the party's effort to retain the land annuities. That Fianna Fáil remained in government during this time demonstrates the efficacy of its altered republicanism as distinct from its earlier form. Under Sinn Féin, relations with Great Britain were antagonistic, violent and abstentionist, and – as Knirck has shown – marked as feminine. Interwar Europe was an age of anxieties, where newly democratised electorates looked to political agents or parties to correct the ills of the present. As such, political organisations enrobed in a masculinist cloak proved appealing to the quaking masses. If we extrapolate this point to Ireland, the more masculine – at least, less feminine – Fianna Fáil republicanism held greater appeal. Take for instance its 'war' stance. This was an intellectual and economic conflict certain to avoid sanguinity and a return to the vagaries of Easter 1916 and its aftermath. The party's aggressive and protectionist stance was reified and returned with slight majorities by the electorate, in turn validating and empowering a masculinist party to assume a defiantly transgressive position in its 'war' with Britain.

Despite the party's view that the Free State constitution and its legal frameworks were mere interregnum between union and republic, Fianna Fáil nonetheless appealed to the legal structures put in place by Cumann na nGaedheal. For example, it is stated in the pamphlet that:

> Six of the most imminent [*sic*] lawyers in Ireland (including five senior counsel), some after months of deliberations, have publicly

stated their opinion that the case for the retention of the Land Purchase Annuities in the Free State is legally sound. The legal advisers of the Government have not replied. Their *silence* is an admission of the *weakness* of the Government's case. Unable to answer the legal case, Cumann na nGaedheal is trying to confuse the issue by raising cries of 'embezzlement' and 'repudiation of just debts'. There is no embezzlement in retaining what is legally and morally one's own.[26]

Note that the pamphlet's author(s) labelled Cumann na nGaedheal as silent and weak, not to mention corrupt – all hallmarks of passivity, cowardice and timidity. Fianna Fáil on the other hand dressed itself in the cloak of activist masculinity by advocating a relatively aggressive means to retain the annuities. As the manly embodiment of Irish nationalism, Fianna Fáil grounded its arguments in legal opinion; consciously or not, further distancing itself from the distasteful aspects of Sinn Féin. In appealing to law (and order), the party demonstrated its ability to achieve its aims through negotiation and diplomacy, led by capable leaders that used intellect instead of emotion. Fianna Fáil was not advocating the *end* of annuity payments per se, but rather sought to change the nationality of the bank to which the monies would ultimately be deposited. Thus, for the landholder, the annuity issue was being reduced to a choice between paying 'us' or 'them'.

Fianna Fáil further strengthened its measured, masculine bona fides by stressing its willingness to recognise the authority and function of parliamentary commissions to justify its aggressive stance. Such was exemplified in the following passage:

Two British Government Commissions – the Childers of 1896 and the Primrose Committee of 1912 – unanimously reported that Ireland had been grossly overtaxed for many years. The Primrose Committee (appointed when Home Rule was in contemplation) recommended that the proposed Irish Parliament should retain the entire proceeds of Irish taxation, and that Ireland should receive from the British Government £3,000,000 a year to pay the existing Old Age Pensions[.] The Committee recommended a further British contribution if this were not found sufficient.[27]

Significant is the notion that the Irish people owed no debt because of their having overpaid on earlier taxation, enough that the advances given to buy farms was already 'Irish' money. Once again, the implication was that Cosgrave's party acted as enablers for Britain's duplicity regarding the draining of wealth from Ireland, not to mention the monies being robbed from the elderly. Lastly, it is worth noting that on the first page of the pamphlet Fianna Fáil presented a laundry list of items for which the annuities would pay. The party claimed, for instance, that the monies saved could solve unemployment, aid in the distribution of land, end emigration, provide for the infirm and elderly and undo any other problem primarily attributed to the British presence in Ireland. It promised nothing less than to offer a corrective to Ireland's economic underdevelopment by its neighbours to the east. Reading such a list, one wonders just how thin Fianna Fáil was willing to spread these monies. However, reality and political rhetoric are never mutually inclusive. Evident in the party's rhetorical aesthetic is the willingness to name – and solve – the crises faced by Ireland.

This choice of 'us' or 'them' underscores the sense that the retention of the land annuities would undo what was presented as a centuries-long corruption of the Irish soil by the British invader and the British enabler in Ireland. The pamphlet reads, in part:

> **The Land Purchase Annuities are unquestionably our property**. On the grounds of natural justice we have a right to them as part of the revenue of the land of our own country.
>
> We have a right to them as partial restitution for the over-taxation of Ireland by Britain (which during the period between the Act of Union and the Treaty amounted to several times the capital value of the annuities), as compensation for the destruction of Irish industries and for the various other financial and economic losses we have suffered as a result of English rule . . .
>
> It is only just that Great Britain should pay for land purchase in Ireland. In the past she confiscated the land of Ireland to reward the soldiers and adventurers who served her against Ireland. When she bought out the interests of the landlords she was merely changing into cash for the descendants the rewards which she had previously given to their ancestors. That is entirely her affair, as the British

Parliament admitted in the Home Rule Act of 1920. It is fantastic to maintain that Ireland is under a moral obligation to recoup England for the wages of her Cromwellian and Williamite soldiers. That, however, is, in effect, the contention of Cumann na nGaedheal.[28]

The retaking and rebuilding of Ireland are recurrent themes in the arguments presented here. The appeal to Irish nationalism that was such an elemental and foundational aspect of Fianna Fáil was also evident. De Valera's party was clearly making the case for a national regeneration that would undo the wrongs of history – the resetting of the primordial order to realign the natural trajectory of Irish history blocked by Cumann na nGaedheal. Moreover, there is something distinctively masculine – or at least male-centric – in the party's defiant stance. From utilising the feminine pronoun 'she' to describe Britain and the associative Cumann na nGaedheal, Fianna Fáil established a gendered binary, where its opposition is not so much female as 'not masculine' (queer) – a topic covered in the next chapter. Nonetheless, Fianna Fáil situated itself as the lone legitimate political agency able to realistically correct Ireland's financial problems, in turn offering itself as the model of active masculine growth. In addition, it rhetorically positioned Britain and Cumann na nGaedheal as conspirators working against Irish interests, portraying one as colonial aggressor and the other as passively enabling the prolongation of the colonial condition, thereby reinforcing and elongating the emasculating effect of Britain's 'theft' of *Irish* land and treasure; and it vacillated between positions that either validated or invalidated the legal frameworks of the Free State in a manner that best suited the party's needs at a given time. This latter point recapitulated Fianna Fáil's reluctance to portray its members as ardent revolutionaries intent on declaring a new Irish republic at the Ottawa Conference, yet provided space enough to advance its politically transgressive cultural nationalism. Played either way, Fianna Fáil found its position bolstered by the electoral victories – however narrow – in February 1932 and January 1933.

Regarding the Cumann na nGaedheal–British axis as advanced by Fianna Fáil, the so-called 'Ultimate Financial Settlement' between Ernest Blythe – Free State minister for finance – and the chancellor of the British exchequer, Winston Churchill, was tantamount to an act of treason. Citing the Boundary Agreement of 1925 – 'relieved of liability in respect of the Public Debt of the United Kingdom',[29] therefore cancelling Ireland's obligation to pay the annuities to Britain – was meant to paint Cumann na nGaedheal as passive and ineffective. However, in what was portrayed as an act of villainous treason, Blythe and Churchill secretly forged an agreement that ensured the payment of the annuities. Additionally, it was claimed that 'Mr. Blythe's agreement was kept secret from the Free State Parliament for eight months after it was signed, and even then Mr. Blythe refused to give the Senate access to the documents, or in any way facilitate enquiry into the transaction'.[30] Therefore, according to Fianna Fáil, the promise to pay the annuities was done in a manner that undermined the Irish cause and gave further proof that Cumann na nGaedheal was working against the interests of the people of Ireland. This supports Girvin's claim that 'Fianna Fáil's charge against Cumann na nGaedheal was that their economic policies, however well intentioned, allowed economic policy to be formulated outside the state'.[31] The pamphlet concluded with the following exhortation underscored by bold typeface: 'Mr. Blythe and his colleagues may believe to be bound by the "Ultimate Financial Settlement". You are not. That Dail has never ratified it. No future Government will be bound by it. The Land Annuities are rightfully ours, and Fianna Fail stands for keeping them in Ireland.'[32] Note the manner in which Fianna Fáil invites the Irish citizen to become actively transgressive by participating in the economic war, further nationalising the party, and, more importantly, wedding policy and aesthetic into an identifiable and relatively appealing participatory ethos.

Fianna Fáil, as the pedagogical model of the Irish Masculine, advanced a discourse regarding the reclamation of Irish land for the Irish, one that was often accompanied by Fintan Lalor's refrain, 'Ireland Free, Ireland Irish'. This does not mean, however, that Fianna Fáil was the originator of land-based nationalist agitation, but it was the first to adapt aspects of agitation to function within the frameworks of the Irish Free State. All of which was buttressed by the socio-economic conditions in Ireland during the interwar years, not to mention the democratic frameworks of the Saorstát. Indeed, Fianna Fáil was aided and emboldened by this long tradition of reclamation efforts to redistribute land to the people of Ireland. As Timothy G. McMahon notes, the issue of land reclamation was part of a larger 'revolution of rising expectations . . . that fuelled the push for full separation from the United Kingdom'.[33] Whereas much of what McMahon argues took place during a period in which popular, 'bottom-up' movements were a larger threat – and indeed, more palpable – Fianna Fáil seized these energies, enveloping the cause into its larger, all-encompassing nationalist schema. Like previous nationalist movements, such as the National League and the Sinn Féin of the 1910s, land reclamation was a central point of contention, but, as will be shown below, it was not Fianna Fáil's *raison d'être* in its attempts to elevate industrial development and economic growth, and as a result improve social conditions in Ireland. Having secured the mythic core and source of decay, Fianna Fáil was able to transition its discourse to focus on the exercise of masculine power during the economic war. Thus the party's nationalist project became pedagogy; its aesthetic, its policy and its polity were intent on modelling for the Irish people how to once again be truly Irish by embracing the past and rushing headlong into the future. And, as the economic war continued, the party melded pedagogy and practice, as Irish men were positioned to physically embody the Irish Masculine.

'THEY CALL THIS PROGRESS': THE AESTHETICS OF THE ECONOMIC WAR

Assertive, masculine economic nationalisms proved advantageous to many political movements in the wake of the Great War and Great Depression.[34] In an Irish context, Fianna Fáil offered an alternative to the liberal/Marxian framework with a blistering attack on the status quo, which the party portrayed as yet another Anglo–Free State construct. Positioning itself as, in a sense, iconoclastic, Fianna Fáil's activist economic rhetoric can be viewed both as a means to rescue Ireland from stagnation, and as a final push to break the centuries-long supplication to England.

Fianna Fáil's desire to foment economic growth by way of a charismatic form of politics is evident in a handbill from 1927. The handbill further offers an introduction to one of the many underlying themes present in the party's economic message and features text divided in two columns: on the left is the header '1918', and on the right, '1927'. 'In 1918,' the text reads, 'The Irish People were faced by a terrible Menace: Conscription. They looked to Eamon de Valera to save them. And he did.'[35] To the right of this somewhat simplistic over-statement is a boastful yet optimistic claim: 'In 1927 The Irish People are again faced by a terrible Menace: Bankruptcy and Starvation. They are looking to Eamon de Valera to save them. And *he* will.'[36] If Fianna Fáil was pedagogical, then de Valera was the professor. In terms of economic policy, during its first decade Fianna Fáil cast itself as a dynamic, manly agent of growth and revival in stark contrast to the inactive, passive Cumann na nGaedheal. A similar message pervaded still another handbill from the same period. Appealing to the 'Workers, Fathers of Unemployed Sons and Daughters', the pamphlet presented readers with two choices: on one side was Cumann na nGaedheal as represented by P.J. McGilligan, Free State minister for industry and commerce, who was quoted as saying: 'It is not the function of the Dáil to provide work, and the sooner that is realised, the better . . . people may have to die in this country in starvation.'[37] On the other side, under the heading 'Party of Work', Fianna Fáil was represented by a quote from de Valera, which read, 'I hold it is the primary duty of a modern state to ensure that every man who is able to and willing to work will have work, so that he may earn his daily bread.'[38] As the economic conditions in Ireland deteriorated – both from historical forces and those aggravated by the onset of global depression in 1929, this passive/active dialectic soon became the central, if not dominant, component of Fianna Fáil's self-portrayal.

An undated and uncategorised Fianna Fáil handbill created to guide electoral mobilisation for James Geoghegan in Longford-Westmeath demonstrates how the party used land redistribution to portray Cumann na nGaedheal as timid in its efforts to fully reclaim Ireland from the British. Extending the land issue beyond the question of annuities, the republicans attempted to portray land reclamation and distribution as an ongoing project to be undertaken with immediacy and aggression. Thus, Geoghegan's opponent was well-intentioned but altogether too slow to act. The handbill was titled *They Call This Progress*, and it was filled with examples of how Cumann na nGaedheal's torpid approach to land redistribution had impacted the farmers of Longford-Westmeath.[39] Raising the issue of untenanted land, the handbill notes that 'From 1923 to 1929 the number of Acres acquired and distributed was . . . 17,374. *The number of Acres yet to be distributed is . . . 32,338. So it will take the Land*

*Commission 21 years to vest all the Tenanted Land, and 11 years to divide
the Untenanted Land in Longford-Westmeath'.*[40] Regarding tenanted land,
the handbill claimed that under Cumann na nGaedheal only 16,268
acres were vested, while 57,585 were yet unvested, costing the farmers of
Longford-Westmeath £3,807 per annum.[41] If one were to analyse only this
portion of the handbill, much could be said about the characterisation
of Cumann na nGaedheal and its inability to initiate genuine land
reformation. However, the handbill specified the amount of money being
lost each year by Geoghegan's potential constituents. Its text continued,
'The Cosgrave Government think nothing of £3,807. *They* give the
Governor-General £3,000 to their army officers to become Cumann na
nGaedheal candidates. *They* give Lord Glenavy a pension of £3,692 6s. 1d.
per year. They give the Automobile Association £3,000 to cover its losses
on motor races in Phoenix Park.'[42] This short passage contains charges
that Cumann na nGaedheal was using what could have been land rent
monies to bolster its own electoral aims, as well as to pay for the pensions
of a *British lord*, not to mention support for decidedly un-Gaelic motor
races in Dublin. Note also how the rhetoric situates Cosgrave and his
ministers as 'they', as being outside the normative Fianna Fáil. The
handbill concluded with this damning statement:

> What does that Government care whether the Longford-Westmeath
> Farmers lose £3,807 a year through the shameful laziness of the
> Land Commission[?]
>   *If you think Longford-Westmeath can do something better with
> £3,807 a year than having it stolen by the Land Commission*
>   WORK AND VOTE FOR JAMES GEOGHEGAN
>   THE FIANNA FAIL CANDIDATE[43]

Essentially, two characterisations of Cumann na nGaedheal can be culled
from this handbill: first, that the party was slow, lazy, inactive, passive and
acquiescent to Britain; second, that the party blithely wasted Irish monies
on British interests. Conversely, a vote for the Fianna Fáil candidate
equalled a vote for work, both in vocation and in efforts to collectively
undo Cumann na nGaedheal's subservience to Britain.

The transition of land from 'British' control to Irish ownership was the
centrepiece of Fianna Fáil's efforts to 'win' the economic war. In another

election flyer, issued in 1933, Fianna Fáil sought to highlight perceptions that Cumann na nGaedheal was torpid or hesitant in reacquiring and redistributing the land for the Irish citizenry, as well as to promote its own contrasting agenda in advance of the January election:

> The total area of land acquired by the Land Commission during the year ended March 31st, 1931, amounted to 38,570 acres, while the land in process of acquisition on that date amounted to 139,058 acres, and the area of land inspected reached 232,147 acres. Hence, it is clear that at the present rate of progress it will take the Land Commission ten years to complete the acquisition of the lands now on their hands.
>
> But there were over 413,000 acres which were the subject of enquiry by the Land Commission on the same date . . . [and] at the present rate of progress the Land Commission will not have completed their present programme and divided the untenanted land available in less than 21 years.[44]

The handbill continues, noting that beginning in 1929 Fianna Fáil had introduced legislation to finalise the tenancies, but the bill was rebuffed by Free State ministers as being impossible. However, once in government, Fianna Fáil – according to the handbill – was able to streamline the process, resulting in a 'speedy vesting of the lands [so] that to-day practically all the tenants in the Twenty-six Counties have their lands vested and have been placed on an annuity basis with reductions from 5 per cent. to 10 per cent. in their annual payments. Fianna Fail can speed up the work of acquisition and division in the same way.'[45] The message was clear: the party intended to rapidly return ownership of land to the Irish citizenry, not to mention reduce and eventually eliminate the annuity to Britain. This promise to build upon what the party had already done was best summarised by a refrain oft-repeated between 1932 and '37: 'Put out the Laggards. Vote Fianna Fáil.'[46]

Fianna Fáil's plan for land reclamation coalesced with its economic intransigence on the annuity issue. Further, the return of the land to the people was an important aspect of connecting the local to the national – a furtherance of the party's national participatory ethos. In other words, Fianna Fáil was not just advocating for the reclamation of land, but also to aggressively promote legislation that facilitated its usage. For example, an article/party advertisement appeared in the June 1937 edition of the *Fianna Fáil Bulletin*. Titled 'We Couldn't – But We Did', it proclaimed that 'in 1931 we "couldn't mill our own flour" – but With [*sic*] the development of our mills under a Government which said "WE MUST" – the flour imports fell from £1,662,402 [in 1931] to £74,816 [in 1936]'.[47] Most notable is the claim that it was the Fianna Fáil government that was largely responsible for the construction of modern flourmills, which resulted in 4,014 mill workers in 1936 – an increase from the 2,417 employed in 1931.[48] Underscoring these claims was the assertion that 'Fianna Fail Will Keep The Wheels Turning!'[49] The kinaesthetic allusion to speed and movement parallels a fetishisation of futurism commonly seen in the aesthetics of interwar nationalist parties in Europe. Such themes are central to a party that sought to offer a corrective – and alternative – to unrealistic communism and ineffective capitalism. Present throughout the article were examples of activism and aggressive tactics in regard to the Irish economy. For instance, 'Eleven Other Benefits to Farmers' were listed, most of which were designed to counter claims that the economic war was damaging Irish agriculture and industry by stunting trade with England, the largest consumer of Irish-produced goods. The eleventh point claimed that Fianna Fáil had actively pursued new markets in Germany and Belgium, and that 'the export of cattle to these new markets had a beneficial effect on the market price for cattle as a whole by removing part of the surplus of exportable cattle at relatively high prices'.[50] Also highlighted were the benefits of land reclamation legislation that had increased acreage devoted to beet, tobacco, potato, swine and vegetable production; important factors that contributed to the reduction of the land annuities, giving 'relief to the Farmers of over £2,000,000 each year'.[51] Further adding support to the agricultural–industrial nexus was the championing of a government-funded canning factory in Waterford that produced 'canned meat in sufficient quantities to meet the needs of the country, and such products as meat extracts, canned tongue, casings, etc. are also produced . . . The farmers are being relieved of old and useless cows which are being converted into meat meal at Roscrea'.[52] Farmers – and their cattle – were thus an integral part of Fianna Fáil's efforts to depart from the old and outdated and instead move towards the industrialisation of various sectors, including the canned tongue market.

Viewed symbolically, Fianna Fáil's new traditionalism served to model to the Irish electorate *the* way in which the nation could be modern while at the same time maintaining its traditionalist connections to the land. Moreover, the party worked to restore to Ireland a masculinity that had been stripped away by centuries of British control, and, more recently, what it presented as the West Britonism enabled by Cumann na nGaedheal and its heir, Fine Gael.

The notion of proactive, aggressive economic legislation falls in line with the economic theories of John Maynard Keynes. A hallmark of Keynesian economics was the importance of an activist government encouraging economic growth through aggressive policy. This sentiment was not lost upon Minister for Finance Seán MacEntee, who highlighted the following phrase in his personal copy of Keynes's *The Means to Prosperity*: 'But in present circumstances this would be true of only a small proportion of the additional consumption, since the greater part of it could be provided without much change of price by home resources which are at present unemployed.'[53] MacEntee noted in the margins: 'Precisely why the fuller employment of men and machines. At present only partially employed.'[54] As with all economic theories, there was a divergence between dogma and practice, as was seen in Keynes' comments regarding the situation in Ireland, however positive his intonations.[55] As a result, Fianna Fáil defied categorisation within the traditional modernist economic definitions of liberalism and socialism. By navigating the third way between capitalism and socialism, the party cherry-picked elements of both systems without having to raise the banner of either – something that contributed to the decline and marginalisation of Cumann na nGaedheal and Saor Éire. Such a stance demonstrated that Fianna Fáil was not fearful of modernity; in fact, it was quite the opposite. The party, by embracing the third way between capitalism and socialism (as well as between liberal democracy and totalitarianism), was in the vanguard of the welfare states that developed in post-second-world-war Europe. While many nations, such as the United States with Franklin Roosevelt's New Deal, embraced Keynesian-style policy to combat economic depression, Fianna Fáil and its European counterparts used this approach as a means of nation-building and, in the case of Ireland, as a unique means to dissolve its colonial ties.

The theme of using nation-building as a corrective to a colonial past can be seen in another piece of party propaganda from the June 1936 edition of the *Fianna Fáil Bulletin*. Encouraging readers to vote for the party's candidates, the article read in part, 'You have the choice of voting for a party most of whose policy is second-hand[,] Most of whose leaders are far from united in their views[;] or for a party with a definite policy and a record of achievement in *nation-building*. Your help is needed to complete the work.'[56] Implicit are several points, including the notion that the party's opposition was incapable of providing the leadership necessary to increase Ireland's independence. Fianna Fáil presented itself as a party united in message, working for the entire nation and its implied destiny of complete independence. More important, however, is how this electoral message actively invites the reader-voter to be an active participant in the party's achievements. By 1936 we find a party confident in its message and unified in its call for a more dynamic electorate that could actively contribute to Fianna Fáil's nationalist aims.

In the same article, Fianna Fáil trumpeted claims that it was responsible for 'the building of an Industrial Arm'; placing 'as many families as practicable on the Land'; 'Re-Housing the Nation'; providing 'Work or Maintenance for the Unemployed'; ensuring 'The improvement of roads, drainage, water supplies . . .'; and finally, watching over 'The control of prices of essential commodities'.[57] This last point had in fact been advocated at least as early as a party handbill from 1932 that read:

> LISTEN!
> . . . the Dail can and must confine the home market to Irish agricultural produce. Further, if necessary, it can legislate for a fair price. If the Government creates a demand at home for fair-priced Irish produce (which it undoubtedly can) Fianna Fail knows that the Irish farmer will supply that demand!
> And now P.T.O.![58]

The Irish farmer was thus expected to become an avatar for Fianna Fáil – a seminal agent of Irish growth utilising Irish goods grown in – or produced on – Irish soil. In this sense the pupil has worked to satisfy the teacher, and the farmer became a surrogate for Fianna Fáil's national regeneration: Ireland by and for the Irish. Finally, the true realisation of Fintan Lalor's nationalist vision. For the reader of such propaganda there was no doubt about Fianna Fáil's commitment to activist economic policy, with top-down approaches that were part and parcel of its Keynesian leanings. Conversely, take note of how the handbill emasculates Cumann na nGaedheal ministers by characterising them as willingly submitting to the whims of England. Such language serves to accentuate Fianna Fáil's masculinity at the same time as it enfeebles, or queers, the party's opposition.

The advocacy of manly, industrial work was a key element in Fianna Fáil's economic aesthetic. Elevating the status of the Irish worker, yet careful not to come across as Marxian classists, Fianna Fáil forged a connection between the modern labourer and government policy. As seen in the previous chapter, Fianna Fáil also sought to channel the energies of republican women, to reconstitute the notion of Irish femininity and to buttress the party's economic and political aims. In a similar fashion, Fianna Fáil emphasised the importance of manly work and the value of labour to the Irish land and people. An electoral flyer from 1932 addressed the unemployed of Ireland, claiming 'There's work for you. Plenty. Right here at home in Ireland!'[59] Again, Fianna Fáil presented a circuitous logic in which work would make the man, the man would make the nation and Fianna Fáil would make the work. The very next line of the flyer intones that Fianna Fáil was promoting growth, in that the Irish people were now 'Making the clothes, growing the food, building the houses – doing a hundred other things for your fellow Irishmen – doing the work that is to-day being done for us by foreigners. We can do it all ourselves . . . You can do it!'[60] Once more, Fianna Fáil advanced a seamless and symbiotic policy in which the Irish male would produce the goods that the Irish female – or the Belgian or the German – would purchase to stock her Irish home or to feed her children. The next line of the flyer erased any doubt about who would be providing such work: 'THERE IS NO WAY OF ENDING UNEMPLOYMENT EXCEPT BY PROVIDED WORK. THAT'S THE SURE POLICY OF FIANNA FÁIL.'[61] Fianna Fáil presented itself as correcting the inactive bodies of the unemployed, restoring the Irish Masculine into a functional, working body that was manly, virile and Irish.

Fianna Fáil's advocacy of an activist economic agenda was omnipresent in the years leading up to the 1937 election that resulted in the enactment of a new Irish constitution. For example, in a typed summary of a stump speech given by Seán MacEntee during the Dublin campaign, the Fianna Fáil minister demonstrated the importance of a power that elevated action and effective policy above calls for party balance and governmental constraint. The official summary of MacEntee's speech read, in part:

> The Government of a country was a serious business. The task of reviving the economic life of the country was a heavy one. It was one which would never be fulfilled if the workers regarded the present political situation as a child's game of see-saw, in which their primary duty was merely to put someone in the middle to keep a balance, while the other two parties went up and down at the end of the plank. Progress would never be made that way. Let the workers and producers make up their minds that they wanted the Fianna policy [*sic*] and then give the candidates who stood for that policy the swinging majority which would enable them to put it into practical operation without doubt, hesitation, or delay. If they were going to give their succeeding preferences to candidates of the Labour Party, Mr. MacEntee asked his audience to make sure to give them to real labour men.[62]

MacEntee walked a fine line between liberal democracy and socialism – even totalitarianism – in the way he asked for the people to give power to an aggressive, strong-willed party. Further, note the effort to marginalise the Labour Party, insinuating that it was not truly representative of the Irish labourer, exhorting the voter to choose men who were true 'labour' men. MacEntee meant, of course, that his party was comprised of candidates most true to the cause of the labourer, as evidenced by Fianna Fáil's ability to enact legislation through its electability and practicality. Such a policy was to be enacted swiftly without bureaucratic delays resulting from constitutional or party see-sawing. For MacEntee and his peers, active economic policy and aggressive rhetoric were part and parcel of Fianna Fáil's calls to 'Keep the Wheels Turning'.

Like its feminine counterpart, the evolution of the Irish Masculine was played out in the pages of the *Irish Press*. Fianna Fáil's paper afforded the party its most public opportunity to adorn itself in a masculinist cloak, and both party and press were mutually exclusive in this endeavour. For example, a cartoon entitled '"An Claidheamh Soluis": the Sword of Light' from the 5 September 1932 edition of the *Irish Press* depicts a masculine hand holding a medieval sword, whose mere presence causes a man labelled 'surrender', 'disunity', 'bitterness', 'weakness' and 'fear' to flee in dread.[63] Here the party, by way of the *Irish Press*, is presented as an aggressive, but not necessarily violent, counter to the problems of Free State Ireland. A similar cartoon from September 1933 depicts the *Irish Press* as a warrior – presumably of the ancient Fianna – bearing a sword called 'Truth' that stands firm against arrows labelled 'enmity', 'strife' and 'defeatism', and shadowy figures denoted as 'violence', 'dictatorship', 'disunity' and 'hypocrisy'.[64] These images are stark depictions of Fianna Fáil's backward gaze – a gaze that connected the party to the purity of an imagined Gaelic past unsullied by England, the treaty and West Britonism. Moreover, the reference to 'The Sword of Light' has dual meaning – both in the alignment between Fianna Fáil and the Gaelic past, and a more concrete connection to *An Claidheamh Soluis*, a newspaper of the Gaelic League.

Light, as a symbol of enlightenment and provider of sustenance, is present in both images, inasmuch as the party sought to portray itself as the foundation of all life in Ireland. Here, light serves to drive away the darkness brought by external control and discord. It is likely that Fianna Fáil, claiming to be an agent combating enmity, caused a few raised eyebrows, especially among those who claimed that de Valera, among others, was responsible for not only the civil war, but also the violence being perpetrated in the name of an Irish republic by the IRA. Nonetheless, the party's aesthetic need not be anchored in historical truth to be effective. After all, Fianna Fáil's connections to both the ancient Fianna and the Gaelic League were tenuous at best. Most important, however, is that the party was able to successfully and effectively utilise this backward gaze as a foundation for the futurist aspect of its aesthetic – that is, one of action, working to restore to Ireland its masculinist visage. Fianna Fáil, then, offered itself as a model of masculinity: strong, virile, unafraid, protectionist, and worthy namesakes of the Fianna. Moreover, a male chauvinism was present – for this Irish Masculine was also the bearer of light, adorned with a phallic sword, vessels of the purest Gaelic

Bee

NATIONAL EXPRESS

ELECTOR

THE OATH

DISUNITY

PROPAGANDA

HATE

YOUR DUTY TO-DAY——CLEAR THE LINES!

Figure 3.2 Bee, 'Your Duty To-Day – Clear the Lines!', *Irish Press*, 16 February 1932, p. 1. With thanks to Irish Newspaper Archives and *The Irish Press*.

genes. Of course, no member of Fianna Fáil resembled the warrior portrayed in the image – that was never the intent. Rather, it was the Irish Masculine who was to hone his body through work in the fields and in the factories secured and (to be) built through Fianna Fáil policy.

Fianna Fáil also presented itself as a dynamic machine, kinetically advancing the cause of the nation. Such is depicted in an image on the cover of the 16 February 1932 edition of the *Irish Press*, in which a steam-spewing locomotive engine dubbed 'National Express' has its movement hindered by a series of boulders labelled 'The Oath', 'Disunity', 'Propaganda' and 'Hate'[65] (see Figure 3.2). Included in the image is a man – festooned in a fedora and work shirt rolled up to the elbows and labelled as 'Elector' – straining to remove the boulder labelled 'The Oath' from the railroad track. The caption reads 'Your Duty To-Day – Clear the

FIANNA FAIL: "How on earth will I clear that road? ——"

UNEMPLOYED (suddenly appearing): "—— But we're here to help you!"

Figure 3.3 Bee, 'How on Earth Will I Clear that Road?', *Irish Press*, 1 March 1933, p. 1. With thanks to Irish Newspaper Archives and *The Irish Press*.

Lines!'[66] The image is rife with masculine imagery: the train – powerful, modern, sleek, kinetic, harbinger of action, and decidedly phallic; the man – young, powerful, lithe and selfless; together – the forces form a symbiosis in which the 'Elector' enables the movement-cum-progress of the national express-cum-Fianna Fáil; strength enables strength in order to remove the obstacles hindering a clear path towards national regeneration. The image speaks volumes about how Fianna Fáil presented itself as a national movement dependent upon the Irish Masculine to assist in its efforts to speed the wheels towards an Irish Ireland. Of further interest is the choice by the artist to situate the boulder labelled 'The Oath' as the one to be moved first – a recognition of Fianna Fáil's broadside on the nature of the Free State constitution.

Similar in tone is another two-panelled cartoon by Bee – the pseudonym for artist Victor Brown – from 11 March 1933. In the left panel a distraught, lone worker with a spade in hand, and the words 'Fianna Fail' emblazoned across his chest, is tasked with clearing a road of some indeterminate material labelled 'Old Economic Policy'[67] (see Figure 3.3). Viewed on its own, this panel symbolises Fianna Fáil's seeming inability to undo centuries of destructive economic policy instituted by Britain, and later reified by Cumann na nGaedheal. Nonetheless, the man-cum-Fianna Fáil has the tools to clear the road, yet the task is daunting and he asks, 'How on Earth Will I Clear the Road?' Relief comes in the second panel, when an army of unemployed men – dressed in clothing signifying the working class – appear with spades, proclaiming 'But we're here to help you!' This bit of fantasia elucidates a number of ideas: first, and most obvious, is the already-established theme of Fianna Fáil as an active, masculine agent working to correct the problems faced by Ireland; second, is the aspired symbiosis between Fianna Fáil/Éire and the Irish (masculine) worker. This speaks to the party's desire to be national in aim and to create an electorate that embodied Fianna Fáil's nationalist vision that was to be indistinguishable from that of an envisioned republic. The symbol of the worker as soldier recalls other figures of the era, including the young men of fascist propaganda films and photographs, who were mobilised to rebuild the nation. Indeed, the workers here are clothed far more modestly than the sweaty, shirtless men of Italy or Germany. Nonetheless, the message is the same: national party and labourer working together to correct the misdeeds of the past, constructing a clear path towards the future. Themes of growth and consumption of domestic products is present in a cartoon from Bee that appeared in the 11 March 1933 edition of the *Irish Press*. In it, a group of workers marked as 'former employed' march into a seemingly new and fully functional/potent factory where the smoke from the smokestacks combines to spell the words 'Buy Irish'.[68] Here we see the coalescence of Fianna Fáil's envisioned Masculine and Feminine: the party enabled Irish men to reclaim their manhood through work, making domestic products to be purchased in markets by Irish women and consumed in the 'All-Irish home'. Though unstated, there is a subtle message to Irish women, who were implored to buy Irish and 'give the Irish [men] work'.[69] Herein lay an aspect of the national coitus, where corrected forms of masculinity and femininity are able to function and (re)produce.

Figure 3.4 'Strength to Strength', advertising supplement, *Irish Press*, 5 September 1933, p. iv. With thanks to Irish Newspaper Archives and *The Irish Press*.

An anniversary supplement was included in the 5 September 1933 edition of the *Irish Press*. In it, there appeared a full-page image marking growth encountered by the *Press* as indicative of Ireland's economic and agricultural development. Sublimated under a series of articles is an image of an ancient Fianna warrior, armed with a sheathed sword (of light) and adorned in clothing evoking that a of Gaelic warrior chief[70] (see Figure 3.4). The man's left arm supports a banner that reads 'Strength to Strength' – a statement with manifold meaning: past to (Fianna Fáil's) present; *Irish Press* to Fianna Fáil; agriculture to industry. The image of the warrior splits a mural depicting a farmer ploughing his fertile fields, and a modern factory with smokestacks billowing black emissions, indicating function and activity. The connection between past, present and future could not be starker. The text of the image reads: 'Ireland is passing through a period of rapid evolution in the Industrial and Agricultural spheres. The newspaper of the future is that which, by the perfection of its news service and by the confident progressive character of its policy, enriches the life of the Nation'.[71] Indeed, the astute reader – likely a Fianna Fáil acolyte – would understand the implicit connection between party and paper, despite reality belying any semblance of rapid industrialisation in Ireland. Nonetheless, aspirations of growth and the possibility that such development would reach all of Ireland offered optimism for the Irish voter. The theme of engorgement and growth is evident in the text that reads: 'During its second year "The Irish Press" has again broken all records by the rapidity of its progress. Average Net Paid Sales reveal that the daily readers of "The Irish Press" have increased in numbers from eighty-five to one hundred and twelve thousand – or, in terms of families, to indirectly over half-a-million persons daily. Equally, Advertisers – realising that "The Irish Press" controls a great and ever-increasing volume of purchasing power – have enormously increased their appropriations'.[72] In short, the *Irish Press* and Fianna Fáil presented themselves as symbiotic and dynamic forces heralding the dawn of an industrial and agricultural golden age made bright by their sword of light. This is not to say that this was true – there is much to demonstrate that the data offered as evidence of growth were inflated, aspirational or only partly the result of Fianna Fáil policy. The veracity of such claims is beyond the purview of this study. Rather, the purpose is to demonstrate what Dev's party purported in its palingenetic, nationalist aesthetic.

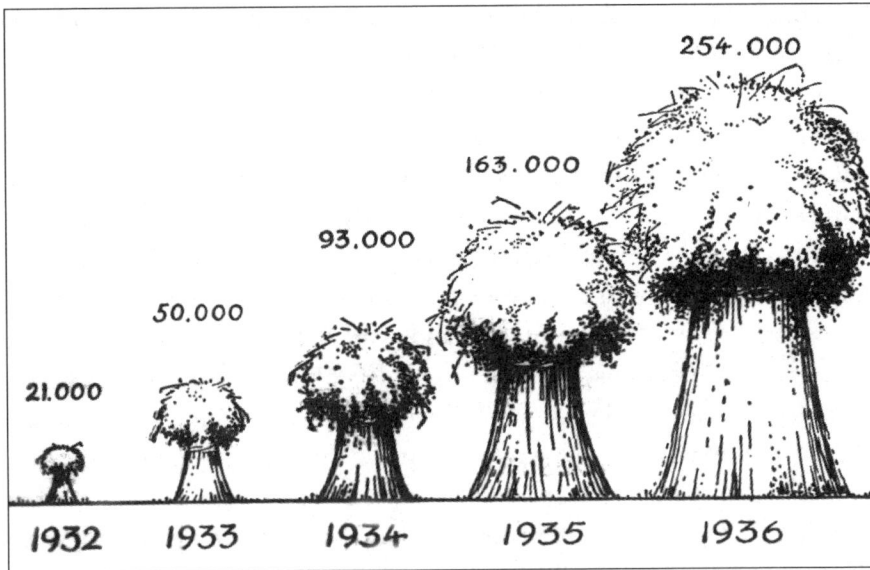

Figure 3.5 'Fianna Fail Achieves "The Impossible"', *Fianna Fáil Bulletin*, June 1937, p. 13.

Much of Fianna Fáil's electoral propaganda was rife with language tinged with allusions to insemination and punctuated by rather phallic imagery – in essence utilising the visual to further blur the lines between party and nation in an effort to 'symbolically ... settle social and economic struggles while it simultaneously promotes the charismatic image of strong and unified political action'.[73] Numerous examples of subliminal, although rather obvious, use of phallic imagery can be seen in propaganda from the *Fianna Fáil Bulletin*. One instance, an infographic entitled 'Fianna Fail Achieves "The Impossible"', depicted five wheat piles, representing acres devoted to wheat production between 1932 and 1937 (see Figure 3.5). The amount of growth – ranging from 21,000 acres in 1932 to 254,000 in 1937 – was marked by increasingly higher piles of wheat.[74] One need not read much further to discover who was responsible for such an increase in output, for the party presented itself as the carrier of the seed that allowed for such an increase. It was noted that 'in 1931 under Fine Gael [*sic*] we were not producing sufficient wheat to give even a crumb of bread per head per day to our population. After only five years of Fianna Fail administration we are producing sufficient to give a third of our requirements'.[75] Exhorting readers to 'Vote Fianna Fail and Reap the Harvest', it was implied that the continued governance of Fianna Fáil would result in the continued insemination of Irish land, further increasing wheat production. Symbolically at least, Fianna Fáil's aesthetic attempted to recapture a masculinity conceivably stripped by British colonisation and by Cumann na nGaedheal's economic weakness and failure to act. Growth, speed and virility were themes espoused by Fianna Fáil in its attempt to establish a newly seminal era for Ireland.

Such themes were not exclusive to agricultural growth, as evidenced in another piece from the June 1937 edition of the *Bulletin*. Highlighting the construction of new factories and workshops, the ad claimed that the party had 'reorganised the economic life of the nation and [that] the success of its industrial policy is ending forever the absolute dependence of our people on foreign made products'.[76] There was no question as to who was responsible for sowing the seed of growth, as the ad further heralded that '800 New Factories and Workshops Give Employment to Over 78,000 People'. An illustration charting the increased net output accompanied the claims that Fianna Fáil was responsible for priming the pump of industrial growth fuelled by an increase in agricultural output, which had resulted from the reclamation and dissemination of land to the Irish farmer. Such statements were not surprising from a party that had advocated in its 1933 election material that 'as principle . . . it is the duty of the State, up to the limits of its power, to provide or induce the provision of work for workless citizens of the State'.[77] Further, the party claimed, 'the work has barely started, however. Much remains to be done and Fianna Fáil will do it. *Sufficient has been accomplished to justify in the full the policy of Fianna Fáil*.'[78] What distinguishes this particular rhetorical thread is the sublimation of the republican party as being completely responsible for the growth of industry and arable land within Ireland. The party positioned itself as one that was enacting policy that led to the regeneration of Irish industry, in direct opposition to those that had stunted growth.[79]

The June 1937 edition of the *Fianna Fáil Bulletin* included a graphic entitled 'Five Years of Industrial Achievement' which underlined the party's record of economic growth since coming to government. This map of Ireland – minus the six northern counties, which are blank – depicts new industries, extension of old industries, 'Turf Co'op Societies', and flour mills.[80] Significant here is the representation of

Figure 3.6 'Fianna Fáil Has a Plan', *Irish Press*, 15 February 1932, p. 5. With thanks to Irish Newspaper Archives and *The Irish Press*.

Fianna Fáil's national reach – that is, that the party presented itself as being responsible for industrial growth in every county in Ireland – and further underscores the party's effort to position itself as a national party

FIANNA FÁIL TAKES THE LAND FROM THE BULLOCK AND GIVES IT BACK TO THE PEOPLE

One of the fundamental aims of Fianna Fáil is to settle as many families as possible on the land.

For this purpose the Land Acts of 1933 and 1936 were introduced and passed—despite the opposition of the Ranchers' friends, Fine Gael.

Result:—Fianna Fáil in the last **3 YEARS** divided **three times** as much land annually as was divided by Fine Gael in its last three years of office.

58,500 ACRES ACQUIRED FOR FORESTRY SINCE 1932

Ireland is the worst afforestated country in Europe. Fine Gael toyed with the problem for ten years. Fianna Fáil made a big effort to reorganise the Forestry Department by opening up new nurseries for young trees; by securing the best technical advice and assistance from abroad; by re-opening the School of Forestry to train young Irish experts; by planting 28,000 acres of land, and by making big experiments in the work in districts hitherto ignored.

The figures planted and the money spent speak for themselves.

FIANNA FÁIL

307,000 acres divided in years 1934—35 1935—36 1936—37

Fine Gael

134,600 acres divided in years 1929—30, 1930—31 1931—32

No. of acres planted in 1931-32 **3,600**

No. of acres planted in 1936-37 **7,200**

The work of planting has only begun. Fianna Fáil is not satisfied with the present rate of progress, but has made a good beginning. The measures it has adopted to reorganise forestry will bear much fruit in the coming five years, and in giving our country a secure supply of timber will give work and wages to increasing numbers and add to the beauty of our scenery.

Total for Afforestation **£154,439**

£60,406

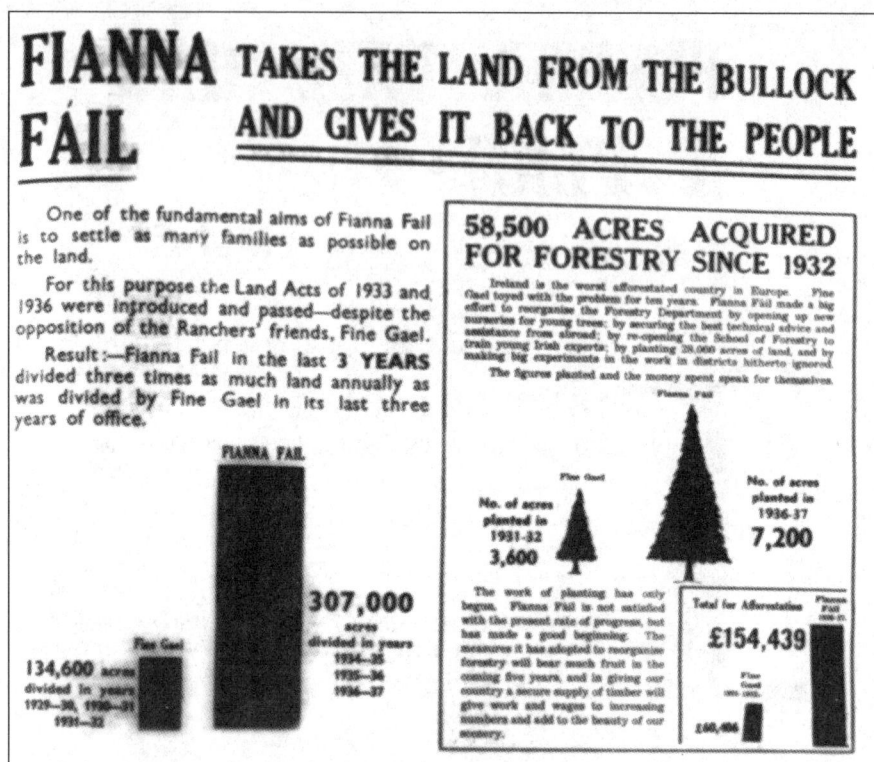

Figure 3.7 'Fianna Fáil Takes the Land from the Bullock and Gives it Back to the People', *Fianna Fáil Bulletin*, June 1937, p. 9.

that coalesced town and country. Moreover, the map can be seen as an effort to unite town and country – and, indeed, agriculture and industry – into a symbiotic entity functioning for the betterment of Ireland. Such is presented as a stark contrast to the party's opponents, whose political and cultural allegiances are called into question. A chart from the same issue notes the areas of increased output: hosiery (the largest, at 236 per cent), boots and shoes, building materials, paper making, apparel, vehicle assembly and repair, engineering and metals, distilling, confectionery and jam, chemicals, paint and fertilisers, mineral waters, wood furniture, cotton, linen, jute, bacon curing, milling, printing, and worsted woollens.[81] Each industry was depicted by a cartoon image, with smaller and larger versions representing 1931 and 1935, respectively.[82] The same graphic includes two charts under the general heading 'The Turn of the Tide', with subheadings for 'Births' and 'Marriages'.[83] The charts depict significant growth beginning in 1931–2 in both areas. Marriages – an indicator of economic and demographic stability – are depicted as having seen the greatest growth, up nearly 2,000 between 1931 and '35. Accurate or not, these charts encapsulate a significant facet of Fianna Fáil's gendered aesthetic: through economic and agricultural growth facilitated by national protection and activist policies, the Irish Masculine and Irish Feminine found that their gender and sexual place were restored – the national coitus between the two had borne fruit in the restoration of marriage and child-bearing. Put another way, these graphs and the associated data are meant to depict actual – though likely imagined – national regeneration transposed onto the bodies of Irish women and men. Speed the wheels, indeed.

Another election flyer underscored the general message that Cumann na nGaedheal had kowtowed to Britain while Fianna Fáil was ready to work to bring manufactures and industry to Ireland:

> While Free State Ministers creep over to England and in all humility, kneel down and beg for the rich man's crumbs, Fianna Fail asks you to consider your own home market. Your Government has no power to regulate or demand a price on the British market.
>
> . . .
>
> And now P[ut]. T[hem]. O[ut]![84]

A similar theme appeared in an electoral ad from the pages of the *Irish Press* which claimed 'Fianna Fáil Has a Plan'[85] (see Figure 3.6). This ad was particularly striking for the connections made between work and security: 'For the worker [Fianna Fáil's plan] means continuous, well-paid employment for an additional 80,000 men, the ending of the downward pressure on wage rates produced by the present huge volume of unemployment, a better standard of living, better houses, better food, better clothes. It means Security.'[86]

In an example of early environmentalist legislation, Fianna Fáil noted the purchase of '58,500 acres acquired for forestry since 1932' – a fact punctuated by an illustration that used a sapling to represent land bought by Cumann na nGaedheal/Fine Gael, and a mighty fir to demonstrate the immense growth under Fianna Fáil[87] (see Figure 3.7). These figures were heralded by the headline: 'Fianna Fail Takes the Land from the Bullock and Gives it Back to the People'. Once again there appeared themes of party-based insemination of the Irish land accompanied by distinctively manly imagery of mighty trees – with Fianna Fáil being the more virile in comparison to Fine Gael's inadequate effort. Not only was Fianna Fáil reclaiming the land for the people, it was also reinvigorating Ireland by actively contributing to the growth of the nation.

'THE ABOLITION OF THE MEMORY OF ALL PAST DISSENSIONS': FIANNA FÁIL AS THE PROTECTORS OF IRISHNESS

The Anglo-Irish economic war – in its essence – was a conflict centred upon the long-festering question of land ownership, annuity payments and market share. To what extent did the Irish 'owe' the British for land rights? Already granted a semblance of political independence, the land annuity payments were framed by Fianna Fáil as the last great vestige of the British colonisation. Further, the complicity of Cumann na nGaedheal (and by extension its later incarnation as Fine Gael) in the payments of the annuities allowed Fianna Fáil to cast itself as the true protectors of the Irish nation – a nation conceptualised as being older and greater than the Free State. A second threat to the nation was the aforementioned global economic depression. Fianna Fáil, like many other nationalist projects, buffered its electoral strength by offering an economic alternative to the nineteenth-century liberal/socialist framework, instead presenting a socio-economic model that vacillated between modern and primordial – agriculture and industry. The nation was to be expressed not through work or class, but through the production and ingestion of national symbols in the guise of Irish factories and Irish-produced goods.

A 1932 party handbill solicited subscriptions by making clear the connection between economic freedom and an independent republic. Noting that the annuity payments stripped Ireland of £5 million per annum, the flier positioned Britain – as well as Cumann na nGaedheal – as the source of Ireland's economic woes. But of particular interest was the sheer number of phrases evoking growth or increased activity – the rhetoric of action and movement and protection – which were associated with Fianna Fáil. The flyer reads:

Because Fianna Fáil stands for the Protection of Irish Industries against unfair foreign competition and thus ensures the production at home of the goods required by the Irish people;

Because Fianna Fáil has endeavoured to benefit Old Age Pensioners and to raise the level of Social legislation;

Because Fianna Fáil has a constructive programme for the development of agriculture, including the derating of Lands and buildings, the provision of a guaranteed market and fixed prices for Wheat, and the direct encouragement of tillage;

Because Fianna Fáil is the only Party which has a clearly-defined policy for dealing with the evil of Unemployment by the provision of work on schemes of public utility;

Because Fianna Fáil desires to abolish the horrors of bad housing by the establishment of a National Housing Board, financed by the Government, and fully empowered to ensure the production of 50,000 houses within a period of ten years;

Because Fianna Fáil stands for the traditional policy of complete Independence and Unity.

You do your part and Fianna Fáil will do the rest.[88]

Fianna Fáil constructed a socio-political narrative that clearly reinforced the notion that the party was there to protect the Irish citizenry from the iniquities of unfair competition, where the more powerful British had stacked the odds in their own favour. A similar document was published at about the same time, aimed to raise money for the Fianna Fáil Headquarters Fund for the constituency of Dublin City North. The letter read in part:

Fianna Fáil is THE Organization of the People – fighting the People's battle . . . It has placed in power a Government pledged to secure the complete political and economic Independence of the Nation. It seeks to unite the People by the abolition of the memory of all past dissensions, and thereby to provide the Government with the moral support so necessary for Peace and ordered Progress.

The work is going ahead. Keep it going. Fianna Fáil will not cease its efforts until it has completed the task for which it was founded.[89]

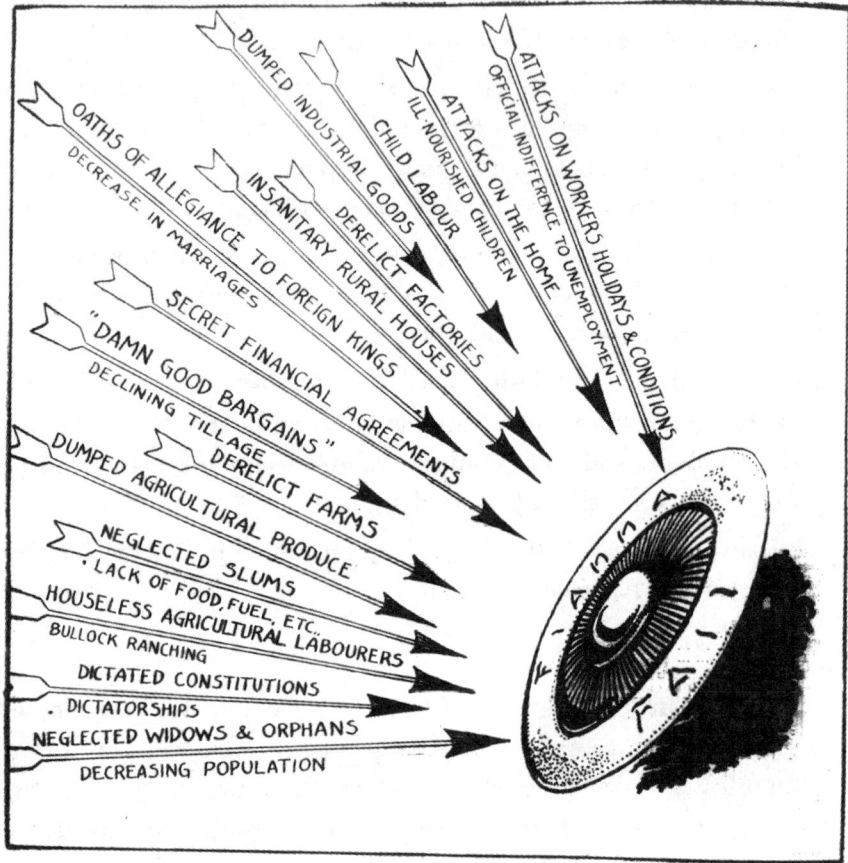

Figure 3.8 'Ward Off the Arrows of Adversity!', *Fianna Fáil Bulletin*, June 1937, p. 16.

In one of the starkest representations of the party's constructed role as protectors of the nation, a *Fianna Fáil Bulletin* cartoon entitled 'Ward Off the Arrows of Adversity!' portrayed Fianna Fáil as an ancient Irish shield guarding the island itself (see Figure 3.8). Accentuated with the name 'Fianna Fáil', the shield represented a connection to the primordial, in the sense that one was to connect the modern republican party to the ancient Fianna. The caption underneath the picture read: 'The Fianna Fail Majority is the Nation's Shield Against National Surrender and Social and Economic Decay'. This notion was more specifically represented in the cartoon as arrows aimed at Ireland, labelled with such phrases as: 'Attacks on Workers Holidays & Conditions, Official Indifference to Unemployment'; 'Attacks on the Home, Ill-Nourished Children'; 'Dumped Industrial Goods'; 'Derelict Factories'; 'Insanitary Rural Houses'; 'Oaths of Allegiance to Foreign Kings'; 'Secret Financial Agreements'; '"Damn Good Bargains"'; 'Declining Tillage'; 'Dumped Agricultural Produce'; 'Lack of Food, Fuel, Etc'; 'Houseless Agricultural Labourers'; 'Dictated Constitutions'; and 'Neglected Widows & Orphans'.[90]

In 1937 Fianna Fáil marked its fifth year in government by trumpeting its economic advances, including, as we have seen, the growth of new industries and farms, as well as the expansion or renovation of old manufactures. As noted in a *Fianna Fáil Bulletin* editorial, 'Fianna Fáil has changed the face of the Country – and provided a strong line of economic defence against World depression and war.'[91] While the struggle over land annuities was a manifestation of its conflict with Britain, the effort to ward off the impact of economic depression enabled Fianna Fáil to further advance its position as protectors of Ireland's journey towards political and economic growth. The article continued, with a 'before' and 'after' snapshot of Ireland's economic status:

> Then – Before 1932 most of our towns were mere distribution centres. The cattle went out – the foreign goods came in. The towns were without modern sewerage and water systems, lined with ugly insanitary shacks. There was nothing for the people to do (except in the large cities) but send out the cattle and sell the foreign goods.
>
> – And Now. With the Coming of Fianna Fail practically every town of size secured a new industry, giving employment, increasing

the spending power of the people, creating a large market for the adjoining farmers, adding to the number of workers in subsidiary trades, building up the revenue of the railway, bringing the breath of life and prosperity to the urban centres. Industries, which had disappeared in the previous decade, were revived – existing concerns extended production – and to-day the wheels are turning with increasing speed and efficiency. Most of these factories produce goods of necessity. No matter what happens outside this island, they provide a bulwark of economic stability to the nation.[92]

Note the consistent use of the gerund verb form: giving, increasing, creating, adding, building; all of which connote action driven by Fianna Fáil policy. In this case, Fianna Fáil – true or not – is presented as turning aspiration into reality. For Fianna Fáil, the economic war was an extension of its overarching autarkic economic policy that included the development and extension of the party's larger, socio-political discourse. While much has been written about the varying level of success of Fianna Fáil's economic programme, little has been done to contextualise its policies as part of a larger, nationalistic thrust, melding the intersections of process and rhetoric. Viewing such activity through the prism of gender and power as part of a nation-building effort elucidates the way Fianna Fáil sought to renegotiate socio-political frameworks in Ireland. The examples given here represent a larger corpus of material demonstrating Fianna Fáil's activist, *masculine* effort to construct an independent Irish republic.

After a half-decade in government Fianna Fáil advanced an even more aggressive rhetoric, and in turn abandoned the largely repressed calls for an independent state. The abandonment of the position taken in the wake of the Ottawa Economic Conference in 1932 had been alluded to but was elevated to the fore in the effort to construct a new constitution for Ireland. A piece of Fianna Fáil propaganda entitled 'The Advance of the Republic' heralded: 'The Next Step Will Be the New Constitution. It will be a Constitution consistent with Ireland's historic claims and one which every Irishman can accept without dishonour. It will consolidate the national advances already made and will place no barrier between the people and the achievement of their ultimate ideal.'[93] The piece further argued, 'Fianna Fail has already made ten decisive irrevocable steps to National Independence. Steps that no party dare retrace, a definite advance towards ending all foreign control.'[94] As evidence, the ad trumpeted the abolition of the oath, forging 'a peaceful method [that] exists for resolving all political differences', the marginalisation of the governor-general and Senate, the holding of the annuities for the people of Ireland, and a 'Programme of Economic Self-Sufficiency [that] is far advanced'.[95] Indeed, Fianna Fáil was speeding the wheels – at least rhetorically, anyway.

CHAPTER 4

'Queering' John Bull: Fianna Fáil and republican heteronormativity

I n June 1932 a papal legation visited Ireland as part of that year's Eucharistic Congress, and were, upon landfall, greeted by a delegation of Fianna Fáil ministers led by party founder Éamon de Valera. Because Fianna Fáil had been in government for only a few months, the Eucharistic Congress had largely been organised under the auspices of Cumann na nGaedheal, yet de Valera's party seized the opportunity to turn the congress into a Fianna Fáil spectacle. De Valera was to greet the delegation in Dublin Castle – the symbol of British colonialism described in the *Irish Press* as 'that stout Birmingham Tower that had looked down on ages of sufferings, even to our own day'.[1] The *Irish Press* also noted the significance of the former prisoner, now president, greeting the delegation within the castle's walls: 'He whom the holders of Dublin Castle had pursued was now within those walls, not as prisoner, but as master.'[2] Wearing a standard business suit, as opposed to the more formal coats with tails and top hats preferred by the opposition, de Valera spoke, saying *'Míle míle fáilte romhat, a Ard-Fhlaith na hEaglaise, a fhear-ionaid an Athar Naofa, go talamh iath-ghlas na hÉireann!'*[3] (see Figure 4.1). De Valera continued briefly in Irish before addressing the audience in Latin. His message was that this was first an Irish and Catholic Ireland, rejecting British influence. A member of the papal legation recalled their entrance into Dublin harbour, where he saw that a 'group of men in dark coats and soft hats whom we had taken for detectives' waited to meet them.[4] These 'detectives' were representatives of the Fianna Fáil government.

De Valera's opening remarks were significant, in the way he positioned the burgeoning Irish state as being on a par with notable Christians who

Figure 4.1 'Eamon de Valera and the Papal Legation', *The Irish Press*, 21 June 1932, 1. With Thanks to Irish Newspaper Archives and *The Irish Press*.

had struggled with oppression in the past. Clearly de Valera was referring to Britain when he stated in Latin:

> My eminent lord, the records of centuries past bear eloquent testimony to the loving zeal with which the Apostolic See has ever honoured our nation. That special affection was ever the more amply given, in proportion to the sufferings of Ireland. Repeatedly, over more than three hundred years, our people, ever firm in their allegiance to our ancestral faith and unwavering even unto death in their devotion to the See of Peter, endured in full measure unmerited trials by war, by devastation and by confiscation. They saw their most sacred rights set at naught under an unjust domination. But repeatedly also did the successors of Peter most willingly come to our aid, in the persons of Gregory XIII, Clement VIII, Paul V, Urban VIII, Innocent X and many others of the line of Roman Pontiffs to the present day.[5]

Fianna Fáil's spectacle had essentially begun with the above statement, which effectively placed Britain and, by implication, the pro-Treaty Cumann na nGaedheal outside of the acceptable norms of Catholic Ireland. From windows adorned with Irish-manufactured candles, to streets lined with 'Episcopal purple'[6] and nationalist green, to de Valera's snubbing of the governor-general, Fianna Fáil's machinations regarding the occasion of the visit by the papal legation served to illustrate the means by which the party marginalised that which did not fit within its gendered nationalistic binary.[7]

Finín O'Driscoll has referred to the visit by the papal legation as an 'event [that] transcended the religious celebration to become a manifestation of triumphant Irish catholic [*sic*] nationalism'.[8] The Eucharistic Congress was more than just an attempt to express the nation's Catholicity; additionally it afforded Fianna Fáil three important opportunities. First, it enabled the party to demonstrate that it had completely shed its outward associations with physical force insurgency as a means to garner a republic. When combined with the peaceful transfer of power from Cumann na nGaedheal in early 1932, Fianna Fail's hospitality towards the Vatican's legation demonstrated that the party had accepted the pope's anti-revolutionary position. Second, the congress gave Fianna Fáil its first opportunity to publicly defy elements of British authority from a position of governmental authority, from their choice of clothing, to de Valera's greeting statement made in Irish, to the barbed tone of his statements as they related to Ireland's history of subjugation to Britain. Further, the choice to have a state reception for the delegation in the grounds of Blackrock College – de Valera's alma mater – avoided 'the embarrassment of the state function being associated with the Vice-Regal Lodge or with the representative of King George V'.[9] Finally, Fianna Fáil was able to demonstrate that it was capable of seizing the reins of the Free State so as to fashion it in the party's own image as an active, masculine party diametrically opposed to the dandyish, fey Cumann na nGaedheal. Thus, the Eucharistic Congress of 1932 marked the first opportunity for Fianna Fáil publicly to reify its gendered constructs of acceptability as well as to define what would not fit within its envisioned Ireland.

The previous chapters have explained how Fianna Fáil established heteronormative means of inclusion within its envisioned republic.[10] From the clear definitions of feminine agency within the republican movement to the idealised notion of manliness with which the party cloaked itself, Fianna Fáil essentially sexualised Ireland. This is not to say, however, that the party was explicitly concerned with *coitus* per se, but rather that it utilised gendered tropes as the basis for reconstituting republicanism. Much has been said about Fianna Fáil's efforts to define what was inclusive in light of its corrective discourse, but this raises the question as to what did not fit in its republican aesthetic. In her definition of gender, Judith Butler has argued that it is 'a construction that regularly conceals its genesis; the tacit collective agreement to perform, produce, and sustain discrete and polar genders as cultural fictions is obscured by the credibility of those productions – and the punishments that attend not agreeing to believe in them'.[11] It is the contention here that while Fianna Fáil was largely successful in constructing agreeable gendered frameworks, it also queered those elements of society and politics that could not be reconciled with its nationalist aesthetic. Politically, these efforts were specific to Ireland's postcolonial condition, where the Irish cultural nationalist ideal clashed with the legacies of British colonialism.

Nikki Sullivan has written that 'queering popular culture, then, involves critically engaging with cultural artefacts in order to explore the way in which meaning and identity is (inter)textually (re)produced'.[12] As demonstrated above, there was little distinction between politics and popular culture in Fianna Fáil's vision of Ireland, for the party's aestheticisation of politics in the Irish Free State left the two mutually interdependent. Sullivan has argued further that the queer 'could be described as moments of narrative disruption which destabilize heteronormativity and all the meanings and identities it engenders, by bringing to light all that is disavowed by, and yet integral to, heteronormative logic'.[13] The effort to queer was not unlike what Edward Said described as 'othering', and the similarities speak to anti-hegemonic aspects of Fianna Fáil's nationalist efforts.[14] While not explicitly taking action against homosexuals per se, queering as defined here was tantamount to Fianna Fáil clearly delineating the 'other' as lacking gender. More than anything, this effort was about establishing a rhetorical narrative in which opponents of Fianna Fáil republicanism were portrayed as neutered and impotent, therefore asexual, neither as active agents of republican industriousness (male) or of passive-aggressive support (female).

For all of its efforts to withdraw Ireland from the British Empire, one fact remained immutable for Fianna Fáil: no amount of party aesthetic or gendered discourse could fully remove the remnants of British influence in Ireland. While the purpose of the previous chapters was to examine Fianna Fáil's effort to construct a nationalist discourse of heteronormativity, the present chapter seeks to briefly cite examples of how it reconciled remnants of Britishness in Ireland by relegating them to a tertiary status outside of the party's masculine and feminine ideal. Politically, the party affected a rhetoric that effectively disarmed the pro-treaty Cumann na nGaedheal and its successor party, Fine Gael, by portraying them as submissive to the whims of London, and thereby emasculating them. Culturally, Fianna Fáil sought to solidify the primacy of Irishness, by affording favoured status to those expressions deemed most suitable to the party's envisioned Ireland.

'THEY NEVER LOOK OUT THE WINDOW': QUEERING CUMANN NA NGAEDHEAL

Cumann na nGaedheal's efforts to feminise the republican cause led Fianna Fáil to advance its own logical, masculine political rhetoric. Cumann na nGaedheal was, of course, better positioned to shape opinions as the party of majority, which was largely due to the spoils of victory in the early Free State. As the 1930s progressed, Fianna Fáil benefited from a similar process, enabling it to direct Ireland's socio-economic and political trajectories. As such, the republican movement had come full circle. The renascent movement under the guise of Fianna Fáil had gained legitimacy because of its ability to combat Cumann na nGaedheal's 'othering' efforts, and now de Valera's party worked to define what was acceptable and what was not. Thus, to cement its status as the new fulcrum in Ireland, the party queered not only its political opposition, but also those tropes associated with British rule.

Apart from depicting their opponents as passive and ineffectual leaders of Ireland, Fianna Fáil's rhetoric was rife with allegations that Cumann na nGaedheal/Fine Gael were cowardly supplicants bending to the will of Britain. In the early 1930s, Fianna Fáil's internal strategy document *Scheme of Election Organisation* stated:

> The next matter is the personalities of the candidates of other parties. Although it is very inadvisable to indulge in personal attacks on opponents, nevertheless it is quite legitimate to examine their

public records and draw attention to anything which would make them undesirable as a public representative. In this connection it is important to note the necessity of examining and dealing with the position of special classes or economic interests in relation to those candidates.

Needless to remark, the nature of our opponents' campaign will have a direct influence on ours. The literature issued by, and speeches made on behalf of our opponents, should, therefore, be carefully noted and all false allegations and misrepresentations dealt with.[15]

Fundamental to Fianna Fáil's efforts to 'correct' Ireland was the notion that both Britain and the Irish Free State had somehow shifted the nation away from its true destiny. Elements of this strategy were evident as early as 1927. Thus, a handbill from that election claimed that it was:

Now or Never!

The scales of Justice is [*sic*] badly balanced, and you will shortly be asked to cast your vote for one side or other. We confidently appeal to you to cast your vote on the side of JUSTICE and RIGHT. There are only two sides – they are:

For Ireland: Those who love Ireland and would serve her.

Against Ireland:

Imperialists. Unionists. Free Masons [*sic*]. Job-hunters. Ex Black and Tans. Bailiffs. Those Who gave away Six Counties. Those who agree to pay Six Millions yearly to England. Ex-Judges.

Could we doubt your answer?[16]

Fianna Fáil's rhetorical flourish blackened its domestic opponents, depicting 'those who agree to pay', i.e. Cumann na nGaedheal, as akin to imperialists, unionists and Freemasons, supplicants to the British, and it built on rhetoric already current in the mid-1920s. Daly has argued that 'the Cumann na nGaedheal government was forced to adopt a pro-British attitude on political matters and a conciliatory economic policy', and Fianna Fáil pounced on this opportunity.[17] Pointedly, another Fianna Fáil handbill portrayed Cumann na nGaedheal as cowards who agreed to 'pay Pensions to the "Black and Tans" for Destroying Your Homes and

Shooting Down Your Countrymen', and who colluded to 'Pay an Annual Tribute of Over £5,000,000 to England'.[18]

The accusation that Cumann na nGaedheal consistently acquiesced to the whims of Britain continued to appear in propaganda that emerged from the office of Fianna Fáil minister Frank Aiken. Another pamphlet, for instance, depicted Cumann na nGaedheal as inherently anti-Irish, and therefore pro-British, having 'stopped at nothing to bring about the downfall of Fianna Fail'.[19] Thus, in a pamphlet, likely to have been printed in 1932, with the lengthy title '*Fianna Fail Kept Their Promise, A Survey of the Great Work Done in Louth, How Drogheda Fared: Great Industrial Revival*', Fianna Fáil depicted itself as 'gallant', pro-Irish, and advocates of policy commensurate with the wishes of the Holy See.[20] In regards to the church and Fianna Fáil's economic programme – namely its housing schemes – the text claimed that 'documentary proofs of this, the age-long policy of the Popes, is found in all the decrees issued by the Holy See from the reign of Innocent III to Pope Pius VII'.[21] The logic being presented was that Cumann na nGaedheal was being rather ungodly regarding housing, and therefore had no place within the devoutly Catholic Ireland. This rhetorical strategy aligned with Fianna Fáil's anti-British clothing choices worn at the Eucharistic Congress in 1932. Both Cosgrave's party and the Seanad (Senate) were equated with 'Exporters, importers, the various personages, political and financial, who have made it their aim for months past to play the part of England and hamper the onward march of the nation'. Following many accusations of Cumann na nGaedheal dishonesty, the pamphlet alleged that:

> Cosgrave has been most accommodating to every country but his own. He, being a broad-minded man, accommodated himself, too, in a generous way to all the requirements of the alien. He will ever be remembered by the Masonic Lodges as one who was a 'Good Sport' and struggled 'manfully' to make capitalistic Imperialism respectable to the 'ignorant Irishry'. He will be remembered as the 'traitor' statesman who made 'a damned good bargain' over the enslaved bodies of half a million Irish Nationalists, sealing his shameful bargain with the annual tribute of 5¾ millions of Irish money.
>
> Despite this opposition, despite the lying Press, despite the whole machinations of *West Britonism*, Fianna Fáil got to work.[22]

These damning accusations, recalling turn-of-the-century Gaelic revival denunciations of West Britonism, solidified Fianna Fáil's assertions that Cosgrave and his party were simply British puppets perpetuating the colonial ties that had been so detrimental to Ireland. Further, the language contained in the pamphlet insinuated that Fianna Fáil, as the opposition, was involved in a struggle of sorts with Britain, whereas Cumann na nGaedheal assumed the position of the passive to Britain's active, thereby sexualising the Anglo-Irish Free State association.

By the time Fianna Fáil had secured a place within the political dialectic of the Free State, it had begun championing associations between the treaty – and therefore the Free State and Cumann na nGaedheal – and Britain. This association placed Cumann na nGaedheal/Fine Gael outside of its republican vision and was reinforced in electoral literature and other party publications. For example, a Fianna Fáil handbill from 1927 presents Cumann na nGaedheal as benefiting from its associations with Britain – via the treaty – in a manner that undermined Ireland. The handbill, in large, bold letters, queries: 'Why wouldn't they? The Free State Ministers are Enthusiastic Upholders of the "Treaty". Why Wouldn't They Be? Since they came into power they have netted the following sums in personal salaries:– Mr. Cosgrave (12,000) [. . .]'.[23] After listing other notable members of the government, the flyer closes with the refrain: 'If the jobs secured by both Ministers and Deputies for their relatives and friends are added, we need not wonder at the eagerness with which these men appeal for re-election nor at the bitterness with which they malign all who stand in their way.'[24] By intoning that a 'Vote for the Fianna Fáil Candidates [would] End this Colossal Jobbery!'[25] the Irish voter was meant to accept the notion that members of Cumann na nGaedheal were underhandedly – so very unmanly – reinforcing their supplication to Britain for their own political and economic gain. As such, the treaty's supporters and the Free State regime were somehow engaged in an illicit relationship with John Bull.

Themes of Cumann na nGaedheal's impotency took on a more explicitly sexual tone when contrasted to the activist economic policies of Fianna Fáil. One such example came from a 1932 party leaflet that decried Cumann na nGaedheal's inability to 'even make their own policy a success!'[26] But as early as 1927, a flyer accused Cumann na nGaedheal of 'Five Years of Poverty and Panic',[27] and Cosgrave and his party of being 'Unable to answer the damning facts and figures' of what Fianna Fáil claimed to be five years of ineffectual – impotent – rule.[28] The most interesting aspect of this pamphlet is towards the end, where the phrase – underscored in bold print – 'It was Panic' is used no less than seven times to illustrate how Cumann na nGaedheal submitted to the whims of British control because of its insecurities.

> **It was Panic** which drove them to attack the Four Courts in 1922, and thus start the Civil War . . .
>
> **It was Panic** which made them surrender to Britain and the Carsonite leaders on the Boundary Question, and, by agreeing to Partition, hand over the defenceless Six-County Nationalists and Catholics to the Orangemen . . .
>
> **It was Panic** which made them enter into the Secret Financial Agreement of March, 1926, by which £5,000,000 a year of the impoverished Irish people's money was handed over to the British Treasury . . .
>
> **It was Panic** which made them agree at the Imperial Conference that the Free State Army should become the tail of the British Army whenever 'these islands' were attacked. 'It is perfectly obvious', Mr. Desmond Fitzgerald (now Minister for Defence), said on February 17th last, 'That our Army must co-operate with the British Army' – thus involving this nation in every British War . . .
>
> That is the National Record of the Free State party – a Record not of courage, but of **PANIC**![29]

Many of the points raised in this piece of propaganda appeared again in a speech made by Frank Aiken on 30 July 1932 in Market Square in Dundalk, where he claimed, among other things, 'Unfortunately Cumann na nGaedheal were either foolishly or deliberately playing England's game. Their talk about the illegality of the Free State's claim to the annuities was playing into Britain's hands, and furnishing arguments which Britain herself would be ashamed to put forward.'[30] To put it simply, Fianna Fáil – like 'true men' – did not panic. They did not submit themselves to the will of the colonial oppressor.

The themes explored above are seen further in visual representations of Cumann na nGaedheal/Fine Gael in Fianna Fáil party propaganda. One example necessitates a return to the cartoon that appeared in the January 1937 *Fianna Fáil Bulletin*, 'Time Marches On!', discussed in Chapter 3. In this case, using queering as a prism, the themes of Britishness and subjugation to the crown are readily apparent. In the reading from the previous chapter, the picture was representative of Fianna Fáil's efforts to couch the party as a masculine endeavour, bringing economic rebirth via industrial growth to Ireland, while William Cosgrave mourns the loss of decay[31] (see Figure 3.1). Viewed through the perspective of queering, the image elicits a different response, for the artist took care to highlight that Cosgrave, in his dandy attire – coat with tails, spats and coiffured hair – was juxtaposed with the idealised, yet faceless, Irish workers adorned in the clothes of the labouring man. More important was the depiction of Cosgrave bowed down, in a pose that explicitly depicts mourning, but that implicitly evokes images of sexual passivity to the active master (a grotesque representation of John Bull), who was adorned in a similar fashion. This visual essentially recapitulated the rhetoric explored above.

Indeed, many representations of Cumann na nGaedheal/Fine Gael ministers highlighted their dandyish attire – a critique that was not only meant to depict them as snobbish and out of touch with the Irish working man, but that also evoked connotations of them as servants, or perhaps poseurs, dressing up in the pastiche of the British upper class. It also spoke to the recurrent accusation that members of Cumann na nGaedheal had actively profited from their association with the crown. These themes were readily apparent in a dual-panelled cartoon from the 9 June 1932 edition of the *Irish Press*, where Patrick McGilligan, minister for external affairs, industry and commerce, and Cosgrave stand beside a stereotyped 'Higher Civil Servant'[32] (see Figure 4.2). Certainly, it was widely appreciated that many civil servants in the 1920s had retained their positions from prior to the formation of the Free State, and thereby could be readily portrayed as having a British lineage. In the 'Then' panel, the three stand in a room, dressed in rather clubbish attire, ignorantly turning their backs on the unemployed Irish workers, adorned in simple suits and newsboy hats most associated with workingmen, who stand outside the window. The unnamed 'Higher Civil Servant' stands

Figure 4.2 Bee, 'They Never Look Out the Window', *Irish Press*, 9 June 1932, p. 1. With thanks to Irish Newspaper Archives and *The Irish Press*.

butler-like beside Cosgrave and McGilligan, who are labelled as 'The Ministers', and are quoted as saying: 'The Country is so prosperous!' The 'Then' panel, which was meant to be representative of Cumann na nGaedheal's time in government, was juxtaposed with a 'Now' panel that emphasised Fianna Fáil's activist economic policy, surprising the ex-ministers because their trusted civil servant has had his salary reduced. Such is shown by the civil servant who appears unaffected by the image of the once idle workingmen busily at work, but expresses shock because Fianna Fáil 'Cut my £1,600!'[33] As such, the artist quite literally positioned Cosgrave and his supporters outside of the heteronormative Ireland where the workingman laboured in factories and on construction sites thanks to the seed planted by Fianna Fáil's economic policies. Further, in reference to the title 'They Never Look Out the Window', the artist was certain to place the civil servant and Cumann na nGaedheal ministers inside a building, enclosed in their own world outside Fianna Fáil's

Figure 4.3 Bee, 'At Downing St. They Turned on the Radio and Smiled Again', *Irish Press*, 3 September 1932, p. 1. With thanks to Irish Newspaper Archives and *The Irish Press*.

heteronormativity. Their light-coloured pants would most certainly have been ruined by the dirt and grime of construction had they ventured outside.

Another cartoon from 1932 by the same artist, Bee, depicted a roomful of British ministers sitting around a table at Downing Street, where 'they turned on the radio and smiled again'[34] (see Figure 4.3). Divided into two panels, the cartoon on the left depicts British Prime Minister Ramsay MacDonald conferring with his colleagues, who include his second in command Stanley Baldwin seated at the far right of the panel. 'Gentlemen,' MacDonald declares, 'we cannot unseat this new Irish Government. Lets [*sic*] come to terms.'[35] Before the cabinet can accede to the prime minister's wishes regarding the recently triumphant Fianna Fáil, Baldwin says, 'Hold on a little while – something may happen yet.'[36]

Situated ominously behind the four men – all of whom are dressed in formal coats and ties, one adorned with a banker's monocle, all with expressions of consternation – is a large wireless radio. In the next panel, the following phrases are emitted from the radio: 'Mr. Cosgrave: "England is Right"'; 'Mr. Blythe: "De Valera has no case"'; 'Mr. McGilligan: "The Land Annuities are Britain's"'; 'Mr. Fitzgerald-Kenny: "England must get them"'; and most threatening from the perspective of Irish farmers, 'Mr. Desmond Fitzgerald: "Pay or – "'.[37] As these words are transmitted, the British cabinet is seen to reply, 'Saved Again!'; 'Attaboy!'; and 'Ha! Ha!', while a smug Baldwin concludes, 'What did I tell you!'[38] Bee's cartoon clearly defined the pro-British aspects of Cumann na nGaedheal's policy in regard to its opposition of Fianna Fáil's economic war against Britain, which had begun in earnest in June 1932 when de Valera announced the party's plan to withhold payment of the land annuities. Further, the cartoon was printed shortly after the private discussions with Baldwin at the Ottawa Conference, and less than three months before the January 1933 election, thus providing another example of Fianna Fáil's nationalist project. If, as argued in the previous chapter, Fianna Fáil was to represent the masculine, and was properly supported by appropriate feminine behaviour – as shown in Chapter 2 – then there was no place for Cumann na nGaedheal within the male/female heteronormative binary. Cosgrave and his supporters, therefore, were positioned outside of the acceptable republican realm.

The run-up to the 1933 general election resulted in some of the most aggressive masculinist aggrandisement of Fianna Fáil's electoral aesthetic as well as the most overt queering of Cumann na nGaedheal and Fine Gael. Such is evident in the political cartoons of Bee and in Fianna Fáil political advertisements printed in the *Irish Press*. In this particular election cycle, Cumann na nGaedheal and William Cosgrave are portrayed as thieves robbing Ireland to curry favour with Britain,[39] as children disrupting Irish progress, and as duplicitous opportunists adorning themselves in Fianna Fáil pastiche in an attempt to remain relevant after electoral defeats. In short, they are men without honour – 'beta' men serving their 'alpha' masters. Moreover, the 1933 election afforded Fianna Fáil the opportunity to run on its record of accomplishments, both real and aspired. For example, in a Fianna Fáil advertisement in the 12 January

Figure 4.4 Bee, 'Make it a Man's Answer This Time!', *Irish Press*, 24 January 1933, p. 1.
With thanks to Irish Newspaper Archives and *The Irish Press*.

1933 *Irish Press*, readers were asked, 'Who Makes England's Case?'[40]
The ad answers: 'Since Fianna Fáil came into office, the Cosgrave party
have been persistently endeavouring to undermine the Irish case for the
retention of the Land Annuities. Their preposterous contentions and
pseudo-arguments, [are made] on Britain's behalf.'[41] It continues, further
enquiring, 'Can we be bound to an annual tribute, which is relatively
heavier than the amount demanded from Germany by the Allies after
the World War by a Secret Agreement[?]'.[42] The tone here – indicative of
that of this election cycle – is that of a fighter seeking to make the final,
knockout punch against a weak, unworthy opponent.

Violent undertones are present in a Bee cartoon from 24 January 1933.
In it, the 'Irish people' – represented by a generic man in a contemporary
business suit – is in the process of landing a solid punch to the face of
another man labelled 'British Interference'. The caption reads, 'Make it
a Man's Answer This Time!'[43] (see Figure 4.4). Further, the man getting

Figure 4.5 Bee, 'Ireland's Strong Man', *Irish Press*, 21 January 1933, p. 1. With thanks to Irish Newspaper Archives and *The Irish Press*.

IRELAND'S STRONG MAN.
In July, 1931, Mr. Cosgrave asked Britain to apply the Hoover Moratorium to €250,000 of the five million he paid her each year. Britain refused—and Mr. Cosgrave did not tell a soul.

punched is holding what appears to be a truncheon in one hand – symbolic, perhaps, of British violence perpetuated on the Irish by the Royal Irish Constabulary and the British Army – and in the other a set of pliers representing 'Economic Squeeze'.[44] Viewed alone, this might appear to be a pretty standard example of a nationalist party transgressing its colonial power. However, the complete picture includes two young boys – adorned in short pants and noted as being from the 'Cosgrave Party' and the 'National Centre Party' – declaring the act of defiant violence as a 'Shame!'[45] This depiction of Cosgrave's Party as being a child reifies the queering of Fianna Fáil opposition, as these are immature boys, not even old enough to be seen as young men, for they give no indication that they are anywhere near adulthood, and therefore unable to offer anything to

Figure 4.6 Bee, 'Mr. Cosgrave', *Irish Press*, 14 January 1933, p. 1. With thanks to Irish Newspaper Archives and *The Irish Press*.

MR. COSGRAVE : Let me in; let me in; I'm Fianna Fáil, too.
(*Mr. Cosgrave has adopted the Fianna Fáil policy of halving the Annuities*)

the nation. This cartoon follows a 21 January 1933 Bee cartoon in which Cosgrave is depicted as child-sized and is slightly bent over waiting in position for a whipping from a generic British politician who states, 'I'm going to give you the trouncing of your life, young man – but don't tell anybody'[46] (see Figure 4.5). Cosgrave, sarcastically called 'Ireland's Strong Man', replies, 'Not a Soul.'[47] There is much to analyse here: Cosgrave's submissive position and willingness to accept a beating from Britain implies passivity and deceitfulness in honour of a foreign master; Cosgrave – and by extension his party – as an immature and impotent entity; a dandy, dressed in British parliamentarian drag, perhaps an indication of his own aspirations, and in direct contrast to Fianna Fáil's 'bankers'. The gendering here is clear, with Fianna Fáil emasculating its rivals to accentuate its own masculinity.

THE CHANNEL SWIMMER.
MR. COSGRAVE (*having borrowed a few Fianna Fáil lifebelts*) : " I may be able to keep my own head above water on Tuesday with these—but, alas, my poor party."

Figure 4.7 Bee, 'The Channel Swimmer', *Irish Press*, 19 January 1933, p. 1. With thanks to Irish Newspaper Archives and *The Irish Press*.

A 14 January 1933 advertisement from the *Irish Press* is emblazoned with the title 'Fianna Fáil was Right All the Time – Even Mr. Wm. Cosgrave, Ex.-T.D., admits it NOW!'[48] The ad declares that 'after eleven months in opposition and one week's tour of the country Mr. Cosgrave has discovered that the burden of the Land Annuities is too heavy for the farmers and "beyond their ability to pay"'.[49] This notion of Cosgrave coming round to Fianna Fáil's position on the annuities – and, in turn, its relationship to Britain – was manifest in a Bee cartoon from the same issue of the *Irish Press*. Here, Cosgrave – his coiffure and signature suit discernible despite his back being turned towards the viewer – is seen banging on the door of the Dáil, imploring, 'Let me in; let me in; I'm Fianna Fáil, too'[50] (see Figure 4.6).

And finally on 19 January 1933, Bee depicted Cosgrave as 'The Channel Swimmer' bedecked with a number of life preservers labelled: 'Annuities Halved'; 'More Tariffs'; 'Waste to Be Cut Down'; 'New Industries'; 'Work'; 'No Secret Agreements'; 'Less British Dumping'; 'Farmers First'; 'Tillage'; and, surprisingly, 'End Partition'[51] (see Figure 4.7). Cosgrave is essentially saving himself and his party via an overcompensation of life preservers that just happen to be representative of Fianna Fáil policy. In this regard, Cosgrave defines his agency through mimesis and submission to who he views as authoritative. Therefore, he is depicted as having no masculine traits – that he is effective-cum-potent when he adorns the cloak of his master. From this perspective, Fianna Fáil, by way of Bee, demonstrates Cosgrave's acquiescence to the effectiveness and potency of de Valera's party.

In February 1936, the *Fianna Fáil Bulletin* reprinted an article from the magazine *New Statesman and Nation* under the headline '"Irish Housekeeping": British Writer on the Results of Fianna Fáil's Economic Policy'. The article highlighted the assertion that 'The Cosgrave regime, it is true, for ten years carried good marks in the British Press by a docile acceptance of previous conditions. Ireland's role was to concentrate on animal husbandry, to supply Great Britain with meat, butter and eggs, importing in exchange most of the necessaries [*sic*] and luxuries of life'.[52] While the piece did not originate with Fianna Fáil, its inclusion certainly reiterated the party's rhetorical portrayal of Fine Gael as having been subservient to Britain. Within sixteen months, however, the *Bulletin* trumpeted Fine Gael's 'slow conversion' to Fianna Fáil's economic approach. The article, entitled 'The Education of Fine Gael', heralded:

> The slow conversion of Fine Gael to the greater part of the Fianna Fail Economic Programme is proof of the overwhelming support of the people for the policy of National Self-Sufficiency and Security. Equally it reveals the negative outlook of the Opposition and is the proof of their utter failure to think constructively or nationally.
>
> Three leaders have left Fine Gael. The desperate and unscrupulous attempt to create a Fascist movement fizzled out in miserable wire-cutting and free-falling. Then followed the conversion – a conversion too late to deceive the Irish people.[53]

Much of the article discussed 'The slow and Pitiful Surrender to Fianna Fail' and demonstrated Fianna Fáil's growing confidence that it was now the hegemonic force that was driving the push towards a new nation. Further, this article serves as a marker of how the rise of Fianna Fáil had transformed Cumann na nGaedheal from a party with its own ideology into one that was essentially reacting – and thereby acquiescing – to the new republican hegemony.[54] Most interesting, however, was the depiction of Fianna Fáil as the 'National Educators' who would 'teach Fine Gael that the people of this country want a Government that will lead them to prosperity through constructive effort and not a party which encourages their oppressors by prophecies of disaster – nor a party which threatens to 'knock the hell out of them'.[55]

'GAEL', 'CELT' AND 'SOCARO': FIANNA FÁIL AND GAELIC SPORT

One final, explicit form of queering the British is present in the juxtaposition between the violent, aggressive forms of Gaelic athletics and the more proper British sports. Mike Cronin cites the creation of the modern *Aonach Tailteann* – 'the Irish olympiad [*sic*], of 1924, 1928 and 1932' – as a cultural nation-building event advocated by Cumann na nGaedheal.[56] Emerging at roughly the same time as the Gaelic Athletic Association, the *Aonach Tailteann* drew support from across the nationalist spectrum, including Sinn Féin and the 'outlawed Dáil Éireann ... [which] began arguing for the renewal of the games, and leading figures such as Eamon de Valera threw their weight behind the campaign'.[57] John Turpin notes that the advocacy of the *Aonach Tailteann* by the new Free State government represented a 'manifestation of Cultural Revival ideology ... attempting to create a modern political entity, distinct from Britain, with its own cultural events and emblems'.[58] Despite this sentiment, Cronin adds that Cumann na nGaedheal was 'hesitant to fund *Aonach Tailteann*, at any level considered excessive'.[59] Support for the games disintegrated when Fianna Fáil 'was not prepared to continue funding a festival whilst government loans remained unpaid. Also, the government viewed the whole event as one that had been set up by their political opponents and which represented the Irish

state as imagined by the leadership of Cumann na nGaedheal.'[60] Not
surprisingly, Fianna Fáil instead aligned itself with the GAA, which was
still republican-nationalist in origin, but as a private body it remained
largely free from associations with the Free State. Further, and more
importantly, the types of sport endorsed by the GAA were more in line
with the nationalist vision advanced by Fianna Fáil.

Although Fianna Fáil was not the first to claim the Gaelic Athletic
Association as its own, the very fact that it was able to envelop the anti-
British facet of the GAA into its own rhetoric speaks to the party's success
at aligning itself with its nationalistic predecessors.[61] Patrick F. McDevitt
has noted that 'male supporters of Gaelic games often connected images
of British men with those of women or neutered men. The feminisation of
the enemy here displays male Irish attitudes not only toward British men
but also toward women and themselves.'[62] McDevitt further noted that
Gaelic sport 'reinforced the image of political unity, namely a brotherhood
of Gaels which, with their women in concomitant subordination,
would reclaim their lost nation from a feminized oppressor'.[63] Thus, it
is of no surprise to find members of Fianna Fáil – many of whom had
previously participated in GAA-sponsored competitions – making
appearances at GAA events, promoting the uniquely Irish-manly and
Irish-feminine elements of such sports as Gaelic football, hurling and
camogie.[64] Following the period in which elements of Irish nationalism
became associated more with the perceptively Anglophilic Cumann na
nGaedheal-run Free State, Fianna Fáil's rhetorical alignment with the
GAA was akin to McDevitt's description that 'the growth of hurling
and Gaelic football as propagated by the GAA was instrumental in the
restructuring of an Irish nationalist manhood. The power to oppose
British games and reclaim independence of action one sphere at a time
marked the first dramatic steps toward greater freedom from English
control.'[65]

As demonstrated in the previous chapter, Fianna Fáil's economic
rhetoric was rooted in the ability to paint Cumann na nGaedheal, and
later Fine Gael, as passive and therefore outside of the acceptable
gendered norms of the Free State. At first blush, such an effort appeared
similar to the process described by McDevitt, but in this era the queering
of Britain evolved due to the political transformation that had resulted

from the creation of the Saorstát. McDevitt's description of the GAA as an anti-imperialist organisation held true in an era when republicanism was synonymous with physical-force insurgency, yet, in the formative era, Fianna Fáil republicanism was as much hegemonic as it was anti-hegemonic. Therefore, the alignment by Fianna Fáil with the Gaelic Athletic Association was as much about the queering of Britishness and its perceived remnants within the new Ireland as it was about the reification of its gendered nationalist frameworks. Where aestheticisation of Fianna Fáilism was tantamount to a corrective force, its alignment with the GAA was representative of its effort to create a general distaste for lingering Britishness in the new Ireland.

Along with its prominent page devoted to women, the *Irish Press*'s coverage and promotion of GAA sport was nothing less than ground-breaking. The level of primacy granted to hurling and Gaelic football helped to elevate national awareness of these sports in Ireland, which in turn 'proved very popular and obliged the *Irish Independent* to respond in kind'.[66] Granted, such English-associated sports as rugby, football and horse racing were covered also; however, they were afforded a secondary status on the sports pages of the *Irish Press*. Quite literally, Fianna Fáil utilised its house organ to visually construct a sense of preference regarding sport in Ireland. A fine example can be found in the sports page from the 3 September 1932 issue, where authors 'Gael' and 'Celt'[67] covered the upcoming All-Ireland hurling final. Contrasted with a large image depicting the members of the Kilkenny and Clare hurling sides were much smaller stories covering results in the Walker Cup – where the poor showing by the British was highlighted in the headline – and the Free State soccer league.[68] Equally significant was the positioning of these latter articles on the fringes of the page, while the eye was directed to the prominent, central photographs and headlines dedicated to Gaelic sports.

Although it is not uncommon to find rhetoric evocative of militaristic engagement in the coverage of all sports, the sportswriters of the *Irish Press* made certain to elevate connections to the traditional aspects of Gaelic sports. One such example is the noms de plume adopted by the sportswriters: 'Gael' and 'Celt' covered GAA sports, while 'The Sport' and 'Socaro' covered horse racing and soccer, respectively. Take for example the article entitled 'The G.A.A. Provides Living Example of Perpetual Motion', where the author, Celt, wrote that 'scarcely has one county or inter-county competition concluded than another is started and, when championship activities die down, the National Leagues come into operation'.[69] The implication was that the reiteration of Irish cultural nationalism as represented by traditional sport was incessant; therefore, the unceasing cycle of manly action and movement were a constant salvo in the nationalist press. The elevation of Gaelic sport to a level of primacy by Fianna Fáil fit well within its dualistic, palingenetic discourse, for the party forged a nexus between the traditional and the modern. This was done by using elements of modernity – mass-produced newspaper, heraldry by a modern political machine and eventually radio broadcasts of major fixtures – and combining them with elements of a primordial Ireland, however imagined. By associating with Gaelic sport, as well as by using its political and cultural strength to influence popular tastes, Fianna Fáil was in a position to incorporate games into its notions of heteronormativity. Anglo-tinged sports, while certainly popular, were relegated to a peripheral presence within Fianna Fáil's envisioned Irish republic.

This chapter has demonstrated how Fianna Fáil defined what was inclusive and what was not. As the previous chapters have shown, Dev's party sought to correct perceived crises in an unbalanced Ireland by working to define what was acceptable and unacceptable as it related to masculinity and femininity – a corrective to anxieties inherited from colonialism and conflict. Such is the theme of a cartoon entitled 'Breaking the Chains' from Bee included in the 25–6 March 1932 edition of the *Irish Press*. The image features a man, standing tall, shirtsleeves rolled to the elbow, the word 'Ireland' written across his chest, stance defiant; the iron shackles around his wrists, labelled as 'Oath', are broken.[70] Behind him is a group of men and women, arranged in a manner resembling a mountain, who are labelled 'The Irish People'. The caption quotes Dr Daniel Mannix, archbishop of Melbourne: 'The Irish have stood upon their feet.'[71] Most interesting is the intermixing of women and men as representatives of the Irish people. In most instances, Fianna Fáil's aesthetic segregated the sexes, but here the depiction of a freed Ireland – embodied as a male – is constituted of men and women. And though the people depicted are melded together in some form, the viewer is still able to discern that the men and women are dressed in professional clothing – the men in the types of suits worn by Fianna Fáil when greeting the papal legation, and the women in demure yet seemingly modern clothing. In short, Ireland has been liberated from Britain by Fianna Fáil, in turn freeing Irish women and men. As this and the previous two chapters have demonstrated, these, the 'Irish people', were situated as the bedrock of a renascent Ireland. Absent from this, the depiction of Ireland, is the fey, duplicitous and Anglophilic Cumann na nGaedheal/Fine Gael, for they were not to be included in the national coitus, as they were symbolically desexualised. As such, Fianna Fáil, in a sense, turned the tables: where the party's early success was dependent upon its adherence to the rule of law and its ability to shed the feminised stigma of Sinn Féin, now – at least in its electoral aesthetic – Fianna Fáil had constituted new definitions of gender that ensured that its republican ideal was the basis of such definitions. Excluded, and therefore unworthy of propagating this new Ireland? Cosgrave and his party.

CHAPTER 5

Conclusion: 'Ireland is not a bad old place after all!'

The 16 March 1933 edition of the *Irish Press* included another cartoon by Bee, with this one entitled 'Ireland Is Not a Bad Old Place After All!'[1] (see Figure 5.1). The cartoon offers a Fianna Fáil-sanctioned world view. Ireland – peaceful, pastoral and united – is surrounded by pictographic avatars of a globe in crisis: Germany as two men – presumably right wing and socialist – in violent conflict; France as two men in heated discussion; Italy as two soldiers – one national and one fascist – marching together in lock-step; South America [*sic*] represented by two '*banditos*' firing guns at one another; the USA beset by an unsteady economy as characterised by a bank with weakened columns; and Japan, as militant aggressor, beating a Chinese national with a club.[2] Racist and essentialised characterisations aside, Bee does touch on the crises that were undoubtedly familiar to regular readers of the *Irish Press*. Ireland is situated in the middle of this chaos, where a male farmer – the Irish Masculine – works in solitude (save for his two horses), ploughing his land. The rays of a new day provide the light for the worker, and in some ways situates Ireland as the fulcrum of a global heliocentrism, where the Irish nation – now governed by Fianna Fáil – is the epitome of peace, calm and progress among a world of chaos. Such a presentation underscores the aspirational vision put forth by Fianna Fáil: a modern, yet traditional nation; united and peaceful despite its recent history; independent and free, where the new day represents hope and optimism. And how did this happen? Fianna Fáil. The party is presented here as restoring order and providing Ireland an opportunity to flourish in the face of its own history and in the context of a world at

Figure 5.1 Bee, 'Ireland Is Not a Bad Old Place After All!', *Irish Press*, 16 March 1933, p. 1. With thanks to Irish Newspaper Archives and *The Irish Press*.

its own throat. Indeed, this view is aspirational and far from truthful. Yet this envisioned Ireland as constructed by Fianna Fáil depicts a party and nation that had transcended the financial and geo-political anxieties, to flourish.

A cartoon from the following week depicted a number of heavily armed soldiers from myriad European nations – clearly demarcated by uniform – marching unguided, with clear looks of confusions on their faces[3] (see Figure 5.2). Foregrounded is the image of an Irish (Masculine) farmer, who, like Cincinnatus, lays down his plough to address (solve) a crisis. A French soldier is told by the Irish farmer, 'Try my way: you'll find it more easily with plough-shares than with swords.'[4] The juxtaposition of a peaceful Ireland and bellicose Europe draws upon the themes of the 16 March 1933 cartoon, yet this one offers a bit more insight into Fianna Fáil's electoral aesthetic than its predecessor. Namely, that Ireland had figured out a way to overcome its own bellicosity to not only flourish

IRELAND (to an armed Europe searching distractedly for peace): Try my way; you'll find it more easily with ploughshares than with swords.

Figure 5.2 Bee, 'Ireland', *Irish Press*, 22 March 1933, p. 1. With thanks to Irish Newspaper Archives and *The Irish Press*.

politically and economically, but in such a way that it could become a beacon for a continent on the verge of – if not searching for – conflict. It can scarcely be believed that Bee, the editors at the *Irish Press* and Fianna Fáil believed that Ireland could effect peace in Europe, or that the nation's agri-economic progress was the missing solution to world peace. Instead, the image falls in line with how the party was presenting itself to the Irish people: as a nation that had settled the violence of the recent past to create a functional, productive and truly Irish nation. The international acclaim presented in these cartoons serves to underscore this envisioned Ireland, no matter how truthful. In this regard, the Irish Masculine – peaceful, traditional and modern, industrious, pious – was the outward face of the modern Irish nation, a role model for the rest of the world. Moreover, while the Europeans are adorned in the attire of the soldier,

Figure 5.3 'Make the Home Fires HOME Fires', *Irish Press*, 22 April 1933, p. 1. With thanks to Irish Newspaper Archives and *The Irish Press*.

the uniform of the Irish Masculine – HIS uniform – is that of the humble and peaceful farmer. Such a vision, however dubious, presented to the Irish citizen-reader provided an alternative vision of Fianna Fáil, where a generic man/Masculine, free of any outward political association, transcended – and corrected – the darkness that was Ireland's past. The Irish Masculine had been freed by Fianna Fáil from the oppression of violence and the remnants of colonialism and thus restored to its/his proper place. This farmer – and as depicted elsewhere, the Irish factory worker – as avatar for Irish masculinity was revitalised as the seminal figure in Ireland, actively working to (re)build, to forge, to sow, to harvest and to procreate.

One month later, on 22 April 1933, another cartoon appeared in the *Irish Press*. The image, by an uncredited artist, depicts an Irish woman dressed in fashionable, yet demure, clothing, modern hairstyle and makeup, sitting in front of a hearth where a roaring fire warms and brightens a seemingly clean and modern home[5] (see Figure 5.3). The apron tied around her waist tells us nothing of her specific vocation, but it does re-emphasise her position as homemaker. Fuelling the fire is Irish turf, and the lone embellishment of the home is a pastoral scene that could easily be Wicklow or any other hilly region of Ireland. She, the Irish Feminine, has a look of contentment and (domestic) peace; she is safe and at home, unencumbered by public engagement with politics, for Fianna Fáil has seemingly made such excitations unnecessary. This, however, is not to say that the Irish Feminine is no longer politically engaged. The cartoon includes the caption 'Make the Home Fires HOME Fires'.[6] The aspired Irish Feminine helps to win the economic war – and thereby support Fianna Fáil's envisioned republic – by not only planning, but by consuming domestically produced Irish turf and, presumably, by wearing the fashions 'made to please'. More than this, the Irish Feminine has opted to eschew the earlier, less desirable variant of republican political activity by turning hers into an all-Irish HOME. This depiction of the Irish Feminine represents Fianna Fáil's envisioned Ireland, where women were returned to the home as caretakers of the familial hearth, yet also subtly and actively political in that they were consumers of Irish goods in support of the economic war and the general march towards an independent Éire. This return to a traditional role elevated the Irish Feminine above the discordant fray of Sinn Féin republicanism. Yet as seen here – and elsewhere in Fianna Fáil's nationalist press – the Irish Feminine was demure and domestic, yet political and modern. The cautious agency imparted by Fianna Fáil was meant as a corrective by way of political organisation and the general march towards a fully independent state. Such was the Irish Masculine and the Irish Feminine. These were the ambitious models to which the people of Ireland were to aspire, situating Fianna Fáil as correcting legacies of conquest and violence, while at the same time assuaging anxieties present in the interwar world – phenomena that the party viewed itself as inheriting and being best suited to rectify. This was Fianna Fáil in the years 1926–38.

Analysing Fianna Fáil's electoral aesthetic through the lenses of gender and historical works on fascism serves to suss out what was on Fianna Fáil's metaphorical mind during the years 1926–38. This study of Fianna Fáil's electoral aesthetic has shown that the party – consciously or not –

constructed, along gendered lines, an appealingly aspirational vision of a peaceful and prosperous Ireland where primordialism and an imagined Irish futurism were reconciled. More than anything else, Fianna Fáil recast republicanism in a new light, where political action and agency were no longer extra-legal and violent; rather, the movement was fully ensconced as a defiantly transgressive party engaged in constitutional struggle to recast republicanism as more appealing to the nation's electorate. The party's electoral aesthetic examined herein shows a party willing to work within existing frameworks only to transgress and undermine Free State structures, in turn viewing the Saorstát as a placeholder for the triumph of the new nation – a nation whose envisioned future was at odds with the political, historical, cultural and economic realities of the time. In this sense, Fianna Fáil's palingenetic aesthetic might have contributed to its electoral successes, including the passage of the 1937 constitution and creation of Éire, but it did not – and realistically, could not – live up to the promise of the party's vision.

The gendered binarism of the Irish Feminine and Irish Masculine martialled by Fianna Fáil does illustrate the party's seemingly contradictory dualism, where the Irish citizen – as the embodiment of the new nation – was to be the physical embodiment of the modern and primordial state. Here, in the conclusion, it should also be noted that Fianna Fáil always depicted itself explicitly as male – never as female. That Fianna Fáil's Ireland had its origins locked into a gendered binarism that was further encoded in the 1937 constitution. Such provides a possible explanation for the furtherance – but not the origins – of heteronormative patriarchy in Ireland, a structure that is finally being dismantled. Indeed, my aim has been to shed light on the electoral aesthetic utilised by Fianna Fáil's 1926–38 iteration, where the need to offer a corrective to Ireland's historical phenomena, and assuage anxieties related to domestic and international affairs, compelled the party to recast republican political agency along gendered lines. Whether this was done consciously or not, the evidence provided herein demonstrates that it was indeed present and effective, in that Fianna Fáil's renascent republicanism translated into electoral success.

Notes

INTRODUCTION

1   Anonymous quote from the *Westminster Gazette*, in Maurice Moynihan (ed.), *Speeches and Statements by Éamon de Valera, 1917–1973* (Dublin: Gill & Macmillan, 1980), p. 129.

2   Irish for Free State. I utilise both Saorstát and Free State interchangeably, solely for stylistic purposes.

3   Éamon de Valera (1930), in *Speeches and Statements by Eamon de Valera, 1917–1973*. Moynihan notes that this passage was found among de Valera's papers and remained unpublished. Nonetheless, it gives insight into the reasons for de Valera's 'new departure' (ibid., p. 129).

4   Given the longevity of Fianna Fáil, there are many works that debate the successes – or lack thereof – of 'Dev's' party. Such debates are left to others and are not to be engaged here. Rather, my aim is to examine the electoral aesthetic of the party between 1926 and 1938.

5   Recent works have explored the efficacy of the Irish Free State under the governance of William T. Cosgrave and Cumann na nGaedheal. Long treated as an internecine period between the more exciting 'decade of revolution' and the Fianna Fáil era, the period between 1922 and 1932 was vital in the creation of an independent Irish state. Jason Knirck's *oeuvre* has done much to direct study on this era. See, for example, Jason Knirck, *Women of the Dáil: Gender, republicanism and the Anglo-Irish Treaty* (Dublin: Irish Academic Press, 2006); Jason Knirck, *Afterimage of the Revolution: Cumann na nGaedheal and Irish politics, 1922–1932* (Madison: University of Wisconsin Press, 2014); Mel Farrell, Jason Knirck and Ciara Meehan (eds), *A Formative Decade: Ireland in the 1920s* (Dublin: Irish Academic Press, 2015). See also Ciara Meehan, *The Cosgrave Party: A history of Cumann na nGaedheal, 1923–1933* (Dublin: Royal Irish Academy, 2010).

6   See, for example, Richard Dunphy, *The Making of Fianna Fáil Power in Ireland, 1923–1948* (Oxford: Clarendon Press, 1995); Joost Augusteijn (ed.), *Ireland in the 1930s: New perspectives* (Dublin: Four Courts Press, 1999); Brian Fallon, *An Age of Innocence: Irish culture, 1930–1960* (London: Palgrave Macmillan, 1998); Terence Brown, *Ireland: A social and cultural history, 1922–2002* (London: Harper Collins, 2004); Brian Girvin, 'The Republicanisation of Irish Society, 1932–48', in J.R. Hill (ed.), *A New History of Ireland. Volume VII: Ireland, 1921–84* (Oxford: Oxford University Press, 2003); John M. Regan, *The Irish Counter-Revolution, 1921–1936: Treatyite politics and settlement in independent Ireland* (Dublin: Gill & Macmillan, 1999); Kevin Boland, *The Rise and Decline of Fianna Fáil* (Cork: Mercier Press, 1982); Gearóid Ó Tuathaigh, 'The Age of de Valera and the Newsreel', in Luke Dodd (ed.), *Nationalisms: Visions and revisions* (Dublin: Film Institute of Ireland, 1999); Declan Kiberd, 'From Nationalism to Liberation', in Susan Shaw Sailer (ed.), *Representing Ireland: Gender, class, nationality* (Gainsville: University of Florida Press, 1997); Desmond Ryan, *Unique Dictator: A study of Éamon de Valera* (London: Barker, 1936).

7   Of course it is rather anachronistic to refer to the period of Irish history between 1919 and 1939 as being 'interwar', for Ireland's somewhat nebulous, or unofficial, role in the Great War

and its neutrality during the 'Emergency' does not necessarily constitute an interwar period. Nonetheless, the purpose here is to situate Ireland within the context of interwar Europe. As such, it is my contention that the term 'interwar' does indeed apply.

8   The Irish title of the 1937 Constitution of Ireland.
9   Michael Mays, *Nation States: The cultures of Irish nationalism* (Lanham: Lexington Books, 2007), pp. 95–6.
10 Alvin Jackson, *Ireland, 1798–1998: Politics and war* (Oxford: Blackwell Publishers, 1999), p. 282.
11 Ibid., p. 283.
12 Dunphy, *The Making of Fianna Fáil Power in Ireland*, p. viii.
13 J.J. Lee, *Ireland, 1912–1985* (Cambridge: Cambridge University Press, 1989), p. 182.
14 James M. Smith, 'The Politics of Sexual Knowledge: The origins of Ireland's containment culture and the Carrigan Report (1931)', *Journal of the History of Sexuality*, vol. 13, no. 2, April 2004, p. 209.
15 Donnacha Ó Beacháin, *Destiny of the Soldiers: Fianna Fáil, Irish republicanism and the IRA, 1926–1973* (Dublin: Gill & Macmillan, 2010). Ó Beacháin's work provides an indispensable look at Fianna Fáil's history from its origins up to the early 1970s. The work is a good starting point for those interested in a deeper history of party organisation and machination.
16 Alan Zink, 'Ireland: Democratic stability without compromise', in Dirk Berg-Schlosser and Jeremy Mitchell (eds), *Conditions of Democracy in Europe, 1919–39* (London: Macmillan Press, 2000), p. 263.
17 Ibid.
18 Ibid., p. 275.
19 Alvin Jackson, 'The Two Irelands', in Robert Gerwarth (ed.), *Twisted Paths, Europe 1914–1945* (Oxford: Oxford University Press, 2007), p. 74.
20 Ibid.
21 Gavin Foster, *The Irish Civil War and Society: Politics, class, and conflict* (London: Palgrave Macmillan, 2015), pp. 2–3.
22 Mel Farrell, *Party Politics in a New Democracy: The Irish Free State, 1922–1937* (London: Palgrave Macmillan, 2017), p. 7.
23 Ibid., p. 8.
24 Aidan Beatty, *Masculinity and Power in Irish Nationalism, 1884–1938* (London: Palgrave Macmillan, 2016), p. 13.
25 Timothy Ellis, 'De Valera's Gains: The masculine body in Irish political cartoons, 1922–1939', *Éire/Ireland*, vol. 54, nos. 3 & 4, fall/winter 2019, p. 61.
26 Beatty, *Masculinity and Power in Irish Nationalism*, p. 170.
27 Ellis, 'De Valera's Gains', p. 62.
28 Mosse, George L., *Nationalism and Sexuality: Respectability and abnormal sexuality in modern Europe* (New York: Howard Fertig, 1985), p. 1.
29 Ibid., p. 64.
30 Ibid., p. 16.
31 Ibid.
32 Joan Wallach Scott, 'Gender: A useful category of historical analysis', in Joan Wallach Scott (ed.), *Feminism and History* (Oxford: Oxford University Press, 1996), p. 167.
33 Philippa Levine, 'Introduction: Why gender and empire?', in Philippa Levine (ed.), *Gender and Empire* (Oxford: Oxford University Press, 2004), p. 7.
34 Roger Griffin, 'The Reclamation of Fascist Culture', *European History Quarterly*, vol. 31, no. 4, 2001, p. 610.
35 Michel Foucault, *The History of Sexuality. Volume I: An Introduction*, trans. Robert Hurley (New York: Vintage Books [1978], 1990), p. 11.

36 Ann Taylor Allen, *Women in Twentieth-Century Europe* (London: Palgrave, 2008), pp. 22–3.

37 Maryann Gialanella Valiulis, 'Virtuous Mothers and Dutiful Wives: The politics of sexuality in the Irish Free State', in Maryann Gialanella Valiulis (ed.), *Gender and Power in Irish History* (Dublin: Irish Academic Press, 2009), p. 107.

38 Mac an Ghail, Máirtín and Chris Haywood, *Gender, Culture and Society: Contemporary femininities and masculinities* (London: Palgrave, 2007), p. 29.

39 Mosse, *Nationalism and Sexuality*, p. 16.

40 Michel Foucault, 'The Subject and Power', *Critical Inquiry*, vol. 8, no. 4, 1981, pp. 782–3.

41 Lutz P. Koepnick, 'Fascist Aesthetics Revisited', *Modernism/modernity*, vol. 6, no. 1, January 1999, p. 56.

42 Knirck, *Women of the Dáil*, p. 2. See also Louise Ryan, '"Drunken Tans": Representations of sex and violence in the Anglo-Irish war (1919–1921)', *Feminist Review*, no. 66, 'Political Currents', autumn 2000, pp. 73–94; Elizabeth Frances Martin, 'Painting the Irish West: Nationalism and the representation of women', *New Hibernia Review/Irish Éireannach Nua*, vol. 7, no. 1, spring/ earrach 2003, pp. 31–44.

43 Knirck, *Women of the Dáil*, p. 15.

44 Kiberd, 'From Nationalism to Liberation', p. 20.

45 Robert O. Paxton, *The Anatomy of Fascism* (New York: Vintage Books, 2005), pp. 12–13.

46 Mike Cronin has done considerable research on the Blueshirts, and his works on the movement continue to be the definitive works on the subject. Cronin argues that the Blueshirts had certain fascist traits – they declared themselves to be as much – yet they 'were not instinctively anti-democratic and . . . the only result of such posturing was to enable Fianna Fáil to present themselves as the saviours of democracy'. Mike Cronin, *The Blueshirts and Irish Politics* (Dublin: Four Courts Press, 1997), p. 39. Cronin contends that the Blueshirts 'should be seen as a popular organisation which attempted to challenge the changes which de Valera envisaged for Ireland. More importantly the Blueshirts galvanized the opposition to form a single block to combat Fianna Fáil.' Ibid., p. 197. See also Fearghal McGarry, 'General O'Duffy, the National Corporate Party and the Irish Brigade', in Augusteijn, *Ireland in the 1930s*, pp. 117–42, and R.M. Douglas, *Architects of the Resurrection: Ailtirí na h-aiséirghe and the fascist 'new order' in Ireland* (Manchester: Manchester University Press, 2009).

47 Lee, *Ireland*, p. 182.

48 Ibid.

49 Ara H. Merjian, 'Fascism, Gender, and Culture', *Qui Parle*, vol. 13, no. 1, fall/winter 2001, p. 4.

50 Mark Antliff, 'Fascism, Modernism, and Modernity', *The Art Bulletin*, vol. 84, no. 1, March 2002, p. 148.

51 The phrase 'third way' comes from Ruth Ben-Ghiat, who argued that fascistic impulses were driven by a need to not only find an alternative to the liberal/Marxian binary, but 'formed part of a larger attempt to reconceptualize "modernity" as a condition that would allow for the retention of specificity at both the personal and national level'. Ruth Ben-Ghiat, 'Italian Fascism and the Aesthetics of the "Third Way"', *Journal of Contemporary History*, vol. 31, no. 2, April 1996, p. 293. Ben-Ghiat adds that this 'third way' was manifest in European fascisms as an 'attempt to fashion a doctrine that would correct the "materialism" of both liberalism and socialism' (p. 294). See also Fearghal McGarry, 'General O'Duffy, the National Corporate Party and the Irish Brigade', in Augusteijn, *Ireland in the 1930s*, pp. 117–42, and Douglas, *Architects of the Resurrection*.

52 Lee, *Ireland*, p. 183. Lee also referred to interwar Ireland as 'Gaelic Weimar' (ibid., p. 184).

53 Ibid., p. 181.

54 Walter Benjamin, 'The Work of Art in the Age of Mechanical Reproduction', in *Illuminations: Essays and reflections*, trans. Harry Zohn (New York: Schocken, 1969), p. 241.

55 Koepnick, 'Fascist Aesthetics Revisited', p. 55.

56 Ibid., p. 56.

57 *Parliamentary Debates*, 5th ser., vol. 335, May 1938, cols. 899–900.

58 MacDonald, Speech to the House of Commons, 5 May 1938, *Parliamentary Debates*, Commons, 5th ser., vol. 335, 1938, cols. 1071–185. Serving the constituencies of Bassetlaw (1929–35) and Ross and Cromarty (1936–45), MacDonald was the secretary of state for the dominions from 1938 to 1940, a term that was followed by a stint as minister of health, which lasted from 1940–1, http://hansard.millbanksystems.com/people/mr-malcolm-macdonald.

59 Churchill, Speech to the House of Commons, 5 May 1938, *Parliamentary Debates*, Commons, 5th ser., vol. 335, cols. 1071–185. At the time of the debate, the future prime minister served the Epping constituency and had no ministerial duties, http://hansard.millbanksystems.com/people/mr-winston-churchill.

60 Gallacher, Speech to the House of Commons, 5 May 1938, *Parliamentary Debates*, Commons, 5th ser., vol. 335, cols. 1071–185. Gallacher was an MP for Fife Western and served from November 1935 to February 1950, http://hansard.millbanksystems.com/people/mr-william-gallacher.

CHAPTER 1. FIANNA FÁIL'S IMMODEST INNOVATION, 1926–31

1   Mary MacSwiney, 'Letter from Mhaire Nic Shuibhne', *c.*1927, Mary MacSwiney Papers (hereafter MacSwiney Papers), UCDA, P48a/42, p. 50. MacSwiney (1872–1942) was arguably the most important and influential feminist republican activist of the twentieth century. She was active in Cumann na mBan and Sinn Féin, serving as an outspoken critic of the treaty. Following de Valera's departure to create Fianna Fáil, MacSwiney became the figurehead of Sinn Féin, working tirelessly to resuscitate its republican vision. Brian Murphy, 'Mary MacSwiney', in James McGuire and James Quinn (eds), *Dictionary of Irish Biography*, Volume 6 (Cambridge: Cambridge University Press, 2010), pp. 192–4. In the wide swathe of sources, Mary MacSwiney's name is spelled a number of different ways in both English and in Irish. For simplicity, I will use the spelling used by University College Dublin for labelling its collection of MacSwiney's papers. However, when citing sources directly, the original will be used.

2   On the decline of Sinn Féin during this period, see Peter Pyne, 'The Third Sinn Féin Party: 1923–1926', *The Economic and Social Review*, vol. 1, no. 1, 1969. Pyne notes that the split with Sinn Féin in 1926 marked the end of the 'Third' Sinn Féin party and the creation of the 'Fourth Sinn Féin party, which existed from 1926 on . . . [and] soon retired from active political life, its small membership feeling more at home in devotion to activities of a social, cultural and propagandist nature' (p. 30). A history of a longer span of Irish republicanism can be found in Joost Augusteijn, 'Political Violence and Democracy: An analysis of the tensions with Irish republican strategy, 1914–2002', *Irish Political Studies*, vol. 18, no. 1, 2003, pp. 1–26.

3   Here I mean progressive in the historical sense; that is, a movement to progress and evolve Irish republicanism.

4   Eunan O'Halpin, 'Politics and the State, 1922–1932', in J.R. Hill (ed), *A New History of Ireland, Volume VII* (Oxford: Oxford University Press, 2003).

5   For an overview of Sinn Féin electoral policy, see Mel Farrell, '"The Tide Had Definitely Turned": The Irish Party, Sinn Féin, and the election campaigns in Longford, 1917–18', *New Hibernia Review*, vol. 21, no. 3, autumn/fómhar 2017, pp. 83–104.

6   O'Halpin, 'Politics', p. 87.

7   Bill Kissane, *Explaining Irish Democracy* (Dublin: UCD Press, 2002), pp. 165–6.

8   Juan Linz, cited in Kissane, *Explaining Irish Democracy*, pp. 165–6.

9   Kissane, *Explaining Irish Democracy*, pp. 165–6.

10 Ibid., p. 193.

11 Much work has been done to draw comparisons between political developments in Ireland and Finland during this time, namely in how the two nations navigated their independence from empire/union while at the same time reconciling the memory of recent violence. Though it is outside the scope of this project, much work can be done to further situate Ireland in the period 1919–32 in a larger, European-wide sense. For more on this see: Risto Alapuro, 'Coping with the Civil War of 1918 in Twenty-First Century Finland', in Kenneth Christie and Robert Cribb (eds), *Historical Injustice and Democratic Transition in Eastern Asia and Northern Europe: Ghosts at the table of democracy* (London: Routledge, 2002), pp. 169–83; Ulla-Maija Peltonen, 'Civil War Victims and the Ways of Mourning in Finland in 1918', in ibid., pp. 185–97; Mandy Lehto, 'Remembering the Finnish Civil War: Confronting a harrowing past', in ibid., pp. 198–209; David Kirby, *A Concise History of Finland* (Cambridge: Cambridge University Press, 2006), pp. 150–96; and Bill Kissane, 'Democratization, State Formation, and Civil War in Finland and Ireland', *Comparative Political Studies*, vol. 37, no. 8, 2008, pp. 969–85. Regarding Ireland and Finland in the 1910s and '20s Kissane argues that 'both civil wars were the products of frustrated democratic transitions. The sudden shift to inclusive elections had given mandates for radical change, but the imperial powers were not willing to devolve legislative power until conservatives had a majority', ibid., p. 981. This connotes that both Finland and Ireland were not created by nationalist revolution, but by the acquiescence of the imperial power. Recent work has situated the influence of this period in a larger, global sense. The myriad essays in John Crowley et al. (eds), *Atlas of the Irish Revolution* (Cork: Cork University Press, 2018), demonstrate the value of viewing Ireland through a wider lens.

12 Knirck, *Afterimage of the Revolution*, p. 21.

13 Knirck, *Women of the Dáil*, p. 1.

14 Ibid., p. 19.

15 R.V. Comerford, 'Republicans and Democracy in Modern Irish Politics', in Fearghal McGarry (ed.), *Republicanism in Modern Ireland* (Dublin: UCD Press, 2003), p. 16.

16 Roy Foster, *Modern Ireland, 1600–1972* (London: Penguin Books, 1988), p. 538.

17 Kissane, *Politics*, p. 189.

18 Donnacha Ó Beacháin, 'Elections and Political Communication', in Mark O'Brien and Donnacha Ó Beacháin (eds), *Political Communication in the Republic of Ireland* (Liverpool: Liverpool University Press, 2014), p. 25.

19 Mel Farrell, 'A "Cadre-Style" Party? Cumann na nGaedheal organization in Clare, Dublin North, and Longford-Westmeath, 1923–1927', *Éire/Ireland*, vol. 47, nos. 3 & 4, fomhar/ geimhreadh (fall/winter) 2012, p. 109. Indeed, Farrell is talking about Cumann na nGaedheal here, and I agree with his assertion that the party was very much a mass party. However, as I show, Fianna Fáil was better at this and bigger.

20 Lee, *Ireland*, p. 152. More specifically, Lee credits Gerry Boland and Seán Lemass as the architects of such a programme.

21 *Document #2* was Éamon de Valera's alternative to the treaty that ended the Anglo-Irish war. The document can be distilled to the phrase 'external association', which proposed that Ireland become independent from Britain yet retain an association not unlike that of a dominion.

22 Kissane, *Explaining Irish Democracy*, p. 193.

23 Mhaire Nic Shuibhne, undated letter, MacSwiney Papers, UCDA, P48a/41, p. 50. Although undated, this letter was likely written in 1927: 'Within the last twelve months . . .', ibid.

24 Mary MacSwiney, Letter to Micheal Ua Domhnaill, Castlegregory, 25 April 1927, MacSwiney Papers, UCDA, P48a/43, p. 31.

25 Máire Nic Shuibhne, Letter to unnamed 'Professor', 16 May 1929, MacSwiney Papers, UCDA, P48a/45, p. 4.

26 Translated as 'Dear Friend', this is a common Irish greeting in letters and is considered a sign of great respect. I have chosen to include these greetings when citing these letters – as the

dialogue between de Valera and MacSwiney wore on, the greetings became colder and more distant, a remarkable fact considering that the two were once close allies in the republican cause. Further, the growing distance between them is indicative of the growing distance between the movements as a whole.

27 MacSwiney to de Valera, 11 May 1927, MacSwiney Papers, UCDA, P48a/43, p. 49. The emphases are my own.

28 Ibid.

29 Printed material of this period often omitted the *fada* in Irish words. If a *fada* is omitted in any quoted material in this book, it is as per the original.

30 De Valera, letter to MacSwiney, 15 May 1927, MacSwiney Papers, UCDA, P48a/43, p. 50. The different spelling of MacSwiney and de Valera's names are reflective of the original text. It should be noted here that, over the years, de Valera was wildly inconsistent in the spelling of his own name. The emphases are my own.

31 Donal K. Coffey, 'The Need for a New Constitution: Irish constitutional change, 1932–1935', *Irish Jurist*, vol. 48, 2012, pp. 275–302. Coffey uses Fianna Fáil's rhetoric of 'the rule of law' as a starting point for an analysis of the structural legislation that led to the writing of the 1937 constitution.

32 Philip Pettit, 'From Republican Theory to Public Policy', in Mary Jones (ed.), *The Republic: Essays from RTÉ Radio's The Thomas Davis Lecture Series* (Cork: Mercier Press, 2005), pp. 136–7.

33 Of course, I do not mean to align myself with such thinking; rather, this language is meant to represent the gendering of political language of the time.

34 Éamon de Valera, 'A National Policy', in Moynihan, *Speeches*, p. 133. The emphasis is my own.

35 Frank Gallagher (1893–1962) was a veteran of both the war of independence (Anglo–Irish war) and civil war and served time in prison following the latter. Upon release, Gallagher served as editor of the anti-treaty papers the *Irish Bulletin* and *The Nation*, later serving as a key figure in creating propaganda for Fianna Fáil. Gallagher served as editor-in-chief of the *Irish Press* upon its creation in 1931 and, upon leaving the paper, undertook the post of deputy director of Radio Éireann (RTÉ). Diarmaid Ferriter, 'Frank Gallagher', in *Dictionary of Irish Biography*, Volume 4, pp. 8–9. See also Graham Walker, '"The Irish Dr Goebbels": Frank Gallagher and Irish republican propaganda', *Journal of Contemporary History*, vol. 27, no. 1, January 1992, pp. 149–65.

36 Frank Gallagher, *Fianna Fáil, Pamphlet #2* (Dublin: Wood Printing Works, *c.*1927), p. 2. Hereafter cited as *Pamphlet #2*.

37 Ibid., p. 1.

38 Ibid., pp. 3–4.

39 Ibid., pp. 4–5.

40 Ibid., p. 5.

41 Ibid., p. 4.

42 Ibid., p. 28. The emphases are my own.

43 Ibid., p. 29. The emphasis is my own.

44 Ibid., p. 30.

45 Ibid.

46 Éamon de Valera, Statement by Éamon de Valera, T.D., at 2nd Annual Ard Fheis of Fianna Fail, as President of That Organisation, de Valera Collection, UCDA, P155/2048.

47 Ibid.

48 For a succinct history of this time period, see O'Halpin, 'Politics', pp. 86–126.

49 Dunphy, *The Making of Fianna Fáil Power in Ireland*, p. 131.

50 O'Halpin, 'Politics', p. 121.

51 *Fianna Fáil Bulletin*, 25 July 1927, de Valera Collection, UCDA, P150/2038.

52 Ibid.

53 Dunphy, *The Making of Fianna Fáil Power in Ireland*, p. 132.

54 Éamon de Valera, untitled letter, 10 August 1927, de Valera Collection, UCDA, P155/2042. Below the text, de Valera wrote: 'Draft which I laid before meeting of the Fianna Fáil deputies on day on which decision to try to enter Dail taken'. The finalised version of this declaration was signed by forty-one of forty-two Fianna Fáil deputies at midnight on 10 August 1927.

55 Ibid. The emphasis is my own.

56 Cumann na nGaedheal, *The Shadow of the Gunman: Keep it from your home. Vote for Cumann na nGaedheal*, 1932, NLI, EPH F53, https://www.irishtimes.com/news/politics/class-warfare-and-shadowy-gunmen-how-the-2020-election-echoes-1932-1.4163679.

57 Cumann na nGaedheal, *Fianna Fail's Game. Don't let them cheat you! Vote for Cumann na nGaedheal*, NLI, EPH, F473.

58 Ibid.

59 The image used by the Gramophone Company was based on an 1898 painting by British painter Mark Barraud, 'Dog Looking at and Listening to a Phonograph'. Charles Bernstein notes that Barraud's painting 'is iconic of the uncanniness of the human voice emanating from a machine unattached to a human body. Dogs, beloved by their owners for their ability to distinguish specific human voices from other sounds in the environment, are the adequate symbol of transhuman voice recognition . . . [and] one of the most striking features of the image is Nipper gazing affectionately into the Victrola's large horn, sometimes imagined to be an ear but which more pertinently can be imagined as a mechanical throat and mouth.' Charles Bernstein, 'Making Audio Visible: The lessons of visual language for the textualization of sound', *Text*, vol. 16, 2006, p. 279.

60 Cumann na nGaedheal, *HIS Master's Voice: Make your voice heard by voting for Cumann na nGaedheal*, 1932, NLI, EPH F474.

61 Cumann na nGaedhal, *Don't let this happen. Vote for Cumann na nGaedheal*, 1932, NLI EPH F45.

62 Ibid.

63 Ibid.

64 Cumann na nGaedheal, *Presented by the artist to the nation. De Valera is now working on another Canvas (s) but what about the price? Vote for Cumann na nGaedheal*, 1932, NLI, EPH F38.

65 Cumann na nGaedheal, *The dead who died for an 'Empty Formula'. Was it worth it? Vote for Cumann na nGaedheal*, 1932, NLI, EPH F43.

66 Ibid.

67 Two examples: Liam Mellows (1892–1922), a socialist, was executed by firing squad in December 1922 by order of the Free State government in retribution for the assassination of treatyite Seán Hayes; see Marie Coleman and William Murphy, 'William Joseph ("Liam") Mellows', *Dictionary of Irish Biography*, Volume 6, pp. 477–9. Erskine Childers (1870–1922), a close associate of de Valera, was executed by the Free State government on 24 November 1922 following his conviction on a firearms possession charge; see M.A. Hopkinson, 'Erskine (Robert) Childers', *Dictionary of Irish Biography*, Volume 2, pp. 498–501.

68 Cumann na nGaedheal, *The dead*.

69 Cumann na nGaedheal, *No goods taken from window! Supplies from goods stores only!* 1932, NLI, EPH F57.

70 Ibid.

71 Ibid.

72 Cumann na nGaedheal, *Senor De Valera*, c. 1927, NLI, EC POL/1930–40/6.

73 Ibid. Fifty-seven is a reference to the number of Fianna Fáil candidates returned in the 1927 general election. John Coakley and Michael Gallagher (eds), *Politics in the Republic of Ireland* (London: Routledge, 2003), p. 368.

74 Frank Aiken (1898–1983) became active in the republican movement following the Easter
    rising, and in 1923 was elected as a Sinn Féin candidate for the constituency of Louth. Aiken's
    loyalty remained with de Valera upon the formation of Fianna Fáil, serving as minister for
    defence after the party's 1932 electoral triumph. He was known as having a particularly anti-
    British disposition and was 'the most anglophobic [*sic*] of de Valera's ministers'. Ronan
    Fanning, 'Francis Thomas ("Frank") Aiken', *Dictionary of Irish Biography*, Volume 1, pp. 52–6.
    This tendency towards Anglophobia is likely responsible for the claim that he would sneer at
    the British lion.

75 Apart from de Valera, Seán MacEntee (1889–1984) had one of the oldest republican lineages,
    dating back to his involvement with the Volunteers in 1914, to his participation in the Easter
    rising, up through his service in the Volunteer executive. As a member of Sinn Féin, MacEntee
    was never elected to the Dáil. This changed when he was elected to the Dáil as a Fianna Fáil
    candidate for County Dublin in 1927. After the 1932 Fianna Fáil victory, MacEntee served
    as minister for finance and played a vital role in the passage of the External Relations Act.
    Deirdre McMahon, 'Sean (John) Francis MacEntee', *Dictionary of Irish Biography*, Volume 5,
    pp. 995–8. The reference to 'Johnny Magintee' and his effervescence was certainly meant to
    call into question his political stability.

76 The comparison of Seán Lemass (1899–1971) to a tightrope performer is likely due to the fact
    that he was slow to speak out against the treaty in 1922. In 1924, Lemass' republican credentials
    were solidified when he was elected to the Dáil as a Sinn Féin candidate for Dublin South.
    He is also credited with urging de Valera to form Fianna Fáil, reputedly talking the leader out
    of possible retirement from politics. As such, Lemass was a founding member of the party,
    served as minister for industry and commerce after 1932 and was instrumental in the passage
    of the Control of Manufactures Acts (1932 and 1934). He would serve as Taoiseach from 1959
    to 1966. Ronan Fanning, 'Seán Lemass', ibid., pp. 433–4.

77 Ibid. This is a reference to the British notion that, to become head of government, one must
    successfully climb a greased pole/poll.

78 Cumann na nGaedheal, *The Empty Formula*, c. 1927, NLI, EC POL/1930–40/6.

79 Angela Bourke, *The Burning of Bridget Cleary: A true story* (London: Pimlico, 1999), p. 44.

80 Bee, 'Ex-Unionist', *Irish Press*, 15 February 1932, p. 1. Bee's mention of Cosgrave's not being
    returned was a reference to Cumann na nGaedheal's loss to Fianna Fáil in the 1932 general
    election.

81 Fianna Fáil, *Unscrupulous Propaganda*, c. 1927, NLI, EC.

82 Ibid.

83 Ibid.

84 Éamon de Valera, 'Mr De Valera's Introductory Speech at the Opening of the Ard Fheis of
    Fianna Fáil, November 24th, 1926', de Valera Collection, UCDA, P155/2047. The highlighted
    elements reflect the original document. The highlighting is significant, as this is the paper
    from which de Valera delivered his address.

85 Gallagher, *Pamphlet #2*, p. 6.

86 Ibid.

87 Ibid., p. 7.

88 Éamon de Valera, 'Éamon de Valera's Closing Speech at the Ard Fheis of FIANNA FÁIL, Nov.
    25th, 1926', de Valera Collection, UCDA, P155/2048.

89 Ibid.

90 Éamon de Valera, 'Statement by Éamon de Valera, T.D.', de Valera Collection, UCDA,
    P155/2048, p. 2. The emphasis is my own.

91 Ibid.

92 Éamon de Valera, 'Statement from the 1932 Fianna Fail Ard Fheis, 9 November 1932', de Valera
    Collection, UCDA, P150/2053.

CHAPTER 2. 'BRIGHT DAYS ARE COMING! IN QUAKER GREY': FIANNA FÁIL AND THE
CONSTRUCTION OF THE IRISH FEMININE

1   For a history of the *Irish Press*, see Mark O'Brien, *De Valera, Fianna Fáil and the* Irish Press: *The truth in the news?* (Dublin: Irish Academic Press, 2001).

2   'Morning in the Irish Home', *Irish Press*, 7 June 1933, p. 5.

3   Margaret Ó Hógartaigh, *Kathleen Lynn: Irishwoman, patriot, doctor* (Dublin: Irish Academic Press, 2006), p. 110.

4   These are matters that the editors couched as being of most interest to the paper's female readers at the time. Indeed, any of its readers might have culled interesting or meaningful content from this part of the paper. As such, it is not my intention to imply that such domestic activity should be aimed exclusively at women. This part of the paper was as much geared towards women as the sports page was directed at men. A glance at any contemporary newspaper will demonstrate that this still holds true.

5   The *Dundalk Examiner/An Scrúduightheoir* began publication on 20 September 1930, under the direction of Fianna Fáil member Frank Aiken. In the fourteen months prior to the launch of the *Irish Press*, each edition of the *Dundalk Examiner* included a page devoted to 'Matters Feminine'. The bulk of the articles with by-lines were credited solely to 'Marie' and were surrounded by recipes, serial stories, and advertisements geared towards women. The articles also focused on women's fashion and domestic advice, much like those that later appeared on the women's page in the *Irish Press*. One distinction in the *Examiner* was the paper's implicit advocacy of Irish tweed and its importance in the fashion choices of Irish women – at least in the sense that it promoted such clothing as vital to the development of home industries, a suggestion that precipitated the many articles that later appeared in the *Irish Press* in which patriotism was connected to consumerism. See *Dundalk Examiner/An Scrúduightheoir*, 20 September 1930, p. 6. The paper was actually purchased by a group led by Aiken and relaunched in 1930. The *Examiner* was certainly a model for the *Irish Press* in that it had a similar layout and similar aims, and its intended goals included the advocacy of 'The Unity and Independence of Ireland', 'The restoration of the Irish Language [*sic*] as the spoken language of the people', 'The development of a distinctive National life in accordance with Irish tradition and ideals', 'The making of Ireland self-supporting and self-contained economically', and 'The making of the financial and material resources of the country subservient to the needs and welfare of the people' (ibid). In addition to the cultural aspects that precipitated the *Irish Press*, the *Dundalk Explorer/An Scrúduightheoir* had an agro-economic bent that aligned to Fianna Fáil's platform, but one that also served its readership in the largely agricultural region of County Louth. In this sense, the *Dundalk Explorer/An Scrúduightheoir* also foreshadowed the economic ideas advanced in the *Fianna Fáil Bulletin*.

6   Anne Dolan, 'The Irish Free State', in Thomas Bartlett (ed.), *The Cambridge History of Ireland. Volume IV: 1880 to the Present* (Cambridge: Cambridge University Press, 2018), p. 333.

7   Ibid.

8   Knirck, *Women of the Dáil*. Most notable among Sinn Féin's ranks was Mary MacSwiney, with whom de Valera had a close professional relationship. As Knirck points out, MacSwiney and other female members of Sinn Féin – and of Cumann na mBan and Inghinide na hÉireann – tended to be the public face of anti-treaty republicanism after the establishment of the Free State. Their adherence to pre-Free State revolutionary rhetoric enabled Cumann na nGaedheal to label Sinn Féiners as reactionary, illogical and violent. In essence, the republican movement had been feminised.

9   I deliberately use the term 'Éire' here, as it is reflective of the aspirational tone set forth by Fianna Fáil and is not meant to reflect the historical accuracy of the term's usage. I use the term to demonstrate that the party envisioned Irish women consuming Fianna Fáil's particular vision of Ireland, thus distinguishing it from such terms as 'Ireland' or 'Irish Free State'.

10 Éamon de Valera, quoted in Maryann Gialanella Valiulis, 'Engendering Citizenship: Women's relationship to the state in Ireland and the United States in the post-suffrage period', in Maryann Gialenella Valiulis and Mary O'Dowd (eds), *Women and Irish History: Essays in honour of Margaret Mac Curtain* (Dublin: Wolfhound Press, 1997), p. 174.

11 Éamon de Valera, 'The Ireland That We Dreamed Of', in Moynihan, *Speeches*, p. 466. The full reference to 'comely maidens' in de Valera's radio broadcast from 17 March 1943 read as follows: 'That Ireland which we dreamed of would be the home of a people who valued material wealth only as the basis of right living, of a people who were satisfied with frugal comfort and devoted their leisure to the things of the spirit – a land whose countryside would be bright with cosy homesteads, whose fields and villages would be joyous with the sounds of industry, with the romping of sturdy children, the contests of athletic youths and the laughter of comely maidens, whose firesides would be forums for the wisdom of serene old age.' Ibid.

12 Nancy J. Curtin, 'A Nation of Abortive Men: Gendered citizenship and early Irish republicanism', in *Reclaiming Gender: Transgressive identities in modern Ireland* (New York: St Martin's Press, 1999), p. 37.

13 Caitriona Clear, *Women of the House: Women's household work in Ireland, 1926–1961* (Dublin: Irish Academic Press, 2000), p. 7.

14 Maryann Gialanella Valiulis, 'Virtuous Mothers and Dutiful Wives', p. 101.

15 Ibid., p. 102.

16 Ibid., p. 109.

17 Caitriona Clear, 'Women in de Valera's Ireland, 1932–48: A reappraisal', in Gabriel Doherty and Dermot Keogh (eds), *De Valera's Irelands* (Cork: Mercier Press, 2003).

18 Smith, 'The Politics of Sexual Knowledge'.

19 Tom Inglis, 'Origins and Legacies of Irish Prudery: Sexuality and social control in modern Ireland', *Éire-Ireland*, vol. 40, no. 3, fall/winter 2005, p. 20.

20 Éamon de Valera, quoted in David McCullagh, *De Valera Rise* (Dublin: Gill Books, 2017), p. 391.

21 Ibid., p. 104.

22 Louise Ryan and Margaret Ward (eds), *Irish Women and Nationalism: Soldiers, new women and wicked hags* (Dublin: Irish Academic Press, 2004), p. 2.

23 Ibid., p. 5.

24 Martin, 'Painting the Irish West', p. 32.

25 Seán MacEntee, quoted in O'Brien, *De Valera*, p. 56.

26 Ibid., p. 8.

27 Ibid., p. 32.

28 Eve Morrison, 'The Bureau of Military History and Female Republican Activism, 1913–23', in Valiulis, *Gender and Power*, pp. 64–5.

29 'Women Are Clever!' *Irish Press*, 15 September 1931, p. 3.

30 Ibid.

31 'I'm Glad I'm Not Beautiful', *Irish Press*, 14 September 1931, p. 3.

32 Ibid. The emphasis is mine.

33 'Shall We? A Quintet That Shows How the Wind Blows', *Irish Press*, 14 September 1931, p. 3.

34 Ibid.

35 'Old-Time Touches in New Decorative Schemes', *Irish Press*, 21 October 1931, p. 3.

36 Ibid.

37 The *Irish Press* women's page is ripe for study by a scholar of class, and I acknowledge the lack of a larger classist analysis A deeper study in this regard might elucidate how Fianna Fáil envisioned class divide in Ireland between 1926 and 1938.

38 Ibid.

39 'The Vogue of the Demure', *Irish Press*, 24 October 1931, p. 3. The story notes: 'Simplicity [is] the Hallmark of the New Frocks. There is a pleasing simplicity about the new frocks for house and business wear . . . Our sketch [actually, a photograph] shows a delightful little dress for day wear featured in midnight blue jersey cloth – a popular material this season – trimmed with the smart diagonal cross-overs. It is supported by geometrically placed buttons, a black patent leather belt, while it achieves a Quakerish demureness with its white collar in Irish linen of fine weave.' Ibid.

40 Emily Dowling, '"At Home in the Country": A town-dweller looks back', *Irish Press*, 22 September 1931, p. 3. This is a rare example of an author's by-line appearing in print.

41 Ibid.

42 Ibid.

43 Ibid.

44 'Modern Furniture in the Home', *Irish Press* 25 September 1931, p. 3.

45 Ibid.

46 'Modern Furniture in the Home: Your kitchen – bathroom – hall', *Irish Press*, 9 October 1931, p. 3.

47 Karen Steele, *Women, Press, and Politics during the Irish Revival* (Syracuse: Syracuse University Press, 2007), p. 117. Constance Markievicz (1868–1927) was a key figure in the Irish theatre, as well as serving a prominent role in Sinn Féin and such feminist organisations as Inghinidhe na hÉireann, Bean na hÉireann, and later Cumann na mBan. Markievicz served in the Easter rising and remained active in the republican cause, most notably as a founding member of Fianna Fáil. Senia Paseta, 'Constance Georgine Markievicz', *Dictionary of Irish Biography*, Volume 6, pp. 361–3.

48 There did appear one article in September of 1931 in which readers were encouraged to 'Go to Irish nurseries for roses of distinction'. The reasoning for this was not the promotion of Irish industry, but rather because of the unmatched beauty and global acclaim of Irish roses, as growers shipped 'rose trees all over the world and some of them are at present flowering as far away as Argentina'. 'The Woman Gardener: Go to Irish nurseries for roses of distinction', *Irish Press*, 30 September 1931, p. 3.

49 'The Woman Gardener: Harmony between house and garden', *Irish Press*, 5 January 1932, p. 3.

50 Ibid.

51 Ibid.

52 'The Woman Gardener: Grow your own vegetables', *Irish Press*, 30 March 1932, p. 3.

53 Ibid.

54 'The Virtues of Herbs: Old-fashioned recipes', *Irish Press*, 8 July 1932, p. 3.

55 'The Woman Gardener: Still much to be done', *Irish Press*, 1 August 1932, p. 3.

56 'The Woman Gardener: Work to do now', *Irish Press*, 18 August 1932, p. 3.

57 'The Woman Gardener: Thinking ahead', *Irish Press*, 17 June 1932, p. 3.

58 'The Woman Gardener: Jobs for July', *Irish Press*, 4 July 1932, p. 3.

59 C. O'R., 'An Irish Home in Adrigole', *Irish Press*, 7 September 1933, p. 5.

60 Ibid.

61 Ibid.

62 Ibid. In English, 'Be fearful and you are not in danger'. Translation is my own.

63 'Fashions in Irish Tweed', *Irish Press*, 17 October 1931, p. 3.

64 Ibid.

65 'The Vogue of the Demure'.

66 'Two Brown Ensembles', *Irish Press*, 7 November 1931, p. 3.

67 'The Longer Wrap', *Irish Press*, 11 November 1931, p. 3.

68 'Coats With a Military Air', *Irish Press*, 18 November 1931, p. 3. Of particular interest is the advertisement for Swan Pens, located to the right of this article, that implored readers to 'Buy British'.

69 'Fashions to Please', *Irish Press*, 6 April 1934, p. 5.

70 The examples given are meant to be representative.

71 Steele, *Women*, p. 130.

72 Ibid., pp. 130–2.

73 E.R.C., 'Dress Hints for the "Sturdy" Woman', *Irish Press*, 30 January 1932, p. 3.

74 'Bright Days Are Coming!' *Irish Press*, 10 March 1932, p. 3.

75 'Your Uniform', *Irish Press*, 28 March 1932, p. 3.

76 'The Housewives' Outfit', *Irish Press*, 19 October 1931, p. 3.

77 Ibid.

78 'Does Beauty Mean Nothing to You?', *Irish Press*, 9 June 1933, p. 6. The emphasis is mine.

79 'Win the Economic War – by Planning!', *Irish Press*, 4 August 1933, p. 5.

80 'Breakfast in the Irish Home', *Irish Press*, 10 June 1933, p. 5.

81 'Irish Paints for Brightening the All-Irish Home', *Irish Press*, 21 June 1933, p. 5.

82 'Look for this Trade Mark', *Irish Press*, 24 June 1933, p. 5.

83 'For Your Medicine Cabinet . . . These All-Irish Preparations', *Irish Press*, 22 July 1933, p. 5.

84 'The Irish Ideal Home', *Irish Press*, 6 December 1934, p. 5.

85 May LaVerty, 'At the Sales, Bargain Hunting: A game of skill', *Irish Press*, 16 January 1936, p. 5.

86 Fianna Fáil, *A Brief Outline of the Aims and Programme of Fianna Fáil*, de Valera Collection, UCDA, P150/2048, p. 7. The first ard fheis took place on '24ad. Agus 25ad. Lá de m.ína Sam. na, 1926' (November 24th and 25th) (ibid).

87 The economic war (1932–7) began when de Valera refused to pay land annuities to Great Britain. Although this topic will be covered in greater depth in the next chapter, it is worth mentioning that economic self-sufficiency and protectionism were key components of de Valera's plan for victory.

88 Éamon de Valera, 'Call for National Discipline. Mr de Valera's Stirring Ard-Fheis Address. Economic Programme', undated newspaper clipping, UCDA, de Valera Collection, P155/2054.

89 'Fireside Industries', *Irish Press*, 26 February 1935, p. 5.

90 Ibid.

91 'Progress of W.I.D.A., Mannequin Parade in March', *Irish Press*, 28 February 1935, p. 5.

92 Ibid.

93 Very little has been written about the origin and history of the WIDA. Much of what I have discovered was reported tangentially in the *Irish Press* and *Fianna Fáil Bulletin*. Of note is a short film clip from British Pathé that documented 'Some of the Irish creations at the Mannequin Parade held under the auspices of the Women's Industrial Association'. Titled 'Mannequins "wear Irish"' (http://www.britishpathe.com/video/mannequins-wear-irish), the film, credited as being filmed in 1933, shows women and children modelling clothes ranging from the modern fashions discussed above to more modest clothing. Included, of course, was a bride adorned in a gown of virginal white. See also D.A.J. MacPherson, *Women and the Irish Nation: Gender, culture and Irish identity, 1890–1914* (New York: Palgrave Macmillan, 2012), p. 140.

94 A.K., 'All Irish Dress Parade', *Irish Press*, 13 March 1935, p. 5. Although it is not clear as to why the event did not occur as planned, there was a reference to the 'wheels of transport [not turning] at all', thus postponing the event. However, in an article from 27 March, there was mention of a transport strike that derailed the event that was to have been held earlier in the month. 'Parading the Dresses of Spring', *Irish Press*, 27 March 1935, p. 5.

95 'Parading the Dresses of Spring'.

96 'Mannequins "wear Irish"'. See also MacPherson, *Women and the Irish Nation*, p. 140.

97 'Handsome Women in Handsome Clothes', *Irish Press*, 8 May 1935, p. 5.

98 Ibid.

99   Ibid.

100   Éamon de Valera, quoted in McCullagh, *De Valera Rise*, p. 392.

101   Sheila O'Brien, 'Irish Linen and Crochet Combine in This Cosy Cover', *Irish Press*, 18 February 1935, p. 5. Another interesting element of this article is the assertion that this pattern was 'specifically designed and made for *The Irish Press*'.

102   Maire, 'Turtle Neck Jumper. In Stock Stitch. Worn With Tweeds', *Irish Press*, 26 February 1934, p. 5.

103   'An Irish Apple a Day?', *Irish Press*, 23 November 1934, p. 5.

104   Ibid.

105   'Camogie: Irishwomen's national game', *Irish Press*, 4 April 1934, p. 5. Camogie is the female version of hurling, a sport of Irish design and one advocated by the Gaelic Athletic Association. For a study on the role that youth played in Nazi culture, see George L. Mosse, *Nazi Culture: A documentary culture* (New York: Schocken Books [1966], 1981), pp. 263–318.

106   D.F., 'What Shall We Do with Our Girls?', *Irish Press*, 13 December 1933, p. 5.

107   Ibid.

108   Ibid.

109   Ibid.

110   Ibid.

111   Clear, 'Women', p. 107. Clear also examines the restricting of factory employment by women in *Women of the House*, p. 3.

112   Mary E. Daly, 'Women in the Irish Free State, 1922–39: The interaction between economics and ideology', *Journal of Women's History*, vol. 6, no. 4, winter/spring 1995, p. 109.

113   Mary Cullen, 'The Potential of Gender History', in Valiulis (ed.), *Gender and Power*, p. 18.

114   Síghle ní Chinnéide, 'Why Women Must Work', *Irish Press*, 18 January 1935, p. 3.

115   Nan Mahony, 'Why Women Must Work', *Irish Press*, 8 February 1935, p. 5.

116   Daly, 'Women in the Irish Free State', p. 103. Daly's article cites an increase in single women's employment between 1926 and 1936, with single women's participation increasing from 48.6 per cent to 53.3 per cent, and that of married women during the same time remaining stagnant at 5.6 per cent.

117   It is no coincidence that this transformation occurred following the transformation of Cumann na nGaedheal into Fine Gael, marking the end of Fianna Fáil's concern with the so-called 'gunmen'. Now the party of majority, de Valera and his followers became increasingly concerned with governance and, perhaps most importantly, gathering a larger number of supporters for the constitution de Valera was hoping to install in 1936 or 1937. Regarding the shift from anonymous by-lines, one such example is an article from January 1934 entitled 'The Married Woman Worker: A married woman's reply', whose authorial credit is listed only as 'A Dublin Professional Woman'. It is remarkable that many of the same arguments made by ní Chinnéide almost exactly a year later can be found in this article, suggesting that she might in fact be the author of this one too. The main difference between the two pieces was the emphasis placed on the ability of married women to juggle career and family, and that 'she understands dignity of labour'. A Dublin Professional Woman, 'The Married Woman Worker: A married woman's reply', *Irish Press*, 15 January 1934, p. 5.

118   Ní Chinnéide, 'Why Women Must Work', p. 3.

119   Ibid.

120   Ibid.

121   Ibid.

122   'Women Must Work While – Men Must Write – These Letters', *Irish Press*, 24 January 1935, p. 5.

123   Sean Gearoid Traynor, 'The Remedies Are Not Modern', *Irish Press*, 24 January 1935, p. 5.

124   A Reader, 'Marking Time', *Irish Press*, 24 January 1935, p. 5.

125 Sighlé ní Chinnéide, 'The Working Woman Controversy', *Irish Press*, 4 February 1935, p. 5. Of note is the English spelling of ní Chinnéide's name in the article, where she was listed as Miss Kennedy.

126 Nan Mahony, 'What Career Would You Choose?', *Irish Press*, 8 February 1935, p. 5.

127 Ibid.

128 Annie M. Smithson, 'Careers for Women. No. 1: The Nursing Profession', *Irish Press*, 9 February 1935, p. 5.

129 Josephine Redington, 'Careers for Women. No. 2: Domestic Economy Teaching', *Irish Press*, 18 February 1935, p. 5. Essentially, the duties of a domestic economy teacher included the instruction of cooking, sewing, etc. Redington was credited as being principal of the Irish Training School of Domestic Economy in Kilmacud.

130 A Woman Civil Servant, 'The Ladder of the Civil Service', *Irish Press*, 23 February 1935, p. 5. This particular article did not include the 'Careers for Women' heading but was still a part of the series.

131 Katharine S. Cruise O'Brien, MA, 'Careers for Women. No. 4: Technical Teaching', *Irish Press*, 2 March 1935, p. 5. The article claims that Cruise O'Brien had 'adapted Gregg Shorthand to the Irish language'. As far as can be told, technical teaching was centred upon educating women in such secretarial skills as shorthand and typewriting.

132 Maire Comerford, 'Women of the Land: A woman farmer's point of view', *Irish Press*, 9 March 1935, p. 5.

133 The Bean Tighe, 'The Professional Bean Tighe', *Irish Press*, 23 March 1935, p. 5. This article also excluded the 'Careers for Women' heading.

134 Margaret O'Donnell, 'Working Women. No. 8: The Waitress', *Irish Press*, 30 March 1935, p. 5. Note the altered heading in this particular entry.

135 Roisin Walsh, BA, 'Working Women. No. 9: Librarianship for Girls', *Irish Press*, 6 April 1935, p. 5.

136 John Brennan, 'Careers for Women, The Telephonist', *Irish Press*, 6 July 1935, p. 5. John Brennan, it should be noted, was female.

137 John Brennan, 'Careers for Women, The Drapery Trade', *Irish Press*, 3 August 1935.

138 Mary Hayden, MA, 'University Training for Women', *Irish Press*, 16 March 1935, p. 5; also A Dublin Woman Doctor, 'Working Women. No. 10: The Woman Doctor', *Irish Press*, 13 April 1935, p. 5. The latter article offers the following warning: 'The work of a medical woman is of such grave importance, and makes such severe demands on her energies, both physical and mental, that much consideration is required before recommending the profession to the average girl as a suitable vocation.' Mary Teresa Hayden (1862–1942) was an important figure in the cause of women's rights in Ireland, forming the Irish Association of Women Graduates in 1902 with Hanna Sheehy-Skeffington. Hayden fought for equal access for women in public education and government employment. In addition to her activism, Hayden served as a lecturer in history – later full professor of modern Irish history – at University College Dublin. Diarmaid Ferriter, 'Mary Teresa Hayden', *Dictionary of Irish Biography*, Volume 4, pp. 531–2.

139 'Our New Page Three', *Irish Press*, 21 March 1936, p. 5. Note the reference to the page as 'Page Three', despite its location on page five. This implies that readers still connected the women's page to its original location in the *Irish Press*.

140 Hanna Sheehy-Skeffington (1877–1946) was born in Cork to a politically active family. She was active in the Irish suffragist movement – namely the Irish Women's Franchise League, which she formed along with Gretta Cousins – but refused to join Inghinidhe na hÉireann or Cumann na mBan due to her belief that nationalist organisations were inherently subservient to men. Despite this, she joined Sinn Féin in 1919, rising to a position of prominence within

the organisation, serving as envoy to the League of Nations in Paris (1923) in the hopes that the league would not recognise the Irish Free State. She left Sinn Féin to join Fianna Fáil, serving on its executive board, but left when de Valera opted to enter the Dáil. Following the split, Sheehy-Skeffington expressed support for the Soviet Union and disdain for de Valera's constitution. Maria Luddy, '(Johanna) Hanna Sheehy-Skeffington', *Dictionary of Irish Biography*, Volume 8, pp. 983–4.

141 'Mr. de Valera Outlines the New Constitution', *Irish Press*, 4 November 1936, p. 1.

142 Maryann Valiulis, 'Neither Feminist nor Flapper: The ecclesiastical construction of the ideal Irish woman', in Alan Hayes and Diane Urquhart (eds), *The Irish Woman's History Reader* (London: Routledge, 2001), p. 157.

CHAPTER 3. 'YOU DO YOUR PART, AND WE'LL DO THE REST': FIANNA FÁIL'S AESTHETIC MASCULINITY

1 I use the terms Irish Masculine and Irish Feminine to highlight the idealised version(s) of each gender as presented by Fianna Fáil. Such an idea is not reflective of any explicit use by Fianna Fáil. Rather, the intent is to distinguish between gender normative masculinity and femininity as it existed in 1920s/30s Ireland and the gender constructs that were an essential aspect of Fianna Fáil's regenerative aesthetic.

2 'Time Marches On!', *Fianna Fáil Bulletin*, January 1937, p. 7.

3 Ibid.

4 Ancillary to this was a queering of its political opponents by Fianna Fáil. Such is the topic of Chapter 4.

5 Ibid.

6 Ibid.

7 This notion of an Anglophilic Free State is meant to be reflective of Fianna Fáil's party aesthetic. Indeed, a number of recent studies have demonstrated that Cumann na nGaedheal, and in turn the Irish Free State, were quite successful in their nation-building efforts during the Free State period. It is quite difficult to envision Fianna Fáil even existing without the democratic frameworks and economic foundations created by Cumann na nGaedheal in the years leading up to 1932. Nonetheless, comparison of the relative success of either party's policies is not the purpose here.

8 Walter Adamson, 'Modernism and Fascism: The politics of culture in Italy, 1903–1922', *The American Historical Review*, vol. 95, no. 2, April 1990, p. 362.

9 Girvin, 'The Republicanisation of Irish Society', pp. 130–1.

10 The reader might notice a vacillation between 1937 and 1938 as the end date of this chapter. This is reflective of the difference between my own thesis and Fianna Fáil propaganda that is largely culled from the elections between 1932 and 1937. Having twice triumphed electorally in 1937, much of the party's energies were legislative as opposed to political. As such, my focus is to examine the party's masculine aesthetic in the years leading up to the Éire Confirmation Bill and the end of the economic war, and therefore when promoting my own ideas 1938 will be used as an end date to this particular period.

11 Lee, *Ireland*, p. 178. For an in-depth study on the events that led to the economic war, see Terence Dooley, *'The Land for the People': The land question in independent Ireland* (Dublin: UCD Press, 2004).

12 Mary Daly, 'An Irish-Ireland for Business? The Control of Manufactures Acts, 1932 and 1934', *Irish Historical Studies*, vol. 24, no. 94, Nov. 1984, pp. 246–72. See also Mary Daly, *Industrial Development and Irish National Identity, 1922–1939* (Dublin: Gill & Macmillan, 1992).

13 Daly, 'Irish-Ireland', p. 27.

14 Girvin, 'The Republicanisation of Irish Society', p. 136.

15 Ibid.

16 Daly, 'Irish-Ireland', p. 247.

17 In keeping with the policy of using Anglicised rather than Gaelicised names in the text, all future references to Sean T. O'Kelly shall use such associations, but when referring to his collection of papers at the National Library of Ireland, I shall maintain said entity's usage. Sean T. O'Kelly (1882–1966) began his career as a Gaelic nationalist, serving as national secretary of the Gaelic League, and was a founding member of Sinn Féin. O'Kelly was imprisoned for his role in the Easter rising and, after siding with the anti-treaty side, he travelled to the United States as envoy for de Valera, returning in 1926 to be a founding member of Fianna Fáil. After the 1932 election, O'Kelly served as cabinet minister for public health, vice-president of the Executive Council, as well as tánaiste (deputy taoiseach). Patrick Maume, 'Seán Thomas O'Kelly', *Dictionary of Irish Biography*, Volume 7, pp. 615–19.

18 Kevin O'Rourke, 'Burn Everything but Their Coal: The Anglo-Irish economic war of the 1930s', *The Journal of Economic History*, vol. 51, no. 2, June 1991, p. 357.

19 The Ottawa Economic Conference of 1932 marked the beginning of the transformation of Britain's empire from a military-political entity into an economic union where the playing field was clearly arranged in favour of John Bull. It also afforded members of the empire an opportunity to openly defy and question British policy. The conference took place at a time when the delegation that was to represent Ireland in Ottawa was explicitly and aggressively challenging the nature of Britain's authority over the island. The Ottawa conference had been called to reassert England's primacy in regulating tariff rates, which had grown markedly due to interwar economic anxieties and complicated by nationalist stirrings among the nations united in the empire. The central point of confluence was the Import Duties Act of 1932 that resulted in a 10 per cent increase in import rates. Exempted permanently were colonies, while dominions were granted conditional rights on products coming into their nation from Britain. For more on the conference, see D.K. Fieldhouse, 'The Metropolitan Economics of Empire', in Judith M. Brown and Wm. Roger Louis (eds), *The Oxford History of the British Empire. Volume IV: The Twentieth Century* (Oxford: Oxford University Press, 1999), p. 90.

20 Fianna Fáil, *Ireland's Right to the Land Annuities*, c. 1932, Seán MacEntee Papers, UCDA, P67/134, p. 51. The emphasis reflects that of the original text.

21 Cumann na nGaedheal, *Fight Points for Cumann-na-nGaedheal Speakers and Workers, General Election 1932* (Dublin: Cumann-na-nGaedheal, 1932), p. 20. The emphasis reflects that of the original text.

22 Ibid. Cumann na nGaedheal claimed that 'The first suggestion for the non-payment of Land Annuities seems to have come from a gentleman by the name of Mr. Peadar O'Donnell at a joint meeting on the 18th and 19th of December, 1926, of a body calling itself "the second Dail", and another body calling itself "Comwhailre na dTeachtai", at which Mr. De Valera and his colleagues of the Civil War were present'. O'Donnell was one of the leading leftists in the IRA. His suggestion *was* apparently the germinal point for de Valera's picking upon the annuities issue. See Timothy M. O'Neill, 'Handing Away the Trump Card? Peadar O'Donnell, Fianna Fáil, and the non-payment of land annuities campaign, 1926–32', *New Hibernia Review*, vol. 12, no. 1, spring/earrach 2008, pp. 19–40.

23 Cumann na nGaedheal, *Fight Points for Cumann-na-nGaedheal Speakers and Workers*.

24 Fianna Fáil, *Ireland's Right to the Annuities*.

25 Ibid. The emphasis is my own. Although undated, Fianna Fáil's pamphlet seemed largely intent on justifying actions under way or about to be taken – such as the holding of the annuities, as well as references to Cumann na nGaedheal, which would cease to exist after merging with the Blueshirts and the National Centre Party to form Fine Gael in 1933 – which

indicates that these documents were published after the 1932 election but before the January 1933 election.

26 Ibid. The emphases in this text are my own.

27 Ibid. See also L. Perry Curtis, *Coercion and Conciliation in Ireland, 1880–1892: A study in conservative unionism* (Princeton: Princeton University Press, 1963).

28 Fianna Fáil, *Ireland's Right to the Annuities.* The emphasis in this excerpt reflects the original text.

29 Ibid.

30 Ibid.

31 Brian Girvin, *Between Two Worlds: Politics and economy in independent Ireland* (Dublin: Gill & Macmillan, 1989), p. 89.

32 Fianna Fáil, *Ireland's Right to the Annuities.* Emphasis reflects the original text.

33 Timothy G. McMahon, '"The Land for the People": The Irish revolution as a revolution of rising expectations', in Michael de Nie and Sean Farrell (eds), *Power and Popular Culture in Modern Ireland: Essays in honour of James S. Donnelly, Jr.* (Dublin: Irish Academic Press, 2010), p. 174.

34 Paxton, *The Anatomy of Fascism*, pp. 12–13.

35 Unnamed Fianna Fáil Election Handbill from 1927, Archives of the Fianna Fáil Party, UCDA, P176/827, p. 28.

36 Ibid. The emphasis reflects that of the original text.

37 Unnamed Fianna Fáil Election Handbill, Archives of the Fianna Fáil Party, UCDA, P176/827, p. 22. Although undated, it is likely that this handbill comes from 1927, as the rhetoric and choice of quotes is consistent with what Fianna Fáil advanced in the 1927 elections.

38 Ibid.

39 Fianna Fáil, *They Call This Progress*, NLI EC. Although undated, this handbill is likely to have been produced for the 1932 election, if not an earlier by-election.

40 Ibid. The emphasis reflects that of the original text.

41 Ibid.

42 Ibid. Emphases are my own.

43 Ibid.

44 *Another Generation before Land Purchase is Completed!*, undated Fianna Fáil election flyer, MacEntee Papers, UCDA, P67/350, p. 25. Although undated, the UCD Archives list the document as being from *c.* 1932.

45 Ibid.

46 Ibid.

47 'We Couldn't – But We Did', *Fianna Fáil Bulletin*, June 1937, p. 15.

48 Ibid.

49 Ibid.

50 Ibid.

51 Ibid.

52 Ibid.

53 John Maynard Keynes, *The Means to Prosperity* (London: Macmillan & Co., 1933), p. 10, UCDA, MacEntee Papers, P67/889.

54 Ibid.

55 Ged Martin cites Keynes' lecture at University College Dublin, where the economist 'shocked some of his audience by expressing sympathy for Fianna Fáil economic policies. Although privately regarding the new government's drive to grow more wheat as "insane", Keynes was attracted to its other developmental plans. He met de Valera, "who impressed me distinctly favourably", and helped pave the way for a visit by Josiah Stamp, a retired senior British civil servant who was an expert in debt negotiations. Stamp in turn found de Valera "very

charming"'. Ged Martin, 'De Valera Imagined and Observed', in Doherty and Keogh (eds), *De Valera's Irelands*, p. 93.

56 Untitled Fianna Fáil election propaganda, *Fianna Fáil Bulletin*, June 1936, p. 8. The emphasis is my own.

57 Ibid.

58 Untitled Fianna Fáil election material, MacEntee Papers, UCDA, P67/350, p. 26. It is likely that the 'P.T.O.' is short for Put Them Out – a reference to the refrain used in 1932 when Fianna Fáil encouraged voters to 'Put the laggards out!'

59 Untitled Fianna Fáil electoral propaganda, MacEntee Papers, UCDA, P67/350/28. Although undated, it is clear that the flyer was intended for use in the 1932 general election.

60 Ibid. The emphasis is reflective of the document.

61 Ibid. The phrase was not only capitalised but presented in a darker and larger font than the rest of the document.

62 Speech for the 'County Dublin Election Campaign', TS, MacEntee Papers, UCDA, P67/350, p. 1.

63 '"An Claidheamh Soluis": the Sword of Light', *Irish Press*, 5 September 1932 p. 1.

64 *Irish Press*, 5 September 1933.

65 Bee, 'Your Duty To-Day – Clear the Lines!', *Irish Press*, 16 February 1932, p. 1.

66 Ibid. Indeed, the image depicts a locomotive operating at full steam, which if real would result in the engine crashing through the boulders. The images presented in this chapter seem to have the ability to defy physics.

67 Bee, 'How on Earth Will I Clear the Road?', *Irish Press*, 1 March 1933, p. 1. For more on the life and artistic contributions of Bee/Victor Brown, see Barry Sheppard's online article 'The Truth in the News: The *Irish Press* cartoons of Victor Brown', https://www.theirishstory.com/2020/04/19/the-truth-in-the-news-the-irish-press-cartoons-of-victor-brown/.

68 Bee, 'Buy Irish – and give the Irish work', *Irish Press*, 11 March 1933, p. 1.

69 Ibid.

70 'Strength to Strength', advertising supplement, *Irish Press*, 5 September 1933, p. iv.

71 Ibid.

72 Ibid.

73 Koepnick, 'Fascist Aesthetics Revisited', pp. 51–2.

74 'Fianna Fail Achieves "The Impossible"', *Fianna Fáil Bulletin*, June 1937, p. 13.

75 Ibid. Although Fine Gael did not exist in 1931, the fact that the party had evolved from Cumann na nGaedheal would not have been lost on the reader in 1937.

76 'Fianna Fail Has Delivered the Goods!', *Fianna Fáil Bulletin*, June 1937, p. 7.

77 Fianna Fáil, *The Wheels Are Moving*, NLI, LOP111 (10). Although undated, this pamphlet appears to have been produced for the 1933 election, as evidenced by references to action 'On December 31st, 1932, [when] 38,011 men were employed on these special works financed out of State funds'. Further, there is a reference to Cumann na nGaedheal, disqualifying any potential usage in 1937.

78 Ibid. The emphasis is my own.

79 In the same pamphlet, Fianna Fáil claimed that 'The famous marble quarries of Ireland which have been closed for years are now reopening'. Additionally, 'The Cumann na nGaedheal and other opposition parties opposed vigorously the policy which produced these new factories. If they should get power, they would reverse it and the factories would have to close again and future development would be stopped'.

80 'Five Years of Industrial Achievement', *Fianna Fáil Bulletin*, June 1937, p. 8.

81 'Increase in Net Output – 1931–1935', *Fianna Fáil Bulletin*, June 1937, p. 9.

82 Ibid.

83 'The Turn of the Tide', in ibid.

84 Untitled Fianna Fáil election poster, MacEntee Papers, UCDA, P67/350, p. 26. Although undated, the UCD Archives list the document as being from *c.* 1932.

85 Fianna Fáil Has a Plan', *Irish Press*, 15 February 1932, p. 5.

86 Ibid.

87 'Fianna Fáil Takes the Land from the Bullock and Gives it Back to the People', *Fianna Fáil Bulletin*, June 1937, p. 9.

88 Fianna Fáil, *Why You Should Subscribe to the Fianna Fáil Collection*, NLI, LO P111, p. 4. Although undated, the rhetoric and tone of the message suggests that this document was from one of the two 1932 elections.

89 Fianna Fáil, *Annual Collection for the Fianna Fáil Headquarters Fund*, NLI, LO P111, p. 6. This letter is also undated, but is most likely from 1932, after the first election, which put Fianna Fáil into a coalition government. The document solicited monies for Seán T. Ó Ceallaigh, Oscar Traynor, Eamon Conney and Cormac Breathnach.

90 'Ward Off the Arrows of Adversity!', *Fianna Fáil Bulletin*, June 1937, p. 16.

91 'Fianna Fail has changed the face of the Country – and provided a strong line of economic defence against World depression and war', *Fianna Fáil Bulletin*, June 1937, p. 9.

92 Ibid.

93 'The Advance of the Republic', *Fianna Fáil Bulletin*, August 1936, p. 8.

94 Ibid.

95 Ibid.

CHAPTER 4. 'QUEERING' JOHN BULL: FIANNA FÁIL AND REPUBLICAN HETERONORMATIVITY

1 'Go And In My Name Say: The Pope Loves Ireland'. Papal Legate's Dramatic Message From Rome', *Irish Press*, 22 June 1932, p. 1.

2 Ibid.

3 Éamon de Valera, 'Welcome to the Pope's Legate, 21 June 1932', in Moynihan, *Speeches*, p. 218. The greeting translated as, 'Many thousand welcomes to the honoured representatives of the Holy Father to the emerald land of Ireland!'

4 Dermot Keogh, *Ireland and the Vatican: The politics and diplomacy of church–state relations, 1922–1960* (Cork: Cork University Press, 1995), p. 96. Keogh also notes that Fianna Fáil wore modern suits – as opposed to the British tradition of wearing formal clothing to parliament – upsetting opposition members, who cited the affront to tradition made by de Valera and his followers (pp. 186–8).

5 'Mr. de Valera's Address Recalls Ireland's Ties With the Holy See – A Welcome in Gaelic', *Irish Press*, 22 June 1932, p. 1. A copy of this speech can also be found in Éamon de Valera, 'Welcome to the Pope's Legate, 21 June 1932', in Moynihan, *Speeches*, p. 219.

6 Ann Kilmartin, 'Trumpets and Drawn Swords', *Irish Press*, 26 June 1932, p. 1.

7 Gillian McIntosh, 'The Centenary Celebrations for Catholic Emancipation', in Augusteijn (ed.), *Ireland*, p. 88.

8 Finín O'Driscoll, 'Social Catholicism in Independent Ireland', in Mike Cronin and John M. Regan (eds), *Ireland: The politics of independence, 1922–49* (Hampshire: Macmillan Press, 2000), p. 131. O'Driscoll also notes that the Eucharistic Congress afforded Fianna Fáil 'further opportunity to claim to be the real and true Catholic political party'.

9 T.P. O'Neill, quoted in Patrick Murray, *Oracles of God: The Roman Catholic Church and Irish politics 1922–37* (Dublin: UCD Press, 2000), p. 262.

10 Heteronormativity can best be defined as the reification of heterosexual norms, which serve to strengthen gendered discourses of normality, as well as to isolate and exorcise the queer from society.

11 Judith Butler, *Gender Trouble: Feminism and the subversion of identity* (New York: Routledge, 1990), p. 140.

12 Nikki Sullivan, *A Critical Introduction to Queer Theory* (New York: New York University Press, 2003), p. 191. Further, Sullivan writes, 'in other words, queer does not function here as a label that one can appropriately or (otherwise) apply to (the essence of) a particular text. Rather than functioning as a noun, queer can be used as a verb, that is, to describe a process, a movement between viewer, text, and world, that reinscribes (or queers) each and the relations between them' (p. 192).

13 Ibid., p. 191.

14 Edward Said, *Orientalism* (New York: Vintage, 1979).

15 Fianna Fáil, *Scheme of Election Organisation*, Aiken Papers, UCDA, P104/1598, p. 6. Although undated, the UCD Archives lists this pamphlet as likely to have been created for the 1932 election – an assessment supported by the nature of the language and tone, namely the following passage, which reads, 'The next point to note is the economic situation in the Constituency and the general occupation of the people. The circumstances of every class and section must be specially considered and plans made for convincing its members that their interests will best be served by the election of a Fianna Fáil Government' (p. 6). Of note is the fact that this pamphlet was underscored by the phrase 'For Private Circulation Only' (p. 1).

16 Fianna Fáil, untitled, undated handbill for 'Boland, Gorry, Tynan', Archives of the Fianna Fáil Party, UCDA, P176/827, p. 24. Although the flyer is undated, the archive has it listed as being from 1927, which is supported by the tone of the handbill. This particular piece of propaganda was likely to have come from Frank Aiken, for work that he is most closely associated with tended to have some element decrying the inclusion of the Freemasons in the Irish Free State. See Fianna Fáil, *Fianna Fáil Kept Their Promise, A Survey of the Great Work Done in Louth, How Drogheda Fared: Great Industrial Revival*, c. 1932, Aiken Papers, UCDA, P104/1575, p. 2. See also Fianna Fáil, *The Economic History of the Land of Erin*, c. 1929, Aiken Papers, UCDA, P104/1582, p. 3. This latter example offers a fairy tale-like story regarding the history of Ireland where the villains include the 'Knights of the Compass and Square and Ring'.

17 Daly, *Industrial Development*, p. 14. Daly also mentions that the position was enhanced by opposition from 'ex-Unionists, a conservative Farmers' party representing larger farmers, and the Labour party'. Although not mentioned, Fianna Fáil – which had not been founded at the time to which Daly refers – was able to identify and exploit the Britishness of Cumann na nGaedheal.

18 Fianna Fáil, untitled, undated election handbill, NLI, LO P111, p. 9. Unique to this material was the association made between Cumann na nGaedheal and Irish soldiers fighting for the British war cause: 'An Irish Army pledged to fight England's Wars at your expense. Your Home and Country subjected to the ravages of a World-War in the interests of British Imperialism and at England's will.' Inaccuracies aside, it is of great interest that there existed propaganda that portrayed Cumann na nGaedheal as the harbingers of violence, a rather fascinating inversion of rhetoric.

19 Ibid.

20 Fianna Fáil, *Fianna Fáil Kept Their Promise, A Survey of the Great Work Done in Louth, How Drogheda Fared: Great Industrial Revival*, c. 1932, Aiken Papers, UCDA, P104/1575, p. 1.

21 Ibid.

22 Ibid., p. 2. The emphasis in the quotation is my own.

23 Fianna Fáil, *Why Wouldn't They?*, NLI, EC. Although undated, the reference to Cumann na nGaedheal ministers and their efforts for re-election makes it clear that this flyer was from one of the two elections held in 1927.

24 Ibid. The names listed include Mrs O'Higgins (widow of the recently assassinated Kevin O'Higgins), Blythe, Fitzgerald, J.J. Walsh, P. Hogan, J.J. Burke and Finian Lynch, who each are

purported to have received £8,500, and the pairs of Eoin MacNeill and Prof. O'Sullivan, Jos. McGrath and Mr McGilligan, and Richard Mulcahy and P. Hughes, which shared the same amount.

25 Ibid.

26 Fianna Fáil, untitled handbill, *c.* 1932, Aiken Papers, UCDA, P104/1601, p. 1. 'Why Britain Created Crisis', *Fianna Fáil Bulletin*, 1 August 1932, p. 4.

27 Fianna Fáil, *Five Years of Poverty and Panic, c.* 1927, UCDA, P176/827, p. 19.

28 Ibid.

29 Ibid. The emphases are reflective of the original text.

30 Fianna Fáil, 'Why Britain Created Crisis'.

31 'Time Marches On!', *Fianna Fáil Bulletin*, January 1937, p. 7.

32 Bee, 'They Never Look Out the Window', *Irish Press*, 9 June 1932, p. 1.

33 Ibid.

34 Bee, 'At Downing St. They Turned on the Radio and Smiled Again', *Irish Press*, 3 September 1932, p. 1.

35 Ibid.

36 Ibid.

37 Ibid.

38 Ibid.

39 This is seen in a cartoon from this period in which Cosgrave is depicted absconding from Ireland to London with a bag filled with £5,000,000. Bee, 'Mr. Cosgrave's method of "Peace in Three Days"', *Irish Press*, 11 January 1933, p. 1.

40 'Who Makes England's Case?', *Irish Press*, 12 January 1933, p. 3.

41 Ibid.

42 Ibid.

43 Bee, 'Make it a Man's Answer This Time!', *Irish Press*, 24 January 1933, p. 1.

44 Ibid.

45 Ibid.

46 Bee, 'Ireland's Strong Man', *Irish Press*, 21 January 1933, p. 1.

47 Ibid. The full text of the caption reads, 'In July, 1931, Mr. Cosgrave asked Britain to apply the Hoover Moratorium to £250,000 to the five million he paid her each year. Britain refused – and Mr. Cosgrave did not tell a soul.'

48 'Fianna Fáil was Right All the Time – Even Mr. Wm. Cosgrave, Ex.-T.D., admits it NOW!', *Irish Press*, 14 January 1933, p. 3.

49 Ibid. The ad also includes the remarkable line 'Fianna Fáil was right in 1923 – Fianna Fáil was right in 1932'. Fianna Fáil, of course, was founded in 1923. Does this mean that Fianna Fáil was co-opting an economic policy of Sinn Féin's as its own, or is the implication that the seeds of Fianna Fáil policy as distinct from Sinn Féin's were present in 1923? It is difficult to make any definitive claim here. The emphasis is my own.

50 Bee, 'Mr. Cosgrave', *Irish Press*, 14 January 1933, p. 1.

51 Bee, 'The Channel Swimmer', *Irish Press*, 19 January 1933, p. 1.

52 '"Irish Housekeeping": British Writer on the Results of Fianna Fáil's Economic Policy', *Fianna Fáil Bulletin*, February 1936, p. 5.

53 'The Education of Fine Gael', *Fianna Fáil Bulletin*, June 1937, p. 14.

54 Girvin, 'The Republicanisation of Irish Society', pp. 132–3.

55 'The Education of Fine Gael', p. 14.

56 Mike Cronin, 'The Irish Free State and *Aonach Tailteann*', in Alan Bairner (ed.), *Sport and the Irish: Histories, identities, issues* (Dublin: UCD Press, 2005), p. 54; Louise Ryan, '*Aonach Tailteann*, the *Irish Press* and Gendered Symbols of National Identity in the 1920s and 1930s', in ibid., pp. 69–84. See also Mike Cronin, 'Projecting the Nation through Sport and Culture:

Ireland, *Aonach Tailteann* and the Irish Free State, 1924–32', *Journal of Contemporary History*, vol. 38, no. 3, 'Sports and Politics', July 2003, pp. 395–411; Cronin, '"Is it for Glamour?" Masculinity, nationhood and amateurism in contemporary projections of the Gaelic Athletic Association', in Wanda Balzano, Anne Mulhall and Moynagh Sullivan (eds), *Irish Postmodernisms and Popular Culture* (Hampshire: Palgrave Macmillan, 2007), pp. 39–51.

57 Cronin, 'The Irish Free State and *Aonach Tailteann*', p. 57.

58 John Turpin, quoted in ibid., p. 58.

59 Ibid., p. 59.

60 Ibid., p. 67.

61 For histories of the GAA, see: Marcus de Búrca, *The GAA: A history* (Dublin: Gill & Macmillan, 2000); Neal Garnham, 'Accounting for the Early Success of the Gaelic Athletic Association', *Irish Historical Studies*, vol. 34, no. 133, May 2004, pp. 65–78.

62 Patrick F. McDevitt, 'Muscular Catholicism: Nationalism, masculinity, and Gaelic team sports, 1884–1916', in Tony Ballantyne and Antoinette Burton (eds), *Bodies in Contact: Rethinking colonial encounters in world history* (Durham: Duke University Press, 2005), pp. 209–10. Although McDevitt's article covers the period between 1884 and 1916, the very fact that the GAA survived beyond the Easter rising – not to mention that it flourishes today – while maintaining its cultural nationalist bent, is of great significance.

63 Ibid., p. 210.

64 For a history of the development of camogie and its inclusion into the GAA, see Mike Cronin, 'More Than Just Hurling and Football: The GAA and its other activities', in Mike Cronin, William Murphy and Paul Rouse (eds), *The Gaelic Athletic Association, 1884–2009* (Dublin: Irish Academic Press, 2009), pp. 227–8.

65 McDevitt, 'Muscular Catholicism', p. 215.

66 Rex Cathcart with Michael Muldoon, 'The Mass Media in Twentieth-Century Ireland', in Hill (ed.), *A New History of Ireland*, p. 683.

67 'Celt' was the *nom de plume* of Patrick James Devlin (1877–1941). As a journalist, Devlin was instrumental in popularising Gaelic sport in Ireland and the United States. In addition to his journalistic endeavours, he was active in the administration of various Gaelic sporting organisations, including the Tailteann Games. A close friend of Michael Cusack, Devlin served as sports editor of the *Irish Press*. John Rouse, 'Patrick James Devlin', *Dictionary of Irish Biography*, Volume 3, pp. 245–6.

68 'Who'll Win Ireland's Hurling Blue Riband?', *Irish Press*, 3 September 1932, p. 8. It should be noted that, generally speaking, the Irish refer to football as soccer – so as to distinguish it from Gaelic football – much in the same way that Americans do to distinguish the sport from American football.

69 Celt, 'The GAA Provides Living Example of Perpetual Motion', *Irish Press*, 7 September 1932, p. 8.

70 'Breaking the Chains', *Irish Press*, 25–6 March 1932, p. 1.

71 Ibid.

CHAPTER 5. CONCLUSION: 'IRELAND IS NOT A BAD OLD PLACE AFTER ALL!'

1 Bee, 'Ireland Is Not a Bad Old Place After All!', *Irish Press*, 16 March 1933, p. 1.

2 Ibid. Bee was not a stranger to racist imagery in his cartoons. Persons from Asia, Africa and the Americas were often depicted using ugly, and racist, imagery. See, for example, the cartoon depicting British colonists in Africa, where two men – one resembling Prime Minister Ramsay MacDonald – are captives of unnamed Kenyans. One of the Britons asks, 'Is there n-no Cumann na nGaedheal party t-t-to get us out of this?' Bee, 'Ye Treaty Breakers',

Irish Press, 15 February 1933, p. 1. Indeed, much could be said about this vis-à-vis the cosy relationship between Britain and Cosgrave's party, but more significant here is the reductive and 'othering' depiction of the Kenyans. They are represented as animalistic and savage – a characterisation not entirely unlike the racialised depictions of the Irish in the British press during the nineteenth century. See, for example, Michael de Nie, *The Eternal Paddy: Irish identity and the British press, 1798–1882* (Madison: University of Wisconsin Press, 2004).

3   Bee, 'Ireland', *Irish Press*, 22 March 1933, p. 1. The image includes a British, a French, a German and an Italian soldier. Such are identified by their uniforms and helmets. Interestingly, the soldiers are not divided by political ideology or by alliance. The image, then, serves to depict a general sense of European disarray distinct from a pacific Ireland.

4   Ibid.

5   'Make the Home Fires HOME Fires', *Irish Press*, 22 April 1933, p. 1. The cartoon has no credited artist, and though the style does resemble the artwork of Bee, he is likely not the creator. Bee's artwork tended to ensure that there was space for his signature.

6   Ibid.

Bibliography

PERSONAL PAPERS AND SPECIAL COLLECTIONS

National Archives of Ireland
Department of the Taoiseach
Office of the Film Censor

National Library of Ireland
Ephemerae Collection
Librarian's Own Collection

National Library of Ireland Manuscripts Collection
Sean T. Ó Ceallaigh Papers

University College Dublin Archives
Archives of the Fianna Fáil Party
Éamon de Valera Papers
Frank Aiken Papers
Kathleen O'Connell Papers
Mary MacSwiney Papers
Seán Lemass Papers
Seán MacEntee Papers

NEWSPAPERS

An Phoblacht
Dundalk Examiner
Fianna Fáil Bulletin
The Irish Independent
The Irish Press
The Nation

GOVERNMENT SOURCES

Bunreacht na hÉireann/Constitution of Ireland (Dublin: Government Publications Sales Office [1937], 2003)
Crowe, Catriona, et al. (eds), *Documents on Irish Foreign Policy: Volume IV, 1932–1936* (Dublin: Royal Irish Academy, 2004)

Crowe, Catriona, et al. (eds), *Documents on Irish Foreign Policy: Volume V, 1937–1939* (Dublin: Royal Irish Academy, 2006)

Dáil Éireann, *Díosboirreachtaí Parlaiminte: Tuairisg oifigiúil* (Parliamentary Debates: Official report) (Dublin: Stationery Office, 1922–)

House of Commons, *Parliamentary Debates*, 5th ser., vol. 335, 1938

Primary Sources: Ephemerae

Cumann na nGaedheal, *No goods taken from window! Supplies from goods stores only!* 1932, NLI, EPH F57

— *Don't let this happen. Vote for Cumann na nGaedheal*, 1932, NLI, EPH F45

— *Fight Points for Cumann-na-nGaedheal Speakers and Workers, General Election 1932* (Dublin: Cumann-na-nGaedheal, 1932)

— *HIS Master's Voice: Make your voice heard by voting for Cumann na nGaedheal*, 1932, NLI, EPH F474

— *Presented by the artist to the nation. De Valera is now working on another Canvas (s) but what about the price? Vote for Cumann na nGaedheal*, 1932, NLI, EPH F38

— *Senor de Valera*, National Library of Ireland, Ephemerae Collection, POL/1930-40/6

— *The Shadow of the Gunman: Keep it from your home. Vote for Cumann na nGaedheal*, 1932, NLI, EPH F53

— *The dead who died for an 'empty formula'. Was it worth it? Vote for Cumann na nGaedheal*, 1932, NLI, EPH F43

— *The hen that took 5 years to lay an egg and then it was empty. Vote for Cumann na nGaedheal*, 1932, NLI, EPH F44(A)

— *Fianna Fail's Game. Don't let them cheat you! Vote for Cumann na nGaedheal*, NLI, EPH, F473

Fianna Fáil, *Statement on the Aims of Fianna Fáil*, 17 April 1926, Éamon de Valera Collection, University College Dublin Archives, P150/2011

— *A Brief Outline of the Aims and Programme of Fianna Fáil*, Éamon de Valera Collection, University College Dublin Archives, P150/2048 (7)

— *Annual Collection for the Fianna Fáil Headquarters Fund*, National Library of Ireland, LO P111 (6)

— *Another Generation before Land Purchase Is Completed!*, Seán MacEntee Papers, University College Dublin Archives, P67/350 (25)

— *Fianna Fáil Kept Their Promise, A Survey of the Great Work Done in Louth, How Drogheda Fared: Great Industrial Revival*, Frank Aiken Papers, University College Dublin Archives, P104/1575 (2)

— *Fianna Fáil, Pamphlet #2* (Dublin: Wood Printing Works, c. 1927)

— *Five Years of Poverty and Panic*, Archives of the Fianna Fáil Party, University College Dublin Archives, P176/827 (19)

— *Ireland's Right to the Land Annuities*, Seán MacEntee Papers, University College Dublin Archives, P67/134 (51)
— *Scheme of Election Organisation*, Frank Aiken Papers, University College Dublin Archives, P104/1598 (6)
— *The Economic History of the Land of Erin*, Frank Aiken Papers, University College Dublin Archives, P104/1582 (3)
— *They Call This Progress*, National Library of Ireland, Ephemerae Collection
— *Unscrupulous Propaganda*, National Library of Ireland, Ephemerae Collection
— *Why Wouldn't They?*, National Library of Ireland, Ephemerae Collection
— *Why You Should Subscribe to the Fianna Fáil Collection*, National Library of Ireland, LO P111 (4)

Primary Sources

Fianna Fáil, *Iubhaile Órga Fianna Fáil, the Republican Party. Concert Souvenir Programme* (Dublin: Fianna Fáil, 1976)

Griffith, Arthur, *The Resurrection of Hungary* (Dublin: UCD Press [1904], 2003)

Harrison, Henry, *The Anglo-Irish Economic War of 1932–1934: The game of 'beggar-my-neighbour' who wins?* (London: The Irish News and Information Bureau, 1934)

Moynihan, Maurice (ed.), *Speeches and Statements by Éamon de Valera, 1917–1973* (Dublin: Gill & Macmillan, 1980)

O'Hegarty, P.S., *The Victory of Sinn Féin: How it won and how it used it* (Dublin: UCD Press [1924], 1998)

Pakenham, Frank, *Peace by Ordeal: An account, from first-hand sources, of the negotiation and signature of the Anglo-Irish Treaty 1921* (Cork: Mercier Press, 1951)

Ryan, Desmond, *Unique Dictator: A study of Éamon de Valera* (London: Arthur Barker, 1936)

Secondary Sources

Adamson, W.L., 'Avant-garde Modernism and Italian Fascism: Cultural politics in the era of Mussolini', *Journal of Modern Italian Studies*, vol. 6, no. 2, 2001, pp. 230–48

— 'Modernism and Fascism: The politics of culture in Italy, 1903–1922', *The American Historical Review*, vol. 95, no. 2, April 1990, pp. 359–90

Alapuro, Risto, 'Coping with the Civil War of 1918 in Twenty-First Century Finland', in Kenneth Christie and Robert Cribb (eds), *Historical Injustice and Democratic Transition in Eastern Asia and Northern Europe: Ghosts at the table of democracy* (London: Routledge, 2002)

Allen, Ann Taylor, *Women in Twentieth-Century Europe* (Hampshire: Palgrave Macmillan, 2008)

Allen, Kieran, *Fianna Fáil and Irish Labour: 1926 to the present* (London: Pluto Press, 1997)

Anderson, W.K., *James Connolly and the Irish Left* (Dublin: Irish Academic Press, 1994)

Antliff, Mark, 'Fascism, Modernism, and Modernity', *The Art Bulletin*, vol. 84, no. 1, March 2002, pp. 148–69

Augusteijn, Joost (ed.), *Ireland in the 1930s: New perspectives* (Dublin: Four Courts Press, 1999)

Bairner, Alan, *Sport and the Irish: Histories, identities, issues* (Dublin: UCD Press, 2005)

Ballantyne, Tony and Antoinette Burton (eds), *Bodies in Contact: Rethinking colonial encounters in world history* (Durham: Duke University Press, 2005)

Barblett, Thomas (ed.), *The Cambridge History of Ireland. Volume IV: 1880 to the Present* (Cambridge: Cambridge University Press, 2018)

Barthes, Roland, *Image, Music, Text* (New York: Hill & Wang, 1966)

Beatty, Aidan, *Masculinity and Power in Irish Nationalism, 1884–1938* (London: Palgrave Macmillan, 2016)

Ben-Ghiat, Ruth, 'Italian Fascism and the Aesthetics of the "Third Way"', *Journal of Contemporary History*, vol. 31, no. 2, April 1996, pp. 293–316

— *Fascist Modernities: Italy, 1922–1945* (Berkeley: University of California Press, 2001)

Benjamin, Walter, 'The Work of Art in the Age of Mechanical Reproduction', *Illuminations: Essays and reflections*, trans. Harry Zohn (New York: Schocken, 1969)

Benton, Sarah, 'Women Disarmed: The militarization of politics in Ireland, 1913–23', *Feminist Review*, no. 50, summer 1995, pp. 148–72

Berg-Schlosser, Dirk and Jeremy Mitchell (eds), *Conditions of Democracy in Europe, 1919–39* (London: Macmillan Press, 2000)

Bernstein, Charles, 'Making Audio Visible: The lessons of visual language for the textualization of sound', *Text*, vol. 16, 2006, pp. 277–89

Bew, Paul, *Ireland: The politics of enmity, 1789–2006* (Oxford: Oxford University Press, 2007)

— *Churchill & Ireland* (Oxford: Oxford University Press, 2016)

Bhreathnach-Lynch, Síghle, 'Cultural Nationalism in Stone: Albert G. Power, 1881–1945', *New Hibernia Review/Iris Éireannach Nua*, vol. 9, no. 2, summer/samhradh 2005, pp. 98–110

Biagini, Eugenio F. and Mary E. Daly, *The Cambridge Social History of Modern Ireland* (Cambridge: Cambridge University Press, 2015)

Biletz, Frank A., 'Women and Irish-Ireland: The domestic nationalism of Mary Butler', *New Hibernia Review/Iris Éireannach Nua*, vol. 5, no. 1, spring/earrach, 2001, pp. 59–72

Bodkin, Thomas (ed.), *Twelve Irish Artists* (Dublin: Victor Waddington Publications, 1940)

Boland, Kevin, *The Rise and Decline of Fianna Fáil* (Cork: Mercier Press, 1982)

Bourke, Angela, *The Burning of Bridget Cleary: A true story* (London: Pimlico, 1999)

Boyce, D. George, *Nationalism in Ireland* (London: Routledge [1982], 1995)

Boyce, D. George and Alan O'Day (eds), *The Making of Modern Irish History: Revisionism and the revisionist controversy* (London: Routledge, 1996)

Bradley, Anthony and Maryann Gialanella Valiulis (eds), *Gender and Sexuality in Modern Ireland* (Amherst: University of Massachusetts Press, 1997)

Braun, Emily, 'Expressionism as Fascist Aesthetic', *Journal of Contemporary History*, vol. 31, no. 2, April 1996, pp. 273–92

Breathnach, Ciara, 'The Role of Women in the Economy of the West of Ireland, 1891–1923', *New Hibernia Review/Iris Éireannach Nua*, vol. 8, no. 1, spring/earrach, 2004, pp. 80–92

Bromage, Mary C., 'De Valera's Formula for Irish Nationhood', *The Review of Politics*, vol. 13, no. 4, October 1951, pp. 483–502

Brown, Judith M. and Wm. Roger Louis (eds), *The Oxford History of the British Empire. Volume IV: The Twentieth Century* (Oxford: Oxford University Press, 1999)

Brown, Terence, *Ireland: A social and cultural history, 1922–2002* (London: Harper Collins, 2004)

Butler, Judith, *Gender Trouble: Feminism and the subversion of identity* (New York: Routledge, 1990)

Capdevila, Luc, 'The Quest for Masculinity in a Defeated France, 1940–1945', *Contemporary European History*, vol. 10, part 3, November 2001, pp. 423–46

Carlson, Julia (ed.), *Banned in Ireland: Censorship and the Irish writer* (Athens: The University of Georgia Press, 1990)

Carroll, Clare and Patricia King (eds), *Ireland and Postcolonial Theory* (Notre Dame: The University of Notre Dame Press, 2003)

Carty, R.K., *Party and Parish Pump: Electoral politics in Ireland* (Waterloo: Wilfrid Laurier University Press, 1981)

Clear, Caitriona, *Women of the House: Women's household work in Ireland, 1926–1961* (Dublin: Irish Academic Press, 2000)

— *Social Change and Everyday Life in Ireland, 1850–1922* (Manchester: Manchester University Press, 2007)

Cohen, Marilyn and Nancy J. Curtin (eds), *Reclaiming Gender: Transgressive identities in modern Ireland* (New York: St Martin's Press, 1999)

Connell, R.W., *Masculinities* (Los Angeles: University of California Press, 2005)

Connolly, Linda, *The Irish Women's Movement: From revolution to devolution* (Dublin: The Lilliput Press, 2003)

Coogan, Tim Pat, *Éamon de Valera: The man who was Ireland* (New York: Dorset Press, 1993)

Cosgrove, Mary, 'Ernie O'Malley: Art and modernism in Ireland', *Éire/Ireland*, vol. 40, nos. 3 & 4, fall/winter 2005, pp. 85–103

Cronin, Michael G., '"He's My Country": Liberalism, nationalism, and sexuality in contemporary Irish gay fiction', *Éire/Ireland*, vol. 39, nos. 3 & 4, fall/winter 2004, pp. 250–67

Cronin, Mike, *The Blueshirts and Irish Politics* (Dublin: Four Courts Press, 1997)

— 'The Blueshirts in the Irish Free State, 1932–1935: The nature of socialist republican and governmental opposition', in Tim Kirk and Anthony McElligott (eds), *Opposing Fascism: Community, authority and resistance in Europe* (Cambridge: Cambridge University Press, 1999), pp. 80–96

— 'Projecting the Nation through Sport and Culture: Ireland, *Aonach Tailteann* and the Irish Free State, 1924–32', *Journal of Contemporary History*, vol. 38, no. 3, 'Sports and Politics', July 2003, pp. 395–411

— '"Is it for Glamour?" Masculinity, nationhood and amateurism in contemporary projections of the Gaelic Athletic Association', in Wanda Balzano, Anne Mulhall and Moynagh Sullivan (eds), *Irish Postmodernisms and Popular Culture* (Hampshire: Palgrave Macmillan, 2007), pp. 39–51

— 'Selling Irish Bacon: The Empire Marketing Board and artists of the Free State', *Éire/Ireland*, vol. 39, nos. 3 & 4, fall/winter 2004, pp. 132–43

Cronin, Mike and John M. Regan (eds), *Ireland: The politics of independence, 1922–1949* (London: Macmillan Press, 2000)

Cronin, Mike, William Murphy, and Paul Rouse (eds), *The Gaelic Athletic Association, 1884–2009* (Dublin: Irish Academic Press, 2009)

Cullingford, Elizabeth, *Yeats, Ireland and Fascism* (New York: New York University Press, 1981)

Curtis, L. Perry, *Coercion and Conciliation in Ireland, 1880–1892: A study in conservative unionism* (Princeton: Princeton University Press, 1963)

Daly, Mary E., 'An Irish-Ireland for Business? The Control of Manufactures Acts, 1932 and 1934', *Irish Historical Studies*, vol. 24, no. 94, November 1984, pp. 246–72

— *Industrial Development and Irish National Identity, 1922–1939* (Dublin: Gill & Macmillan, 1992)

— 'Women in the Irish Free State, 1922–39: The interaction between economics and ideology', *Journal of Women's History*, vol. 6, no. 4, winter/spring 1995, pp. 99–116

— '"Oh, Kathleen Ni Houlihan, Your Way's a Thorny Way!" The condition of women in twentieth-century Ireland', in Anthony Bradley and Maryann Gialanella Valiulis (eds), *Gender and Sexuality in Modern Ireland* (Amherst: University of Massachusetts Press, 1997), pp. 102–26

— 'The Irish Free State/Éire/Republic of Ireland/Ireland: A country by any other name?' *Journal of British Studies*, vol. 46, no. 1, January 2007, pp. 72–91

Davis, Leth, *Music, Postcolonialism, and Gender: The construction of Irish national identity, 1724–1874* (Notre Dame: University of Notre Dame Press, 2006)

Davis, Troy D., 'Éamon de Valéra's Political Education: The American tour of 1919–20', *New Hibernia Review/Iris Éireannach Nua*, vol. 10, no. 1, spring/earrach, 2006, pp. 65–78

De Búrca, Marcus, *The GAA: A history* (Dublin: Gill & Macmillan, 2000)

De Grazia, Victoria, *The Culture of Consent: Mass organization of leisure in fascist Italy* (Cambridge: Cambridge University Press, 1981)

de Nie, Michael, *The Eternal Paddy: Irish identity and the British press, 1798–1882* (Madison: University of Wisconsin Press, 2004)

de Valera, Terry, *A Memoir* (Dublin: Currach Press, 2004)

Debord, Guy, *Society of the Spectacle* (Detroit: Black & Red, 1983)

Dennison, S.R. and Oliver MacDonagh, *Guinness, 1886–1939: From incorporation to the Second World War* (Cork: Cork University Press, 1998)

Doherty, Gabriel and Dermot Keogh (eds), *De Valera's Irelands* (Cork: Mercier Press, 2003)

Dooley, Terence, *'The Land for the People': The land question in independent Ireland* (Dublin: UCD Press, 2004)

Douglas, R.M., *Architects of the Resurrection: Ailtirí na h-aiséirghe and the fascist 'new order' in Ireland* (Manchester: Manchester University Press, 2009)

Dunphy, Richard, *The Making of Fianna Fáil Power in Ireland, 1932–1948* (Oxford: Clarendon Press, 1995)

Dwyer, T. Ryle, *Big Fellow, Long Fellow: A joint biography of Collins and de Valera* (Dublin: Gill & Macmillan, 1998)

Ellis, Timothy, 'De Valera's Gains: The masculine body in Irish political cartoons, 1922–1939', *Éire/Ireland*, vol. 54, nos. 3 & 4, fall/winter 2019, pp. 61–93

English, Richard, *Radicals and the Republic: Socialist republicanism in the Irish Free State, 1925–1937* (Oxford: Clarendon Press, 1994)

Fallon, Brian, *An Age of Innocence: Irish culture, 1930–1960* (London: Palgrave Macmillan, 1998)

Fanning, Bryan, *Racism and Social Change in the Republic of Ireland* (Manchester: Manchester University Press, 2002)

— *The Quest for Modern Ireland: The battle of ideas, 1912–1986* (Dublin: Irish Academic Press, 2008)

Fanning, Ronan, *The Four-Leaved Shamrock: Electoral politics and the national imagination in independent Ireland* (Dublin: National University of Ireland, 1983)

— *'Raison d'État and the Evolution of Irish Foreign Policy',* in Michael Kennedy and Joseph Morrison Skelly (eds), *Irish Foreign Policy, 1919–1966: From independence to internationalism* (Dublin: Four Courts Press, 2000), pp. 308–26

— *Éamon de Valera: A will to power* (Cambridge, MA: Harvard University Press, 2015)

Farragher, Sean P., *Dev and His Alma Matter: Éamon de Valera's lifelong association with Blackrock College, 1898–1975* (Dublin and London: Paraclete Press, 1984)

Farrell, Brian (ed.), *De Valera's Constitution and Ours* (Dublin: Gill & Macmillan, 1988)

Farrell, Mel, 'A "Cadre-Style" Party? Cumann na nGaedheal organization in Clare, Dublin North, and Longford-Westmeath, 1923–27', *Éire-Ireland*, vol. 47, nos. 3 & 4, fomhar/geimhreadh (fall/winter) 2012, pp. 91–110

— *Party Politics in a New Democracy: The Irish Free State, 1922–37* (London: Palgrave Macmillan, 2017)

Farrell, Mel, Jason Knirck, and Ciara Meehan (eds), *A Formative Decade: Ireland in the 1920s* (Dublin: Irish Academic Press, 2015)

Feeny, Brian, *Sinn Féin: A hundred turbulent years* (Madison: University of Wisconsin Press [2002], 2003)

Ferme, Valerio C., 'Redefining the Aesthetics of Fascism: The battle between the ancients and the moderns revisited', *Symposium*, vol. 52, no. 2, summer 1998, pp. 67–84

Ferriter, Diarmaid, *Judging Dev: A reassessment of the life and legacy of Éamon de Valera* (Dublin: Royal Irish Academy, 2007)

Finnegan, Richard B. and James L. Wiles (eds), *Women and Public Policy in Ireland: A documentary history, 1922–1997* (Dublin: Irish Academic Press, 2005)

Fitzpatrick, David, *Politics and Irish Life, 1913–1921: Provincial experience of war and revolution* (Dublin: Gill & Macmillan, 1977)

Foster, Gavin M., *The Irish Civil War and Society: Politics, class, and conflict* (London: Palgrave Macmillan, 2015)

Foster, R.F., *Modern Ireland, 1600–1972* (London: Penguin Press, 1989)

— *W.B. Yeats: A life. Volume I: The Apprentice Mage, 1865–1914* (Oxford: Oxford University Press, 1997)

— *W.B. Yeats: A life. Volume II: The Arch Poet, 1915–1939* (Oxford: Oxford University Press, 2003)

Foucault, Michel, *The History of Sexuality. Volume 1: An Introduction*, trans. Robert Hurley (New York: Vintage, 1978)

— *Power/Knowledge: Selected interviews and other writings, 1972–1977*, edited by Colin Gordon and translated by Colin Gordon et al. (New York: Pantheon Books, 1980)

— 'The Subject and Power', *Critical Inquiry*, vol. 8, no. 4, 1981, pp. 782–3

Frazier, Adrian, 'Queering the Irish Renaissance: The masculinities of Moore, Martyn, and Yeats', in Anthony Bradley and Maryann Gialanella Valiulis (eds), *Gender and Sexuality in Modern Ireland* (Amherst: University of Massachusetts Press, 1997), pp. 8–38

Garnham, Neal, 'Accounting for the Early Success of the Gaelic Athletic Association', *Irish Historical Studies*, vol. 34, no. 133, May 2004, pp. 65–78

Garvin, Tom, *1922: The birth of Irish democracy* (Dublin: Gill & Macmillan, 1996)

Gerwarth, Robert (ed.), *Twisted Paths: Europe, 1914–1945* (Oxford: Oxford University Press, 2007)

Gillespie, Michael Patrick, *The Myth of an Irish Cinema: Approaching Irish-themed films* (Syracuse: Syracuse University Press, 2008)

Girvin, Brian, *Between Two Worlds: Politics and economy in independent Ireland* (Dublin: Gill & Macmillan, 1989)

— 'The Republicanisation of Irish Society, 1932–48', in J.R. Hill (ed.), *A New History of Ireland. Volume VII: Ireland, 1921–84* (Oxford: Oxford University Press, 2003)

Girvin, Brian and Gary Murphy, *The Lemass Era: Politics and society in the Ireland of Seán Lemass* (Dublin: UCD Press, 2005)

Griffin, Roger (ed.), *Fascism* (Oxford: Oxford University Press, 1995)

Griffin, Roger, 'Introduction: God's Counterfeiters? Investigating the triad of fascism, totalitarianism and (political) religion', *Totalitarian Movements and Political Religions*, vol. 5, no. 3, winter 2004, pp. 291–325

— 'The Reclamation of Fascist Culture', *European History Quarterly*, vol. 31, no. 4, 2001, pp. 619–20

Grubgeld, Elizabeth, 'Class, Gender, and the Forms of Narrative: The auto-biographies of Anglo-Irish women', in Susan Shaw Sailer (ed.), *Representing Ireland: Gender, class nationality* (Gainesville: University Press of Florida, 1997), pp. 133–55

Hachey, Thomas E., 'The Rhetoric and Reality of Irish Neutrality', *New Hibernia Review/Iris Éireannach Nua*, vol. 6, no. 4, winter/geimhreadh 2002, pp. 26–43

Hart, Peter, *The IRA at War, 1916–1923* (Oxford: Oxford University Press, 2003)

Hayes, Alan and Dian Urquhart (eds), *The Irish Women's History Reader* (London: Routledge, 2001)

Hewitt, Andrew, *Fascist Modernism: Aesthetics, politics, and the avant-garde* (Stanford: Stanford University Press, 1993)

Higgins, Roisín and Regina Uí Chollatáin (eds), *The Life and After-Life of P.H. Pearse / Pádraic Mac Piarais: Saol agus oidhreacht* (Dublin: Irish Academic Press, 2009)

Hill, J.R. (ed.), *A New History of Ireland. Volume VII: Ireland, 1921–1984* (Oxford: Oxford University Press, 2003)

Hogan, Gerard, 'De Valera, the Constitution and the Historians', *Irish Jurist*, vol. 40, 2005, pp. 293–320

Hopkinson, Michael, *Green Against Green: The Irish civil war* (Dublin: Gill & Macmillan, 1988)

Horgan, John, *Irish Media: A critical history since 1922* (London: Routledge, 2001)

Horn, David G., *Social Bodies: Science, reproduction, and Italian modernity* (Princeton, NJ: Princeton University Press, 1994)

Howe, Stephen, *Ireland and Empire: Colonial legacies in Irish history and culture* (Oxford: Oxford University Press, 2000)

Hug, Chrystel, 'Moral Order and the Liberal Agenda in the Republic of Ireland', *New Hibernia Review/Iris Éireannach Nua*, vol. 5, no. 4, winter/geimhreadh 2001, pp. 22–41

Inglis, Tom, 'Origins and Legacies of Irish Prudery: Sexuality and social control in modern Ireland', *Éire/Ireland*, vol. 40, nos. 3 & 4, fall/winter 2005, pp. 9–37

Jackson, Alvin, *Ireland, 1798–1998: Politics and war* (Oxford: Blackwell Publishers, 1999)

— *Home Rule: An Irish history, 1800–2000* (Oxford: Oxford University Press, 2003)

— 'The Two Irelands', in Robert Gerwarth, *Twisted Paths: Europe 1914–1945* (Oxford: Oxford University Press, 2007), pp. 60–83

Jones, Mary (ed.), *The Republic: Essays from RTÉ Radio's* The Thomas Davis Lecture Series (Cork: Mercier Press, 2005)

Kennedy, Michael and Joseph Morrison Skelly (eds), *Irish Foreign Policy, 1919–1966: From independence to internationalism* (Dublin: Four Courts Press, 2000)

Kenny, Kevin, *Ireland and the British Empire* (Oxford: Oxford University Press, 2006)

— *De Valera's Irelands* (Cork: Mercier Press, 2003)

Keogh, Dermot, *Ireland and the Vatican: The politics and diplomacy of church–state relations, 1922–1960* (Cork: Cork University Press, 1995)

— *Twentieth-Century Ireland: Revolution and state building* (Dublin: Gill & Macmillan [1995], 2004)

Keown, Gerard, 'Taking the World Stage: Creating an Irish foreign policy in the 1920s,' in Michael Kennedy and Joseph Morrison Skelly (eds), *Irish Foreign Policy, 1919–1966: From independence to internationalism* (Dublin: Four Courts Press, 2000), pp. 25–43

— *First of the Small Nations: The beginnings of Irish foreign policy in the interwar years, 1919–1932* (Oxford: Oxford University Press, 2016)

Keynes, John Maynard, *The Means to Prosperity* (London: Macmillan and Co., 1933)

Kiberd, Declan, 'From Nationalism to Liberation', in Susan Shaw Sailer (ed.), *Representing Ireland: Gender, class, nationality* (Gainesville: University Press of Florida, 1997), pp. 17–28

Kincaid, Andrew, *Postcolonial Dublin: Imperial legacies and the built environment* (Minneapolis: University of Minnesota Press, 2006)

Kirk, Tim and Anthony McElligott, *Opposing Fascism: Community, authority and resistance in Europe* (Cambridge: Cambridge University Press, 1999)

Kissane, Bill, *Explaining Irish Democracy* (Dublin: UCD Press, 2002)

— *The Politics of the Irish Civil War* (Oxford: Oxford University Press, 2005)

Knirck, Jason K., *Imagining Ireland's Independence: The Debates over the Anglo-Irish Treaty of 1921* (Lanham: Rowman & Littlefield, 2006)

— *Women of the Dáil: Gender, republicanism and the Anglo-Irish Treaty* (Dublin: Irish Academic Press, 2006)

— *Afterimage of the Revolution: Cumann na nGaedheal and Irish politics, 1922–1932* (Madison: University of Wisconsin Press, 2014)

Koepnick, Lutz P., 'Fascist Aesthetics Revisited', *Modernism/modernity*, vol. 6, no. 1, January 1999, pp. 51–73

Laffan, Michael, *The Resurrection of Ireland: The Sinn Féin Party, 1916–1923* (Cambridge: Cambridge University Press, 1999)

Laquer, Walter and George L. Mosse (eds), *International Fascism, 1920–1945* (New York: Harper Torchbooks, 1966)

Lee, J.J., *Ireland, 1912–1985: Politics and society* (Cambridge: Cambridge University Press, 1989)

Levine, Philippa (ed.), *Gender and Empire* (Oxford: Oxford University Press, 2004)

Lloyd, T.O., *Empire, Welfare State, Europe: English History, 1906–1992* (Oxford: Oxford University Press, 1993)

Luddy, Maria, *Prostitution and Irish Society, 1800–1940* (Cambridge: Cambridge University Press, 2007)

Lyons, F.S.L., *Culture and Anarchy in Ireland, 1890–1939* (Oxford: Clarendon Press, 1979)

Mac an Ghail, Máirtín and Chris Haywood (eds), *Gender, Culture and Society: Contemporary femininities and masculinities* (Hampshire: Palgrave Macmillan, 2007)

MacCurtain, Margaret, *Ariadne's Thread: Writing women into Irish history* (Galway: Arlen House, 2008)

MacDermott, Eithne, *Clann na Poblachta* (Cork: Cork University Press, 1998)

MacDonagh, Oliver, *States of Mind: A Study of Anglo-Irish Conflict, 1780–1980* (London: George Allen & Unwin, 1983)

Mahony, Christina Hunt, 'Memory and Belonging: Irish writers, radio, and the nation', *New Hibernia Review/Iris Éireannach Nua*, vol. 5, no. 1, spring/earrach, 2001, pp. 10–24

Martin, Elizabeth Frances, 'Painting the Irish West: Nationalism and the representation of women', *New Hibernia Review/Iris Éireannach Nua*, vol. 7, no. 1, spring/earrach, 2003, pp. 31–44

Martin, Peter, *Censorship in the Two Irelands, 1922–30* (Dublin: Irish Academic Press, 2006)

Mays, Michael, *Nation States: The cultures of Irish nationalism* (Lanham: Lexington Books, 2007)

Mazower, Mark, *Dark Continent: Europe's twentieth century* (New York: Vintage, 1998)

McBride, Lawrence W., *Images, Icons and the Irish Nationalist Imagination* (Dublin: Four Courts Press, 1999)

McCaffery, Lawrence J., 'Sean O'Faolain and Irish Identity', *New Hibernia Review/Iris Éireannach Nua*, vol. 9, no. 4, winter/geimhreadh 2005, pp. 144–56

McCullagh, David, *De Valera Rise* (Dublin: Gill Books, 2017)

— *De Valera Rule* (Dublin: Gill Books, 2017)

McDevitt, Patrick F., 'Muscular Catholicism: Nationalism, masculinity, and Gaelic team sports, 1884–1916', in Tony Ballantyne and Antoinette Burton (eds), *Bodies in Contact: Rethinking colonial encounters in world history* (Durham: Duke University Press, 2005), pp. 201–18

McGarry, Fearghal (ed.), *Republicanism in Modern Ireland* (Dublin: UCD Press, 2003)

McGuire, James and James Quinn (eds), *Dictionary of Irish Biography* (Cambridge: Cambridge University Press, 2010)

McMahon, Timothy G., *Grand Opportunity: The Gaelic revival and Irish society, 1893–1910* (Syracuse: Syracuse University Press, 2009)

— '"The Land for the People": The Irish revolution as a revolution of rising expectations', in Michael de Nie and Sean Farrell (eds), *Power and Popular Culture in Modern Ireland: Essays in honour of James S. Donnelly, Jr.* (Dublin: Irish Academic Press, 2010)

Meehan, Ciara, *The Cosgrave Party: A history of Cumann na nGaedheal, 1923–33* (Dublin: Royal Irish Academy, 2010)

Merjian, Ara H., 'Fascism, Gender, and Culture', *Qui Parle*, vol. 13, no. 1, fall/winter 2001, pp. 1–12

Morash, Christopher, *A History of Irish Theatre, 1601–2000* (Cambridge: Cambridge University Press, 2002)

Morris, Ewan, *Our Own Devices: National symbols and political conflict in twentieth-century Ireland* (Dublin: Irish Academic Press, 2005)

Mosse, George L., *Nazi Culture: A documentary history* (New York: Schocken Books [1966], 1981)

— *Nationalism and Sexuality: Respectability and abnormal sexuality in modern Europe* (New York: Howard Fertig, 1985)

— 'Fascist Aesthetics and Society: Some considerations', *Journal of Contemporary History*, vol. 31, no. 2, April 1996, pp. 245–52

Mullin, Katherine, *James Joyce, Sexuality and Social Purity* (Cambridge: Cambridge University Press, 2003)

Murray, Patrick, *Oracles of God: The Roman Catholic Church and Irish politics 1922–37* (Dublin: UCD Press, 2000)

Nash, John, *James Joyce and the Act of Reception: Reading, Ireland, modernism* (Cambridge: Cambridge University Press, 2006)

Nye, Robert A., 'Western Masculinities in War and Peace', *The American Historical Review*, vol. 112, no. 2, April 2007, pp. 417–38

Ó Beacháin, Donnacha, *Destiny of the Soldiers: Fianna Fáil, Irish republicanism and the IRA, 1926–1973* (Dublin: Gill & Macmillan, 2010)

Ó Drisceoil, Donal, *Censorship in Ireland, 1939–1945: Neutrality, politics and society* (Cork: Cork University Press, 1996)

Ó hAllmhuráin, Gearóid, 'Dancing on the Hobs of Hell: Rural communities in Clare and the Dance Hall Acts of 1935', *New Hibernia Review/Iris Éireannach Nua*, vol. 9, no. 4, winter/geimhreadh 2005, pp. 9–18

Ó Hógartaigh, Margaret, *Kathleen Lynn: Irishwoman, patriot, doctor* (Dublin: Irish Academic Press, 2006)

O'Brien, Mark, *De Valera, Fianna Fáil and the Irish Press* (Dublin: Irish Academic Press, 2001)

O'Brien, Mark and Donnacha Ó Beacháin (eds), *Political Communication in the Republic of Ireland* (Liverpool: Liverpool University Press, 2014)

O'Driscoll, Mervyn, 'Inter-war Irish–German Diplomacy: Continuity, ambiguity and appeasement in Irish foreign policy', in Michael Kennedy and Joseph Morrison Skelly (eds), *Irish Foreign Policy, 1919–1966: From independence to internationalism* (Dublin: Four Courts Press, 2000), pp. 74–95

O'Driscoll, Mervyn, *Ireland, Germany and the Nazis: Politics and diplomacy, 1919–1939* (Dublin: Four Courts Press, 2004)

O'Duffy, Eoin, 'The New Corporate Ireland', in Roger Griffin (ed.), *Fascism* (Oxford: Oxford University Press, 1995), pp. 182–5

O'Halpin, Eunan, '"Weird Prophecies": British intelligence and Anglo-Irish relations, 1932–3', in Michael Kennedy and Joseph Morrison Skelly (eds), *Irish Foreign Policy, 1919–1966: From independence to internationalism* (Dublin: Four Courts Press, 2000), pp. 61–73

O'Leary, Philip, *Gaelic Prose in the Irish Free State, 1922–1939* (Dublin: UCD Press, 2004)

O'Neill, Timothy M., 'Handing Away the Trump Card? Peadar O'Donnell, Fianna Fáil, and the non-payment of land annuities campaign, 1926–32', *New Hibernia Review*, vol. 12, no. 1, spring/earrach 2008, pp. 19–40

O'Regan, Maebh, 'Richard Moynan: Irish artist and unionist propagandist', *Éire/Ireland*, vol. 39, nos. 1 & 2, spring/summer 2004, pp. 59–80

O'Rourke, Kevin, 'Burn Everything but Their Coal: The Anglo-Irish Economic War of the 1930s', *The Journal of Economic History*, vol. 51, no. 2, June 1991, pp. 357–66

Painter, Borden W. Jr., *Mussolini's Rome: Rebuilding the Eternal City* (New York: Palgrave Macmillan, 2005)

Passmore, Kevin (ed.), *Women, Gender and Fascism in Europe, 1919–1945* (Manchester: Manchester University Press, 2003)

Paxton, Robert O., 'The Five Stages of Fascism', *The Journal of Modern History*, vol. 70, no. 1, March 1998, pp. 1–23

— *The Anatomy of Fascism* (New York: Vintage Books, 2005)

Pettit, Philip, 'From Republican Theory to Public Policy', in Mary Jones (ed.), *The Republic: Essays from RTÉ Radio's* The Thomas Davis Lecture Series (Cork: Mercier Press, 2005)

Phoenix, Eamon, *Northern Nationalism: Nationalist politics, partition and the Catholic minority in Northern Ireland, 1890–1940* (Belfast: Ulster Historical Foundation, 1994)

Pickering-Iazzi, Robin (ed.), *Mothers of Invention: Women, Italian fascism, and culture* (Minneapolis: The University of Minnesota Press, 1995)

Quinn, Antoinette, 'Cathleen ni Houlihan Writes Back: Maud Gonne and Irish national theatre', in Anthony Bradley and Maryann Gialanella Valiulis (eds), *Gender and Sexuality in Modern Ireland* (Amherst: University of Massachusetts Press, 1997), pp. 40–59

Re, Lucia, 'Fascist Theories of "Woman" and the Construction of Gender', in Robin Pickering-Iazzi (ed.), *Mothers of Invention: Women, Italian fascism, and culture* (Minneapolis: The University of Minnesota Press, 1995), pp. 76–99

Redican, Noel, *Shadows of Doubt* (Cork: Mercier Press, 2008)

Regan, John M., *The Irish Counter-Revolution, 1921–1936: Treatyite politics and settlement in independent Ireland* (Dublin: Gill & Macmillan, 1999)

Reynolds, Simon and Joy Press, *The Sex Revolts: Gender, rebellion, and rock'n'roll* (Cambridge: Harvard University Press, 1995)

Rockett, Kevin, *Irish Film Censorship: A cultural journey from silent cinema to internet pornography* (Dublin: Four Courts Press, 2004)

Ryan, Louise, '"Drunken Tans": Representations of sex and violence in the Anglo-Irish war (1919–1921)', *Feminist Review*, no. 66, 'Political Currents', autumn 2000, pp. 73–94

— *Gender, Identity and the Irish Press, 1922–1937* (Lewiston: Edwin Mellen Press, 2002)

Ryan, Louise and Margaret Ward (eds), *Irish Women and Nationalism: Soldiers, new women and wicked hags* (Dublin: Irish Academic Press, 2004)

Said, Edward, *Orientalism* (New York: Vintage, 1979)

Sailer, Susan Shaw (ed.), *Representing Ireland: Gender, class, nationality* (Gainesville: University Press of Florida, 1997)

Schmid, Ulrich, 'Style versus Ideology: Towards a conceptualisation of fascist aesthetics', *Totalitarian Movements and Political Religions*, vol. 6, no. 1, June 2005, pp. 127–40

Schüller, G., *James Connolly and Irish Freedom: A Marxist analysis* (Cork: Cork Workers Club [1926], 1974)

Scott, Joan Wallach (ed.), *Feminism and History* (Oxford: Oxford University Press, 1996)

— *Gender and the Politics of History* (New York: Columbia University Press, 1999)

Shonk, Kenneth L. Jr., 'Éamon de Valera and the Renewal of Irish Nationalist Republican Discourse, 1926–1932', master's thesis, California State University, Fullerton, 2005

Sisson, Elaine, *Pearse's Patriots: St Enda's and the cult of boyhood* (Cork: Cork University Press, 2004)

Skeffington, Andrée Sheehy, 'A Coterie of Lively Suffragists', in *Writers, Raconteurs and Notable Feminists: Monographs by Alf Mac Lochlainn and Andrée Sheehy Skeffington* (Dublin: Cumann Leabharlann Náisiúnta na hÉireann, 1993), pp. 34–52

Skidelsky, Robert, *John Maynard Keynes, 1883–1946: Economist, philosopher, statesman* (London: Macmillan, 2003)

Smith, James M., 'The Politics of Sexual Knowledge: The origins of Ireland's containment culture and the Carrigan Report (1931)', *Journal of the History of Sexuality*, vol. 13, no. 2, April 2004, pp. 208–33

Smith, M.L.R., *Fighting for Ireland? The military strategy of the Irish republican movement* (London: Routledge, 1995)

Spengler, Oswald, *The Decline of the West. Volume One: Form and Actuality* (New York: Alfred A. Knopf, 1957)

— *The Decline of the West. Volume Two: Perspectives of World-History* (New York: Alfred A. Knopf, 1957)

Steele, Karen, *Women, Press, and Politics during the Irish Revival* (Syracuse: Syracuse University Press, 2007)

Stone, Marla Susan, *The Patron State: Culture and politics in fascist Italy* (Princeton: Princeton University Press, 1998)

Sullivan, Nikki, *A Critical Introduction to Queer Theory* (New York: New York University Press, 2003)

Tanner, Marcus, *Ireland's Holy Wars: The Struggle for a Nation's Soul, 1500–2000* (Yale: Yale University Press, 2000)

Tobin, Daniel, 'Modernism, Leftism, and the Spirit: The poetry of Lola Ridge', *New Hibernia Review/Iris Éireannach Nua*, vol. 8, no. 3, autumn/fómhar, 2004, pp. 65–85

Valiulis, Maryann Gialanella (ed.), *Gender and Power in Irish History* (Dublin: Irish Academic Press, 2009)

Walker, Graham, "'The Irish Dr. Goebbels": Frank Gallagher and Irish republican propaganda', *Journal of Contemporary History*, vol. 27, no. 1, January 1992, pp. 149–65

Ward, Margaret, *Unmanageable Revolutionaries: Women and Irish nationalism* (London: Pluto Press, 1995)

— 'Nationalism, Pacifism, Internationalism: Louie Bennett, Hanna Sheehy-Skeffington, and the problems of "defining feminism"', in Anthony Bradley and Maryann Gialanella Valiulis (eds), *Gender and Sexuality in Modern Ireland* (Amherst: University of Massachusetts Press, 1997), pp. 60–84

Weihman, Lisa, 'Doing My Bit for Ireland: Transgressing Gender in the Easter Rising', *Éire-Ireland*, vol. 39, nos. 3 & 4, fall/winter 2004, pp. 228–48

White, Timothy J., 'The Changing Social Bases of Political Identity in Ireland', in Susan Shaw Sailer (ed.), *Representing Ireland: Gender, class, nationality* (Gainesville: University Press of Florida, 1997), pp. 113–32

Whyndham, Andrew Higgins (ed.), *Re-Imagining Ireland* (Charlottesville: University of Virginia Press, 2006)

Whyte, J.H., *Church and State in Modern Ireland, 1923–1970* (Dublin: Gill & Macmillan, 1980)

Zink, Allan, 'Ireland: Democratic stability without compromise', in Dirk Berg-Schlosser and Jeremy Mitchell (eds), *Conditions of Democracy in Europe, 1919–39* (London: Macmillan, 2000), pp. 263–93

Zuelow, Eric G.E., *Making Ireland Irish: Tourism and national identity since the Irish civil war* (Syracuse: Syracuse University Press, 2009)

Index

Page numbers followed by 'n' indicate notes e.g. 187n. 'FF' denotes Fianna Fáil.